ALL

ETERNITY

LIES

BEFORE ME

Praise for

All Eternity Lies Before Me

"Although I had read the original story of the loss of Alfa Foxtrot 586 when it first came out, this book is a detailed account of the story of the ordeal of the crew of Alfa Foxtrot 586. Loreen Gibbons does a superb job of recounting the story in a gripping manner that brings the reader along with the increasing tensions of the crew as the problems with the Orion unfold. Occasionally switching back to the Grigsby household offers the reader an understanding of what the families face when the fate of their loved ones is unknown. Overall, this story is an example of the teamwork, discipline, and dedication that air crews must demonstrate when the need arises. The months and months of training in the event an emergency should happen is evident in this account. This book should be mandatory reading in the training of these air crews.

Finally, I knew LCDR Jerry Grigsby well. His professionalism and courage in carrying out his duties as Aircraft Commander demonstrate his commitment to his men, and his country. Not leaving the sinking plane until he felt that all the crew were safely out was an act of love. I never understood why Jerry didn't receive the Navy Cross."

—CDR. EVERETT ALVAREZ, USN (RET), CEO ALVAREZ IT LLC, US Navy's First Vietnam POW, author of *Chained Eagle* and *Code of Conduct*

"I think the story and the story-telling are brilliant. Congratulations Loreen!"

—ANDREW C.A. JAMPOLER, Captain USN (Ret), Naval Historian, author of *ADAK: The Rescue of Alfa Foxtrot586*

"LCDR Jerry Grigsby was a true military hero, an inspiration to all. Without his superb skills, none of the fifteen crew members would have survived the ditching of Navy Alfa Foxtrot 586. In 1978, Jerry was the only active P-3 pilot in our squadron with prior experience on the Martin P-5M, the Navy's last flying boat. He knew the extreme winds and waves were not survivable if the ditching had been flown using the rules found P-3 flight manual.

The P-3 manual said flying directly into the waves would be like flying into a mountain. In fact, flying into the waves in gale force winds was the only way to survive that day. By flying into the waves, he was also flying into the wind. Jerry's decision reduced our final landing speed over the water from 115 knots to 70 knots and our wings were level. He also reduced the recommended rate of descent from the manual's suggested 200 feet per minute to 50 feet per minute. His decisions allowed the entire airframe to absorb the shock of landing at the same time at half the speed.

Sadly, when a military hero dies there are few books written by the surviving spouse or family. I am an avid reader. Both of my parents had Masters Degrees in Library Science. This is, by far, the best book I have ever read from that point-of-view."

—Ed Caylor, Co-Pilot Alfa Foxtrot 586, Senior Surviving Officer, Retired Delta Airlines 767 Captain

"*All Eternity Lies Before Me* is Loreen Gibbon's gripping personal account. A testament to love . . . grit . . . and personal resilience—central to the hero Jerry Grigsby proved to the world himself to be—the same key traits that ground all Navy families."

—Kyle Cozad RADM, USN (Ret), former Chief of Naval Education and Training, CEO National Navy Aviation Museum Foundation, author of *Relentless Positivity*

"Americans honor and appreciate military rescue stories. Most involve actions necessary to overcome a determined enemy. But sometimes that enemy can be Mother Nature herself. In this expansive narrative, Loreen Gibbons tells the story of one such rescue, a US Navy P-3 callsign Alfa Foxtrot 586, down in the bitter cold waters of the northern Pacific. With a compelling style, she tells the story from the perspective of the downed crews and then interlaces it with the travail of the families, who wait, hope, and pray. She reminds us that for those who love, time is eternity, and love is the most powerful and still most unknown energy in the world. Bravo Zulu!!"

—DARREL WHITCOMB, COL USAF (RET), Vietnam Forward Air Controller, author of *The Rescue of Bat 21, Combat Search and Rescue in Desert Storm*

"I included the inspiring story of *Alfa Foxtrot 586* in *Leading at The Edge*, and I was delighted to read Loreen Gibbons account of the years that followed for the surviving crew and their families. She skillfully blends themes of tragedy, love, and remembrance in a compelling narrative."

—DENNIS N. T. PERKINS PhD, USMC Company Commander Vietnam, Faculty, Yale School of Management, CEO of Syncretics Group Inc, author of *Leading at The Edge* and *Into the Storm*

"A stunning memoir that not only honors servicemen and their sacrifice, but also highlights the extraordinary strength and resilience of a military spouse. Breathtaking in its honesty, Gibbon's story will stay with you for eternity."

—JULIE TULLY, Navy Wife, author of *Dispatches from the Cowgirl*

ALL ETERNITY LIES BEFORE ME

Hope, Faith, and Love
After the Loss of
Navy Alfa Foxtrot 586

LOREEN GIBBONS

SHE WRITES PRESS

Published 2025
Printed in the United States of America
Print ISBN: 978-1-64742-820-4
E-ISBN: 978-1-64742-821-1
Library of Congress Control Number: 2024916257

For information, address:
She Writes Press
1569 Solano Ave #546
Berkeley, CA 94707

Interior Design by Tabitha Lahr

She Writes Press is a division of SparkPoint Studio, LLC.

Names and identifying characteristics have been changed to protect the privacy of certain individuals.

Since 1775, more than five million young men and women have served in the United States Navy.

For nearly 250 years, the Navy has honored their heroes by naming bases, ships, streets, and buildings for them.

This is the story of one of those heroes: Lieutenant Commander Jerry Grigsby and his legacy as told by his shipmates and family.

The Scene

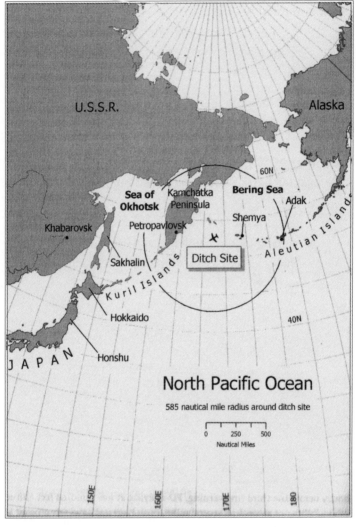

Map used with permission of Naval Institute Press.

The Crew Positions

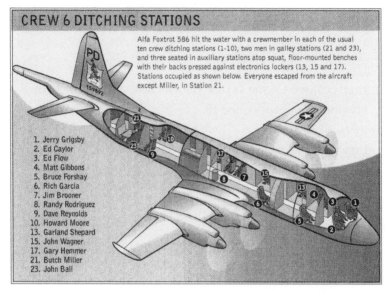

CREW 6 DITCHING STATIONS

Alfa Foxtrot 586 hit the water with a crewmember in each of the usual ten crew ditching stations (1-10), two men in galley stations (21 and 23), and three seated in auxiliary stations atop squat, floor-mounted benches with their backs pressed against electronics lockers (13, 15 and 17). Stations occupied as shown below. Everyone escaped from the aircraft except Miller, in Station 21.

1. Jerry Grigsby
2. Ed Caylor
3. Ed Flow
4. Matt Gibbons
5. Bruce Forshay
6. Rich Garcia
7. Jim Brooner
8. Randy Rodriguez
9. Dave Reynolds
10. Howard Moore
13. Garland Shepard
15. John Wagner
17. Gary Hemmer
21. Butch Miller
23. John Ball

Used with permission of Naval Institute Press.

The Crew

LIEUTENANT COMMANDER JERRY GRIGSBY, Patrol Plane/ Mission Commander, age 36

LIEUTENANT ED CAYLOR, Copilot (also a fully qualified Patrol Plane Commander), age 26

ENSIGN JOHN WAGNER, Third Pilot, age 25

LIEUTENANT (JUNIOR GRADE) MATTHEW GIBBONS, Patrol Plane Tactical Coordinator, age 25

LIEUTENANT (JUNIOR GRADE) BRUCE FORSHAY, Navigator/ Communicator, age 24

LIEUTENANT (JUNIOR GRADE) JOHN BALL, Navigator/ Communicator, PARPRO Rider, age 32

PETTY OFFICER SECOND CLASS ED FLOW, Flight Engineer, age 26

PETTY OFFICER SECOND CLASS BUTCH MILLER, Flight Engineer, age 33

Petty Officer Third Class, Jim Brooner, Sensor 1 Acoustic Operator, age 23

Petty Officer Third Class Howard "Howie" Moore, In-Flight Technician, age 24

Airman Dave Reynolds, Aviation Ordnanceman, age 23

Airman Randy Rodriguez, Sensor 2 Acoustic Operator, age 19

Airman Richard Garcia, Sensor 3, Non-acoustic Operator, age 20

Master Chief Garland Shepard, Guest from Tactical Support Center Adak, age 34

Petty Officer First Class Gary Hemmer, Guest from Naval Facility Adak, age 34

Part One: October 1978

Time is too slow for those who wait,
Too swift for those who fear,
Too long for those who grieve,
Too short for those who rejoice,
But for those who love, time is eternity.

—Henry Van Dyke

The conclusion is always the same:
love is the most powerful and still most
unknown energy of the world.

—Pierre Teilhard de Chardin

Anticipation

Almaden Valley, California
October 26, 1978

Nine-year-old Karen Todd, our neighbor from across the street, tells me about her nightmare as I unlatch the safety lock of the backyard gate to let her go home. Unlike the other outrageous stories she has told me in the past, this one stops me dead.

"A screaming eagle was diving after your husband," she says as she flashes that impish look of hers. Something long forgotten and locked away begins to churn up emotions as I gasp and feel my heart pound in fear. She studies my face and turns away, then wraps her towel around her dripping swimsuit and pads home barefoot across the street.

How did that get into her dream? Does she even know my husband's Navy squadron is called the Golden Eagles? I take a deep breath, pushing my feelings down before letting go of the gate. The safety mechanism takes over, the gate swings shut, and the safety lock clicks into place. All is secure once again. Karen can't possibly know anything about that, can she?

I compose my face before turning back to my daughters, who are almost finished putting away the pool toys. "Scoot upstairs now for a quick shower. We'll have just enough time to eat dinner before your marionette class," I tell them.

From the corner of my eye, I catch a flash of light in the distance that seems to be coming from the northwest. It distracts me and is gone before I can make anything of it. Was it some kind of explosion? A fire? I shiver despite the glorious warmth of this rare Indian summer day and work to dispel the sense of foreboding that is starting to take hold. I turn back to pick up a wet towel as the pool sweep clicks on and begins its journey around the pool, cleaning away the debris of the afternoon swim.

Preflight

The sixties-era Bachelor Officer Quarters (BOQ) for Naval Station Adak perches on the side of Bering Hill, all gray cinder block, with small aluminum-framed windows, surrounded by the rubble of ancient volcanic eruptions and engulfed in a thick gray mist. Even on a rare day when there is some parting of the mist, the gray-green landscape remains almost unrelieved by color; so inhospitable is the climate that nothing much grows here. The occasional view of the airfield below and the tundra and bay beyond reveals even more shades of gray. There is no Indian summer here in the Aleutian Islands.

It is in this dismal landscape that a small subset of the Golden Eagles of Navy Patrol Squadron Nine has been assigned a six-week rotation from their home base at Moffett Field in California. Most count the days until they can go home.

This morning begins for Lieutenant Commander Jerry Grigsby's crew much like any other morning on Adak when the officers—wearing baggy flight suits, lace-up boots, and government-issue parkas—meet in the lobby of the BOQ at 4:15 a.m. Today's crew, however, is an ad hoc crew put together just the day before based on individual qualifications and the needs of the mission. Navy patrol squadrons typically form crews selected by the Commanding Officer to ensure a balance of talent. Normally a crew flies together for months at a time, learning to work together as a team, and your crew members become the only people on the planet who share your work schedule. It is late 1978. The Vietnam War is over, and with manpower cutbacks firmly in place, the Navy's patrol plane community juggles to keep the missions manned.

The duty driver is already waiting for the crew in a faded gray, thirteen-passenger Dodge van with door latches that cannot be trusted. Everyone is in good spirits despite the early hour, and Grigsby, who is putting on his navy-blue watch cap over his red hair, smiles when he overhears Lieutenant (junior grade) John Ball quip, "just another fine Lee Iacocca product," as he and the others climb into the van.

"Glad to have you aboard today, John," Grigsby says, and he means it. He appreciates not only Ball's technical expertise in secure communications but also his lighthearted, irreverent banter and infectious good humor. Ball has been in the squadron for five months and has already established a solid reputation for his attention to detail.

Grigsby is warmed by the camaraderie surrounding him and possesses a deep affection for those who are giving so much of their youth in service to their country. The men continue making light of the rattles and squeaks as they bump their way down the hill through the frigid darkness and into a cloud-shrouded day that holds onto secrets.

Lieutenant (junior grade) Matthew Gibbons, a young Tactical Coordinator who sports a Burt Reynolds–style mustache and who joined the squadron as an Ensign, can tell you something about military budget cuts. His basic flight training in Pensacola had been accelerated by five months because of a need to get Flight Officers to the fleet. After completing the Advanced Air Navigation School, he received his NFO (Naval Flight Officer) wings forty-seven weeks after starting in Pensacola. At Patrol Squadron 9 (VP-9), he flew flight after flight, amassing more than eleven hundred hours in the P-3 Orion turboprop during his first twenty-four months—a feat that normally takes nearly thirty-six months.

Now on Adak, the squadron is on day 160 of a planned six-month commitment—rotating crews, aircraft, and maintenance personnel in and out from Moffett Field. Gibbons is on day 107 of what was originally planned as sixty-seven days for each officer and flight crew member. The command has rotated him from crew to crew because of the ongoing personnel shortage. He is now dubbed an "Adak Centurion," a humorous way of recognizing him for spending one hundred plus days in the Aleutians.

That is how on October 26, this twenty-five-year-old is the senior NFO on this mission. He is the Tactical Coordinator and he oversees everything going on in the plane behind the cockpit. "My flying career is off to a fast start," he sometimes jokes, "but the pay's the same."

It's a quick trip in the van down to the hangar where the crew visits Maintenance Control to find out which airplane has been assigned and to check over the maintenance logs. "What's all this?" Grigsby asks Gibbons as he helps him unload a full shopping bag and a tote bag holding a electric cooking pot. Gibbons is known for his "morale menus." He had stopped by the "Geedunk"—the base mini-mart—last night for supplies to make chili cheese dogs.

The mood becomes attentive and professional in the Tactical Support Center (TSC) as Lieutenant John Eger begins the mission brief at 5:00 a.m. They are scheduled for a 9:00

a.m. takeoff window for a Peacetime Airborne Reconnaissance Program (PARPRO) flight—a special weekly mission to gather intelligence along the coast of the Soviet Union. Some of the crew had attended a pre-briefing the day before and are expecting a routine, long, and tedious patrol. There had not been much recent Soviet submarine activity detected in their patrol area, and with a major storm brewing over the North Pacific and Bering Sea, there wouldn't be much ship traffic to monitor either.

Returning to the hangar, the men grab their flight gear, but Gibbons's helmet is not in his locker and he slams the door shut. He is pissed that someone has taken it. It has an intricate helmet design; he had spent hours decorating it with colored reflective tape. There is no available spare helmet and nothing to be done about it. Now he will have no helmet for the flight. He will wear his navy-blue knit watch cap and use a headset and microphone instead.

They all head to their assigned P-3 aircraft to do the preflight inspection, a series of checklist items to ensure that dozens of systems are working properly. An experienced crew typically takes three hours to go through the entire list, and they do it as though their lives depend on it, which, of course, they do. Training sessions for every conceivable situation have been thorough, repetitive, and ongoing, imprinting it all on their subconscious minds. The men have gotten through months and months of it all because they understand the importance of these missions for national security. Any notions they may have held about the romance of a flying career have long since been quelled.

Lieutenant Ed Caylor, the copilot for this flight, and Ensign John Wagner, the third pilot, conduct the walk-around inspection outside the airplane, checking landing gear, brakes, and propellers. Grigsby, the Mission Commander, is freed to get the weather briefing and file the flight plan. Meanwhile, the ground-based mechanics and the crew's flight engineers are looking at a minor leak on the number one propeller.

Grigsby had piloted this plane up from California several days earlier in a quick turnaround flight after dropping another plane off at Moffett Field, affording him a brief overnight visit with his wife and daughters and earning him the nickname "Quickie" among the other Lieutenant Commanders. Out of respect, no one on his crew would ever let on that they had overheard that good-natured ribbing.

In the post-flight inspection at that time, the ground-based maintenance crew had noted a small leak on the number one propeller. They had deemed it to be within normal operating limits then, and during this preflight today it is tested again, and again it is thought to be well within normal limits. The plane had undergone a thorough maintenance check before leaving California, and the number one propeller had been replaced with a fully reconditioned propeller that had the latest version of propeller control O-rings and cold weather hydraulic fluid. It's still a day much like any other.

Inside the fuselage, preflight activities proceed per the individual crew station manuals. Some crew members, having completed their portion of the preflight checks, get back into the van and head over to the Birchwood dining facility to eat a quick breakfast. They leave Lieutenant (junior grade) Bruce Forshay, Petty Officer Jim Brooner, and Airman Randy Rodriguez to complete the inspections of the navigation and secure communication equipment and the two acoustic sensor stations, as those portions of the preflight have more check-points and usually take more time.

The breakfasts at Birchwood, the only dining hall on Adak open at this early hour, are monotonous but hearty—scrambled eggs, hash browns, toast, bacon, and coffee. After eating, Gibbons purchases a few apples and Eggo waffles for those still back at the airplane.

Ball has had breakfast there this morning as well and has enjoyed a brief visit with his friend Lieutenant (junior grade) Dennis Mette. Grigsby had tracked Ball down the night before and asked him to be an extra navigator as backup for Forshay, who had only just recently completed his training, and to assist Gibbons with the tedious manual encryptions that will be needed for this mission.

Ball had been playing bingo and drinking beer in the Chief Petty Officers' Club when Grigsby approached him about this flight the night before. "I don't think that's a good idea for the morning," Ball replied. "There's that twelve-hour bottle-to-throttle rule, and it's already 7:00 p.m." He was having a good time—about as good as it gets on the rocky outpost that is Adak Island—and Grigsby was aware, but he did a quick calculation in his head and excused Ball from the preflight exercises, telling him to join the crew at 7:00 a.m. in plenty of time for takeoff.

There just was not anyone else in the small detachment qualified to handle that responsibility in the morning.

———————————

Back at the plane, preflight checks are complete and the crew is waiting. A few are having coffee, and others are already at their stations. Over the PA system, Grigsby announces the "planeside" briefing—called that by tradition even though the pre-takeoff briefings are no longer held planeside—and gathers the crew in the cocooning warmth of the fuselage, which is heavily padded with a thick layer of insulation.

Grigsby, soft-spoken and solid, is the sort of officer you would want on your crew. He leads by example. "Today's mission is a PARPRO flight, and we'll be collecting intelligence in the Rough-cut Delta area off the Kamchatka coast. Our call sign for today's flight is Alfa Foxtrot 586."

"We've got two special guests aboard today, Master Chief Garland Shepard and Petty Officer First Class Gary Hemmer. Please make them feel welcome. We'll be flying enroute at twenty thousand feet. The weather forecast for the area is variable winds southwest at thirty knots [35 mph] to northwest at forty knots [46 mph] with moderate turbulence. There'll be rain and snow showers, and we'll be in and out of icing conditions." These weather conditions are far from ideal, but not bad enough to cancel the mission.

Master Chief Shepard is the Command Master Chief of the Adak TSC who chose to fly with this crew to fulfill his monthly flight time requirement. Petty Officer Hemmer is along for an orientation flight to see how the airborne systems work, as he is assigned to the ground-based Naval Facility and charged with tracking submarines using large mainframe computers connected to miles of undersea microphones.

Then it is Gibbons's turn to speak, and he lets everyone know that the preflight data-insertion program has been loaded successfully. "Mr. Forshay and Mr. Ball have cross-checked all fly-to point coordinates. The rules for this flight dictate no approach closer than forty miles to the Soviet coastline. After takeoff, we will build lines on the tactical display at forty-five miles to create a visual reference in the flight station. Mr. Forshay will call out any time we approach within fifty miles of their coast. Petty Officer Garcia will back us up with radar fixes if we get any radar contacts close to the line. We will be monitoring Skyking broadcasts; if you hear our call sign, Alfa Foxtrot 586, write down all the letters you hear." Most of the time, the letters are not meant for them, but if they hear "Alfa Foxtrot 586," that means the coded message is addressed to them. In the event of static or faded signals, it is important to have multiple crew members listening and writing down the letters.

The entity known as Skyking is a conglomerate of long-distance radars, satellites, and additional classified airborne platforms. Today the crew will be playing a game of cat and mouse with the Soviets, and their low-altitude flight will be watched over by one or more high-altitude Air Force or Navy counterparts with the goal of activating some mobile Soviet air defense radar sites.

During the Cold War, it was essential to maintain an updated inventory of enemy air defense network radars. The precise location, characteristics, frequencies, and detection ranges were vitally important if hostilities ever escalated. In the event of a Cold War attack on the United States, the retaliating aircrews would either avoid the radars completely or obliterate them as they struck back deep into enemy territory.

During hostilities, Skyking would provide the Emergency Action Messages to authenticate any attack orders. The Skyking communication system was routine during peacetime, but the structure, formality, and visibility was in place if the situation ever escalated.

The crew is perhaps a little more formal and thorough than usual because there are guests aboard. Forshay lets them know that the inertial navigation systems are aligned and stable and that all preflight secure communications checks are complete. Each man in turn contributes to the briefing: that the number one propeller has been serviced and topped off with fresh hydraulic fluid, that all three sensor stations are up and fully checked out, that the central computer is good to go, and that all sonobuoys are loaded per the buoy load card.

"Assuming we don't find a lot of contacts in this weather, today's flight will be about training in addition to our normal PARPRO responsibilities. Mr. Wagner will get grilled up front as the third pilot, and I will be helping Mr. Ball with his Personnel Qualification System [PQS] on the Tactical Coordinator station. Speaking of PQS, congrats to AX3 Moore who has just passed his eighty-hour PQS review and is no longer flying as an In-Flight Technician [IFT] under instruction. Today is his first tactical mission without a supervising IFT, so try not to break anything." Gibbons then asks if there are any questions.

This briefing time offers an opportunity for the junior enlisted crew to ask the officers questions. Thirteen crew members are scheduled for the flight, and it is important that everyone, including the two guests, be on the same page. Hemmer asks, "What time do you think we'll be back?" When Grigsby replies that it will be about 6:00 p.m., he knows it is shaping up to be a long day.

The two acoustic sensor operators, Brooner and Rodriguez, won't have much to do unless a submarine is discovered in the area, Gibbons reasons, so he asks them to introduce the guests to their stations—the latest-version sensor gear in the Pacific Fleet. These stations are the "ears" of the airplane. They process underwater sounds made by submarines. The computers match known sound "fingerprints" to help identify those submarines.

Grigsby signals the successful completion of the preflight activities by saying, "Okay, everyone, let's get ready to go flying! Let's get above these clouds and see some sunshine." The men go to their assigned stations—Grigsby in the left seat of the wide cockpit, Caylor in the right, and Petty Officer Ed Flow in the flight engineer's seat behind the center console. The others go to stations back in the fuselage, or tube, as it is often called. Then they adjust their headrests in place, fasten seat belts and shoulder harnesses, and put on helmets and fire protection gloves.

More than four hours into their morning, Crew 6 is finally ready to go. "Crew, Set Condition Five, prepare for takeoff," Grigsby says over the PA system while electronics hum along in the background. Condition Five is always set for takeoff and landing, and requires everyone to be in his assigned crew station, helmet on, shoulder harnesses and seat belts fastened. The engine starts are normal, taxi and pre-takeoff checklists are complete, and Grigsby taxies to the end of the runway positioning the plane for takeoff.

The scheduled takeoff time had been set for 9:00 a.m., plus or minus fifteen minutes. They hold on the runway for five minutes to hit that window, otherwise the Fifth Air Force Skyking monitors in Japan will be more than a little annoyed with their lack of adherence to protocols. Deviating from the mission schedule just isn't worth the hassle. As if to under-score the reality of their mission, "Skyking, Skyking, message follows: Lima. X-ray. Alfa. Tango. Romeo. Zulu . . ." pulses over the radio receivers with an encoded singsong voice trans-mission, something Gibbons, Ball, and Forshay expect to hear every fifteen minutes during today's nine-hour flight. Gibbons and Forshay will each write down every message they hear and compare notes to be sure that what they have written is correct. If "Alfa Foxtrot 586" precedes a message, they will decode that message.

Caylor feels a fuming frustration taking hold as he waits for takeoff—a frustration he keeps to himself. His scheduled rotation with the detachment has just ended, and by rights, he should have been on his way home with his own Crew 7, but he is needed here today. He only found out a couple of days ago—had been ordered to stay on by Lieutenant Commander "Iron Mike" Harris, the officer in charge of the detachment. Caylor doesn't like the high visibility nature of these PARPRO missions. No one does. There are too many people watching. You never get a pat on the back for a job well done on these flights. That just isn't part of what happens, but you may well get buried in criticism for a job less than perfectly executed. Yes, he will maintain a professional attitude in the cockpit, as they all will, no one wanting a blot on their record and all wanting to be part of a successful team. At precisely 8:45 a.m. they begin their takeoff roll, and they all anticipate a smooth, routine, and uneventful patrol: What could possibly go wrong?

The Very Heart of Me

Almaden Valley

October 26

*T*he evening is still pleasant after our quick dinner. I let myself out through the family room sliding door thinking about my husband while humming along with the radio: "If you leave me now . . . you take away the very heart of me . . ." Jerry loves to sing, and I picture his red hair and smiling blue eyes. It is almost as though he is right here singing along with me, and I realize I've allowed myself to become lonesome and sentimental. He will be home by Thanksgiving with the rest of his squadron's detachment in Alaska, and he'll be home for Christmas this year as well. I can get through this; I've done it many times before!

Our backyard is something of a sanctuary, a refuge. It is the typical suburban backyard, but the swimming pool is a centerpiece surrounded by an exposed aggregate patio. On one end there is space for a patio table set and a couple of padded deck chairs with a matching ottoman. On the other end, Jerry has built a playhouse for the girls and painted it to match our house. The patio area is surrounded on three sides by a planting of evergreen trees and shrubs. A six-foot-tall redwood fence encloses all of it. Over the top of the fence, I can see tree-covered hills and the Santa Cruz Mountains in the distance.

I sink into one of the cushioned deck chairs fighting back tears and watch as mist from the ocean begins to gather atop Mount Umunhum on the west side of the valley. Are we in for a change of weather? Is this the end of Indian summer? The mist continues to rise, all but obscuring the incessant turnings of the ancient early-warning radar antenna located there, and as I settle into relaxation, I allow a memory to surface, one that has been nagging at the back of my mind ever since Karen went home. It was my first date with Jerry.

————————————

I was not quite seventeen. We went out to a movie and stopped for a chance to talk and to enjoy a Coke at Lou's Drive-In afterward. He walked me to my front door, and I went inside after he said he would be calling me again soon. Everyone was already in bed as I walked across my parents' dark living room in the haze of a pleasant, easy feeling. I was almost past the piano when I felt overcome by a strong sensation of amazing happiness.

The living room faded away in a blur, and, as my mind's eye cleared, something came to me in the way a memory comes, only it was not a memory, and it played in my mind almost like a movie: I was aware I had married him and it had been the best time of my life. I saw myself looking out a picture window watching men in dark suits get out of black cars. I heard crying from across the room, and I knew what the men had come to say—but that was it. That was as far as I could see in my mind's eye, and as my parents' living room came back into focus, I realized I did not find out what the men had come to say even though I felt I must have already known what it was. I did not know how long I stood next to the piano in the dark living room, but I did know that marriage was not on my mind. I was still sixteen after all.

Now, all these years later in 1978, that almost-forgotten vision comes back to haunt me. It is as though there is a realm of intelligence beyond thought; it comes as a quick flash of revelation. I did not know what to make of it then, and I don't want to dwell on it now. Hadn't my mother always chided me for my overactive imagination and my tendency for drama? I force my breathing to become slow and rhythmic as I draw those memories away from my mind. I am intensely conscious of the present moment, highly alert and aware but not thinking—just relaxing and experiencing the view of the distant mountains. I feel a profound inner stillness until the unwelcome ring of the phone pierces through the peace, bringing me closer to my future. The mist crests over the top of Mount Umunhum, and, like a tidal wave in slow motion, a cold, white froth descends toward the valley.

Above the Clouds

Kamchatka Views

October 26

The climb-out from Adak is unremarkable, and Grigsby heads the plane southwest toward the Soviet Union, flying along the predefined track that is designed to be far enough out to sea to remain in international airspace, yet close enough to trigger a Soviet response. Things soon settle down to a predictable routine with the guests sipping on coffee at the acoustic stations. The activities throughout the aircraft have a familiar rhythm, a procedural dependability, and a secure feeling of order and structure. Every phase of the flight has its own tempo and sequence. Up in the cockpit, Grigsby and Caylor quiz Wagner, discussing various aircraft systems. Flow and Miller join in trying to stump the new pilot, but Wagner is up to the challenge.

Back in the tube, Forshay is focusing on the navigation tasks and Ball is seated at the Tactical Coordinator (TACCO) station checking out the myriad switches and menus. At the Sensor Three station, Garcia is busy using the radar to create a 360-degree view searching for surface ship contacts and monitoring the Electronic Support Measures system for any hints of Soviet radar signals.

Airman Dave Reynolds and Petty Officer Third Class Howard "Howie" Moore bond over a game of acey-deucey in the galley. Howie, so new to the squadron that this is only his eighth mission, smiles at Reynolds's offer of friendship in this way. Acey-deucey is a version of backgammon popular among sailors, and learning to play it is almost a rite of passage. This game doesn't require a lot of strategy and plays more like a race. They continue playing until they hit the storm system an hour southwest of Adak with massive waves, tall banks of gray clouds, buffeting winds, and icy rain.

They know it is time to return to their stations and get buckled in. Ball catches Gibbons's eye and says, "Just another fine Adak day," causing both Forshay and Gibbons to laugh. Ball, smart and dependable, can never stay serious for long. They can always rely on his sarcastic sense of humor to lighten the mood. Grigsby decides to stay above the clouds and go down through the storm only when they pick up radar surface contacts to investigate or Soviet search radars tracking them. It's all shaping up to be one more long and tedious patrol that will bring them one day closer to returning home to California.

As they find smoother air, the AWs—Anti-submarine Warfare Operators—enjoy demonstrating their equipment to the guests and talking about the airplane systems. These are all "techie" young men. Brooner, the senior acoustic operator, lets Rodriguez, the newest operator, explain how the new Victor Six Directional Frequency Analysis (DIFAR) system filters out the background noise and shows the submarine sound signature patterns on its display. This newest version of the DIFAR system points directly toward the sounds made by a submarine at great detection distances. By triangulating two or more bearing lines the submarine can be quickly located.

Rodriguez's youthful enthusiasm engages Master Chief Shepard—always called "Master Chief" in deference to his hard-won rank. He has "seen it all" over the past sixteen years. They get into the details of decibels, detection levels, and sensitivity. It helps break up the tedium, Gibbons observes, as he walks a lap through the tube checking on things.

It is a pleasant distraction for Gibbons to be working with Forshay, the squadron's newest Navigator/Communicator. His skill level is already impressive, and Ball is always a lot of fun to have aboard. Ball and Forshay graduated from the Air Force Navigator training program and are very comfortable staying mentally ahead of the aircraft. The three NFOs are content navigating and communicating as they work their way west toward the Soviet Union.

As the flight progresses, they encounter two surface ships: a small Korean fishing boat and a larger Soviet fishing trawler. Flying at high altitude, Radar Operator Garcia finds them both easily with the forward search radar, which feeds direction and distance information directly to the pilots. The plane descends through the weather, and the men perform the standard identification low-altitude flyby. Aviation Ordnanceman Reynolds takes a series of pictures with the Navy-issue Pentax SLR camera to identify the ships by name and country while Forshay logs the contact name, time, position, course, and speed on the computer printout. Gibbons records this information by hand in the post-mission summary report called the RAINFORM Purple, and it never crosses his mind how important this knowledge might be to them later. They all notice and comment on the huge waves below them, feeling sorry for the storm-tossed sailors as they climb back above the storm clouds returning to smoother air and blue skies.

They are above the weather again, and off in the distance to the west, like sentinels of hope, they can see a volcano releasing a faint puff of steam, and near that, another snow-covered peak. This view of the Kamchatka Peninsula with mountaintops floating on top of the clouds in the brilliant blue sky reminds Grigsby of views he has seen of Japan's Mount Fuji. He has his personal Nikon in the cockpit and takes pictures while standing behind Caylor, who is now having a turn in the left seat.

Junior pilots like to fly with Grigsby because he is known to share time in the left seat while at the same time maintaining quiet oversight. Wagner returned late from a flight the day before and swapped third pilot assignments with Van Gamble on the flight schedule in order to fly with Jerry and bond with his new crew. It is important to him to connect with his crew, and he enjoys flying with Jerry. Wagner is now in the right seat, and Reynolds uses the Navy Pentax to take pictures as well. Grigsby makes a call over the PA system for anyone else who wants to see this rare view of the Soviet Union to come on up as there are not many windows back in the body of the plane.

Very few ships are this far out to sea, and the flight continues along the assigned track just fifty miles off the Siberian coast of the Kamchatka Peninsula where the Soviets have located multiple sensitive military installations. Specialists in the Pentagon and Defense Intelligence Agency hope this mission will provoke the Soviet air defense system into activating air search radars and tactical communication systems. American intelligence units have their attention focused on the plane and are watching for any response to its flight. They are recording and triangulating every signal for later analysis while Skyking personnel monitor their progress.

At 10:50 a.m. they decide to shut down, or "loiter," the number one engine to save fuel in case they need to divert to another Aleutian airfield due to the storm. The number one engine is typically shut down to conserve fuel because it is the only engine that does not drive an electrical generator.

P-3 Orion crews routinely fly on three engines as a standard practice on almost all overwater tactical missions.

The pre-loiter checklist is satisfactory, and the number one propeller is successfully feathered. The automatic propeller control advances the blades perpendicular to the air stream, making an X as the propeller blades stop rotating and the turbine engine winds down to a full stop.

The crew members take turns eating lunch. In the morning, they had each ordered boxed lunches through the squadron duty office with the typical choices of fried chicken or bologna sandwiches. Some prefer frozen dinners and have ordered Salisbury steak or spaghetti and meatballs instead. Gibbons, who sometimes reminds Ball of a puppy eager for approval, has warmed up some canned chili, sliced cheese, and hot dogs in his Crock-Pot, giving this routine day a bit of variety. Chili cheese dogs are always a welcome addition to the monotonous choices in the plane's small galley and are a favorite way to chase away the pervasive cold and damp of the Aleutian October. Gibbons wants to ensure these men are well cared for. His father had been an enlisted Aviation Radioman First Class flying in dive-bombers during WWII. He instilled in his son a strong commitment to take care of his sailors. His father's advice was simple and straightforward: "Take care of your sailors, and they will take care of you."

The flight continues southwest, and the cockpit crew continues quizzing Wagner as part of his training on his aircraft systems knowledge.

Unfeathering Number One

Early Afternoon
October 26

They reach the southern turnaround point by 1:00 p.m.—just as the day is about to reveal a few of its secrets. The weather at this location is worsening, and they encounter more clouds. They had been cruising along on three engines, flying between the cloud layers. They had flown along at varying altitudes and distances from the coast to record Soviet radar signals. The number one engine that had the minor propeller leak has been shut down for a couple of hours.

The weather is getting colder, and Grigsby, now in the right seat, makes the decision to restart the engine so that it will produce enough heat to keep ice crystals from building up and damaging the turbine. Caylor, also a fully qualified Patrol Plane Commander, sits behind Wagner on the forward radar cabinet, where it is warm. Wagner is flying from the left seat. He begins a slow descent from 7,000 feet to get below the clouds to avoid the icing conditions. Petty Officer Second Class Butch Miller, now in the flight engineer's seat, begins performing the required restart sequence and reporting each item as completed:

"Unfeathering number one." Both pilots look up automatically as Miller reaches for the red button above his head, pushes the guard away, and pulls the red button out to start the feather pump.

Wagner looks out over his left shoulder as the propeller blades begin to spin slowly clockwise and says, "Rotation."

Gibbons, watching over Ball's shoulder, says, "Hey, John, let's look outside because you never know what you're going to see." Restarting number one happens nearly every flight, and Gibbons is not expecting to observe anything out of the ordinary. This time, however, the propeller seems a beat slower than normal to rotate up to speed. They both assume it is due to the cold weather and think nothing of it.

The tempo of activity picks up in the cockpit as Miller, watching the number one tachometer on the panel of black-and-white gauges, says, "Propeller rotating normally," then, "Ignition," and, as he turns on the fuel and ignition switch, "Light-off" (indicated by the temperature rise inside the jet engine). Everything looks totally normal and routine as the turbine engine warms up at flight idle.

Caylor is standing behind Grigsby. The pilots turn toward the number one prop gauges as Miller scans the engine instruments again, announcing, "Normal start, number one."

Almost textbook perfection. Almost. Everything is fine at first as the restarted engine is warming up. Wagner advances the power lever to match the other engines, the engines and props make a quiet and steady *hum, hum, hum, hum* noise until that noise becomes slightly less steady. One propeller is a bit out of sync and doesn't sound quite right for a couple of beats, but then it goes back to the way it should be. Grigsby notices the change, something a less experienced pilot might not, and is instantly alert, watching and listening. His thought processes speed up while everything around him seems to slow.

The small rpm gauge of the number one prop reads 100 percent rpm—exactly what it should read. In three or four seconds, it twitches ever so slightly, then falls back to 100 percent rpm again. For the next minute, it continues up and back, climbing faster each time. This is highly unusual, indicating there is something different going on inside the propeller control system. Grigsby tells Miller, "If rpm gets to 103.5 percent of normal, pull the emergency handle."

The P-3 is a turboprop aircraft, designed to have fast spinning jet engines connected to large powerful propellers via a "reduction gearbox." The massive props are thirteen feet, six inches in diameter and weigh twelve hundred pounds. A series of shafts and gears reduce the propeller rotation to a constant speed with variable pitch. Power adjustments on the turbine engine change the blade angle to take more or less "bite" out of the air. The prop control mechanism is fully automatic, maintaining the normal propeller rpm at 100 percent as indicated by a small gauge on the instrument panel.

Unlike more-modern planes with jet engines suspended below the wings, the Orion has jet engines installed above the wings within a streamlined, aerodynamic nacelle (the curved panels covering the engine).

Grigsby is the Patrol Plane Mission Commander and in control, but he utilizes a collaborative cockpit management style, telling others what he is thinking and communicating so that everyone is following his actions while learning from them. If rpm reaches 103.5 percent of normal, it becomes a critical emergency. The propeller is not built to sustain that amount of twisting force, and the machinery will eventually break; there is nothing to be done except to try to figure out what is going on and attempt to correct it.

The cockpit crew watches the gauge indicating the prop's accelerating revolutions. When the gauge indicates 103.5 percent of normal, Grigsby orders, "Feather number one."

Miller says, "Check number one." Everyone in the cockpit

is looking to see that his hand is on the correct handle when he yanks the emergency handle straight toward him.

The turbine engine winds down and stops, but the propeller does not, continuing to spin faster and faster, passing through 129 percent of its normal operating speed, the highest the rpm gauge can indicate. The tips of the propeller blades approach supersonic speed. The cockpit crew watches in stunned silence, not comprehending. The practiced and predictable rhythms of the flight have just ended. None have ever seen this before, not in actual flight nor in the flight simulator, but their minds register there is a serious problem. At this rpm, the propeller could tear itself apart.

The sound of the runaway and nearly supersonic propeller has become deafening in the cockpit—a high-volume, staccato *ch-k, ch-k, ch-k* burst accompanied by a shuddering vibration. The nose of the plane lurches up somewhat while the left wing dips down. In an instant the cockpit crew members are thrust from doing their jobs in a predictable and routine manner into a deafening, vibrating, out-of-control experience. It is more than they can take in. Those in the back of the plane are largely in the dark about what is happening up front, although they realize something is far from normal.

Grigsby, shouting from the right seat, says, "I've got the aircraft!" He doesn't change seats with Wagner, and already recognizes that the runaway overspeeding prop has decoupled and is no longer connected to the shut-down engine. He knows instinctively that he must slow the plane, so he pulls back power on all engines, grabs the yoke in front of him with force, and plants his foot firmly on the right rudder pedal, pressing hard. Good pilots know they must aviate, navigate, and communicate, in that order. It is all he can do to aviate, to keep his mind ahead of the plane, and he is aware of this as he pulls back on the yoke to initiate a climb to slow down the plane even further.

Grigsby beckons Caylor toward him and yells into his ear. He is already thinking ahead to a possible emergency scenario and tells Caylor to get Wagner's helmet, but it isn't stored where it's supposed to be. Caylor is out of the cockpit looking for it for a couple of minutes.

The number one prop blades have violently slammed back to a picthlocked blade angle and are now windmilling at 25 degrees. They are no longer creating any forward thrust. The windmilling prop blades now create enormous drag, working against the other three engines, creating a huge amount of turning force to the left. The autopilot is useless. It is taking a substantial amount of physical effort to keep the plane on course and the wings level, and all the while Grigsby is thinking things through. His mind is racing. He is familiar with a similar prop-fails-to-feather situation, but the cockpit annunciator lights are telling a different story.

With a feathered engine and propeller, the number one prop pump warning light and number one oil pressure warning light should be illuminated, but they are dark just like the three good engines, suggesting that oil is still flowing within the reduction gear assembly. Grigsby's hours and hours of repetitive training channel through his subconscious mind in a blink along with all the practical knowledge gleaned during his years of flying. Even his recent instructor pilot training yields no clue to suggest what is causing the problem, and no known emergency scenario seems to fit these indications. Hours in the flight simulator have not shown this combination.

Normal conversation across the wide cockpit is impossible, so Miller moves over across the distance and puts his mouth up next to Grigsby's ear, yelling to be heard over the screaming propeller. Wagner is too far away, on the left side of the cockpit, and can no longer hear or talk to Grigsby. Miller's years of electrical expertise lead him to believe the problem is electrical; the cockpit indicators are signaling contradictory information. The indicators show oil is still flowing even though the emergency handle has been pulled out. No one else can hear the details of what the two are saying to each other, and Grigsby and Miller have a judgment call to make deciding what to do next after completing the emergency shutdown checklist. Do they jump ahead to the fails-to-feather checklist, or do they pause?

Grigsby initiates a climb to slow the prop by slowing the airplane. At 11,000 feet, the rpm of the number one propeller is still dangerously high at 115 percent of normal, but the plane has become somewhat stabilized at 150 knots (173 mph) airspeed, stall speed plus only 10 knots (12 mph), a slow speed more appropriate for landing. He next lowers the wing flaps, effectively increasing wing area and further reducing stall speed. The noise within the cockpit is reduced as well.

Flow, who had been eating lunch, races forward to the cockpit. He is the senior flight engineer and has a great deal of mechanical expertise. Miller turns to tell him that because he doesn't know what has gone wrong, he is not certain what would happen to the rpm if he were to reset the emergency handle. Flow tells Miller he isn't certain either, and no one wants to lose the little bit of control they seem to have.

Caylor comes back with Wagner's helmet and is unaware of decisions already made about pausing next steps. Not that it would matter anyway; he is just as puzzled as everyone else in the cockpit.

At 1:05 p.m. Grigsby orders everyone in the cockpit to fasten seat belts and put on helmets. Five minutes later, Grigsby's muscles are so fatigued from fighting the turning force that he says to Caylor, "Get your exposure suit on and take over as copilot." Once Caylor is ready, Grigsby tells him, "I need you to fly the plane. I know it's a challenge, but I'll show you how." After showing him, Grigsby says, "Your aircraft."

"My aircraft," Caylor acknowledges. Now Grigsby can focus his energy on the mental work needed for the situation. Wagner stays just behind them watching what is going on from a perch on top of the forward radar cabinet. He thinks his help may soon be needed as he watches how fatiguing the stress and strain of piloting is for Caylor and Grigsby.

When We First Met

*T*he phone continues to ring as I head toward the family room sliding door to go inside and answer it. I am still thinking about Jerry, and I remember when he and I first met. It was during the summer before my senior year of high school when I had dropped by to visit my aunt Bev, which I sometimes did to escape the chaos caused by my three little brothers and my high-strung mother. My hair was wound in pink curlers, I wore an old, faded pair of jeans, and I didn't have on any makeup because I didn't expect anyone else to be there. I was embarrassed when I arrived to see two college-age guys visiting with Uncle Bob, so I sat quietly on a swivel rocker listening to the conversation. Before long, I decided it was time to go home. Uncle Bob, who was a pilot for United Airlines, was trying to set the guys up with a couple of stewardesses, but Jerry wasn't interested.

The next time I went for a visit I made sure I was more presentable, my hair nicely done and some makeup on. The guys were there again, and this time I felt more confident and was friendly and talkative. After I left, Aunt Bev asked Jerry what he thought about her niece. He told her he liked her other, quieter niece better, and they had a good laugh when he realized it was the same niece. I still laugh when I think about this, even now. I usually tend to be the quiet version of myself. I guess he already had his sights set on me, but it was a couple weeks later before he asked me out.

Jerry and his friend Don had come to Seattle as part of a church-sponsored summer program to help with a fledgling Baptist church. In return, they would be given help finding a job and a place to live, and Uncle Bob was their sponsor. It was a great opportunity for two young guys from small-town Oklahoma to experience another part of the country.

Aunt Bev asked me if I could help with vacation Bible school. I was surprised because I wasn't Baptist. She said that didn't matter because I would be helping with art projects, serving snacks, and tidying up after the kids went home at noon. I decided I could do that because I was working part-time in the evenings in an infirmary at a retirement home and my mornings were free.

It was during Bible school that Jerry and I started talking and getting to know each other. We talked about books we had read, movies we had seen, hiking and camping trips we had enjoyed. He told me about how he liked being in the college musical Oklahoma, how he enjoyed the singing and the dancing. He was easy to talk to and always upbeat and pleasant. Then one day he asked me if I'd like to go to a movie with him, and things really took off from there.

In Extremis

Forshay, whose Navigator/Communicator (NAVCOMM) station is located across the tube from Ball and Gibbons, can't see the propeller from where he sits. The screaming noise of the propeller travels out and forward, and the cacophony in the cockpit is not as distinct at his station. He gets his first inkling as to the seriousness of the problem when Grigsby requests a divert heading direct to the Shemya Air Force Base, approximately 460 miles away. He glances around at Ball and Gibbons, but both men appear untroubled, their calm demeanor belying the fear they are just beginning to feel. Alfa Foxtrot 586 diverts from its PARPRO track as Grigsby turns the northbound plane to the right and veers east.

Gibbons and Ball continue to watch as the giant, four-bladed propeller spins uncontrollably just outside their observation window. Gibbons then spots something he knows the pilots cannot see from their position: a thin caramel-colored film of what he supposes is cooked hydraulic fluid streaming back from the black number one propeller afterbody onto the gray painted surface of the nacelle. The normal fluid is bright red, much like what you see in a car's automatic transmission, but this looks more like maple syrup. There must be a major leak somewhere inside the gearbox assembly, and the time has come to begin work on an encrypted message for Elmendorf Airways Radio, part of the Air Force Global Radio and Air Traffic Coordination Network near Anchorage, Alaska.

Using a manual encryption book, Gibbons, working with Ball, begins the manual encryption of their message into groups of three letters as dictated by the secure communication protocol due to their proximity to the Soviet Union. Adrenaline is kicking in, altering the perception of time. It's becoming difficult to maintain the level of patience and focus needed for flipping through the codebook. The noise level back in the heavily insulated tube is slightly quieter than in the cockpit; normal conversation is still possible, but even so, the encryption process is slow, tedious, and prone to error, each man verifying the other's work to be sure no mistakes are made in composing the message from the current glossary of words and phrases.

Using the NATO phonetic alphabet, the first message contains twelve three-letter groups: "India Hotel Tango, Lima Juliet Sierra, Victor Golf Bravo . . ." and is broadcast over the Skyking channel. It conveys the first report that they are aborting the mission. This message, when decoded by the Skyking watch team in Yokota, will say only: "Mission abort. Propeller malfunction 51 degrees 50 minutes north, 161 degrees 50 minutes east."

At 1:10 p.m. Gibbons and Ball notice a slight wobble in the arc of the propeller, which gradually worsens. Howie, sitting in the aft observer seat in the back of the plane, can see it as well. Gibbons fears the prop could tear itself apart, throwing one or more blades through the fuselage where he sits, yet his trust in routines practiced until they are automatic sticks even in this stressful situation. He remains outwardly calm as he reports the wobble over the intercom and follows up with a report to Elmendorf through the Skyking channel.

He trusts the cockpit crew to do their jobs, as he has been taught. He remains professional and cool. He has been called a cockeyed optimist in the past, but perhaps he is now in denial, numb to the extreme gravity of the situation. Grigsby, he knows, is among the most experienced of pilots in the squadron. He has even done a tour in the Naval Air Rework Facility in Alameda as a maintenance test pilot taking planes out after extensive overhauls. His faith and confidence in Grigsby are absolute.

Maybe they are all in denial. There is a pervasive air of calm throughout the fuselage. On the other hand, the crew members have all been through the Dilbert Dunker water survival drill, which simulates an airplane crashing into the water. Gibbons remembers being trained to brace for impact, to free himself from shoulder and seat harnesses, and to swim to the surface. He recalls his jitters as he sat in the mock cockpit anticipating the twenty-five-foot drop into the large, deep pool below. He remembers the key to success in that training drill was to learn to control his emotions and let his training take over, as he is doing now. No matter what the situation is, he has learned to control his response to it. He recalls the old Mark Twain quote about fear: "Courage is resistance to fear, mastery of fear, not absence of fear." Deep down inside he knows there is no place for fearful behavior onboard this aircraft today.

Minutes after the malfunction began, Gibbons orders the tactical crew to put on their Quick Donning anti-exposure dry suits in preparation for a possible ditching. A controlled ditching is the conscious decision to put the aircraft into the water. Apart from a few floatplanes and specially designed amphibious planes, most aircraft are not designed to land on water. With hundreds of miles to go, this last resort option is suddenly becoming very real.

The emphasis on ditching is ingrained throughout the maritime patrol community as these aircraft do not have ejection seats. On every flight, either a ditching or bailout drill is practiced. During overwater flights, P-3 crews prefer ditching over bailout as individual crewmen need to make it to their assigned place in one of three life rafts.

Gibbons can hear the discussions in the cockpit over the intercom and wants to be ready. Ball and Brooner distribute the protective packs, each containing a tightly rolled, water-proof, one-size-fits-all coverall. Most have never tried these on before, and an unpracticed dance of putting them on over baggy flight suits and heavy flight boots begins in the narrow aisle within the tube. They open Ziploc-style torso seams that run from the left shoulder to the crotch and force large boots through tight ankle cuffs one at a time, losing their balance as they press their boots into enormous booties. They put their arms into armholes, squeeze hands wearing fireproof gloves past tight rubber wrist cuffs, and finally slide-close the torso seal as they rush back to their ditching stations to put on their helmets and life preserver assemblies. Only then is the scripted harmony of teamwork once again restored.

Ball and Gibbons begin the slow and tedious work of another encryption, and fueled by a sense of impatience and frustration, Gibbons takes over radio transmission from For-shay, saying: "Fuck it! Let's go clear voice!" Unknown to him, his enormous bootie is caught on top of his microphone foot switch, transmitting his voice and the screaming noise from the prop out to the world, jamming the Elmendorf radio chan-nel with 1,000 watts of power. The keyed foot switch is now preventing anyone else from talking and making it impossible for them to hear Elmendorf's incoming radio calls. The noise of the overspeeding prop right outside his window and the internal static drown out any communication.

"Get off the mike!" he yells. "Get off the mike! I can't talk on the radio!" Looking down, he notices his own bootie over the foot microphone switch. Elmendorf Airways had tried calling back several times without success. When Gibbons moves his foot, the noise on the radio goes away and a reply from Elmendorf comes through asking if they are declaring an emergency. "That," Gibbons says, "is affirmative."

Now that Gibbons is doing the radio transmissions, it allows Forshay to focus his full attention on precise navigational updates. The roles of aviate, navigate, and communicate are now distributed to five people. The crew stations on the plane are interfaced to the same computer system and have access to the same readouts. Gibbons has instantaneous access to relevant information of location, course, speed, winds, and altitude:

"Elmendorf, Alfa Foxtrot 586. We're a Papa Three aircraft; we have a propeller malfunction at this time. Present position 52 degrees 22 minutes north, 164 degrees 30 minutes east. Our altitude is one one thousand feet, true airspeed 154 knots, ground speed 194 knots. We are departing direct Shemya. We are not in extremis at this present time."

Grigsby immediately cuts in on the intercom to say they are indeed in extremis— a situation of extreme emergency and possible death. His handling of the emergency has been done with such finesse and calm that Gibbons and the others are not yet fully aware of the magnitude of the danger.

Elmendorf radio frequencies are monitored by multiple Air Force and Navy communication stations in the Pacific region, operating through the Skyking network. Elmendorf comes back: "Requesting your souls on board forward and aft, forward and aft. How copy?"

Gibbons: "Ah, one five. I say again, one five souls on board. We're a Papa Three aircraft, over."

Elmendorf: "Requesting number of souls fore and aft, fore and aft, over."

Gibbons now realizes what they are asking. He assumed that they knew a P-3 had three cockpit positions, and the rest of the fifteen are in the back. He now realizes the distant Air Force radio voices have no idea what a P-3 is.

Gibbons: "Ah, Roger [I understand]. There are three souls fore [in the cockpit] and one two souls aft [in the tube]. Ah, thank you for your assistance, out."

Caylor takes over the stressful job of piloting again from Grigsby in the right seat. Wagner moves to the left seat and fills in as standby after they have put on anti-exposure suits, allowing Grigsby to put on his and walk through the tube to speak with each crew member individually. Passing by Gibbons, he says, "We're going home," as he gives him a reassuring squeeze of the shoulder. Gibbons overhears him tell Master Chief Shepard to take care of Hemmer once the aircraft stops. Master Chief Shepard tells Grigsby the tube is about as squared away as it can be. When Grigsby returns to the cockpit, he takes over the left seat; Wagner goes back through the tube to his assigned ditching station.

Grigsby and Caylor switch back and forth every ten minutes with the strenuous job of piloting the crippled plane. They fly along at a reduced speed to keep the windmilling propeller somewhat slowed down. At this rate, it will take them more than two hours to reach the US Air Force base on Shemya, which is much closer than Adak. They can communicate through the headsets in their helmets, and they are trying to figure out how much longer they can keep the plane in the air.

They can't do anything but head toward Shemya. Caylor now understands that there is no oil going to the propeller gearbox, even though the instrument panel lights and over-head gauges show oil is flowing. These lights are still not on, supposedly indicating there is no problem. Caylor now knows this is not accurate, and realizes Grigsby is aware of it too.

Erratic wind changes from minute to minute make the plane fly slower or faster. The crippled engine has no ability to de-ice and is building up considerable ice weight—possibly a thousand pounds by now—making it more challenging to control the plane. They climb and descend, go left and right to gain some control.

"Iron Mike" Harris, the Patrol Squadron Nine Detachment's officer in charge, is now in the TSC at Adak. They have just received news from Elmendorf with information that Alfa Foxtrot 586 has aborted its mission because of a major propeller malfunction, and he directs the Ready Alert crew to launch an intercept and escort flight to stay with them if they need to ditch their aircraft. For Lieutenants John Eger and John Watkins, the TSC watch team, the focus has shifted into search and rescue coordination.

Fire in the Sky

Thursday Afternoon
October 26

At 1:40 p.m. a fire alarm blares at earsplitting volume and is immediately silenced. Smoke drifts from the number one engine, and Miller pushes the button to direct firefighting compound on the overheated gearbox. The P-3 has one High Rate Discharge (HRD) pressurized fire extinguisher system per engine. In the event of a fire, there is a backup in the adjacent engine that can be transferred for a second chance. The fire goes out, but the wildly spinning propeller is certain to overheat again causing more fresh fires, and there is precious little firefighting compound left. Miller is beginning to feel shaky and tense. His palms are damp. He realizes he is trapped, all of them are trapped, and there is no place of escape out here on the edge of nowhere, no place at all.

> Elmendorf: "Alfa Foxtrot 586, Elmendorf."
> Gibbons: "Elmendorf, Alfa Foxtrot 586,
> go ahead, over."
> Elmendorf: "Roger, sir. I have an ATC clearance.
> You ready to copy?"
> Gibbons: "Go ahead."

He realizes that the Elmendorf Airways radio operator does not have a copy of their flight plan. On tactical missions, the P-3 typically flies "due regard," meaning that with their own onboard radar systems and a full-time radar operator, they need no additional clearance when they change course. They can go anywhere they choose. In this remote and isolated airspace, well below commercial airliners, they are not concerned about air traffic.

> **ELMENDORF:** "Roger, sir. ATC clears Alfa Foxtrot 586 direct Shemya via present position, direct Shemya. Maintain one zero thousand feet. Requesting souls on board. Amount of fuel and time. How copy?"
>
> **GIBBONS:** "Elmendorf, Alfa Foxtrot 586, Roger. We have one five souls on board. Approximately six hours plus zero minutes fuel, and we are presently at eight thousand feet. Trying to maintain eight thousand feet. Request you launch search and rescue aircraft to intercept us. We are presently heading 100 degrees true. Present position 52 degrees 28 minutes north, 165 degrees 16 minutes east. We are three hundred and twenty miles west of Shemya, and we are requesting you launch search and rescue aircraft at this time, over."
>
> **ELMENDORF:** "Roger, copy. Understand requesting an intercept at this time."
>
> **GIBBONS:** "That's a Charlie, Charlie. Thank you. Out."

High-frequency radio channels are subject to noisy static, fade-outs, and distortion as these messages travel over thousands of miles. As a result, radio communications are scripted and always repetitive, giving them an intense quality. It is vital that all involved understand each other fully. At least this ATC clearance informs Shemya to expect them if they can get that far.

Flow takes over responsibility in the flight engineer's seat so Miller can go back aft and put on his anti-exposure suit. Miller knows from his years of experience and training that the plane will never make it to Shemya, and he also knows the junior crew members are not aware of what he has just realized. He also remembers that even though the P-3 is perhaps the safest and most reliable plane in the fleet, it has never survived an open-ocean ditching emergency. It was derived from a civilian airliner and was never designed for a water landing.

Things are not going well for Miller. He was added on to the crew for this flight at the last minute. He had recently had a major quarrel with his wife, Karen, before he left Moffett Field for this detachment, and now he wonders if he will ever see her again so they can try and make things right. Dread grabs ahold of him. He feels like he is suffocating, feels faint and so overcome by his emotions that when Caylor looks up at him as he is leaving and sees his white face and agitation, he is concerned that Miller might be having a heart attack.

Caylor had quarreled with his wife, Barbara, as well. He had been paying tuition for her to get a law degree at Santa Clara University Law School, and had recently discovered she had spent massive amounts of money on illegal drugs, spending down their savings. The fuming frustration he felt before takeoff now erupts into a vengeful spite—a red-hot anger like he has never felt before. He is angry that he is stuck on this flight, with this broken airplane, contemplating a broken marriage. Then a motivating and energizing idea comes to him, and all the energy of his angry passion becomes focused on doing everything he can to get out of this situation alive. He will not have her receiving his death benefits. His plan is to get home as quickly as possible and try to straighten things out. He also feels a deep-down sorrow as he thinks about his beautiful wife, so intelligent and talented. How had it come to this? If he cannot work things out, he will file for divorce, but he won't have her receiving survivor benefits. All this he keeps hidden under his professional demeanor. He has his role to play. He knows Navy life is hard on family life, but still . . .

Miller makes a bit of a recovery and begins helping a small team finish stowing loose equipment into the head — the Crock-Pot, galley oven, coffeepot, other odds and ends — in preparation for a possible ditching, as directed by Gibbons, who has selected the HF radios on the internal public address speakers so everyone can hear that help is being summoned.

Meanwhile, Flow anticipates a second fire. One of the first things he does when he returns to the flight engineer's seat in the cockpit is to break the safety wire that protects the fire extinguisher switch. He also depressurizes the plane so that if it goes into the water the crew will be able to open the escape hatches.

Howie, watching from the aft observer seat, reports a second fire and panic grabs hold of Miller again. Miller's feeling of absolute terror becomes palpable, contagious even, and Ball starts to feel this terror for the first time while they work together.

Ball is aware that the P-3 Orion is not as bombproof as he and the others have been led to believe. His flight training friend, George Nuttelman of Patrol Squadron Eight at Naval Air Station Brunswick, had recently died in an accident when the number one engine and propeller assembly separated from the wing, causing catastrophic failure of the wing structure itself. The engine had gone up and over the wing, taking the wingtip with it. Debris also hit the left part of the tail. The aircraft spun out of control, crashing into the wooded Maine countryside.

Ball and Gibbons had been talking about the recently published preliminary accident summary just yesterday afternoon. Like many naive, confident, and invincible young aviators, Gibbons was convinced that would never happen to them because they had much newer airplanes, only two years old, yet here they were. He was stubborn and clung to the notion that the P-3 was still the safest aircraft in the fleet.

Gibbons sees sparks fly out of the nacelle and a bright yellow glow around the edges of the access panels. Flow directs the fire-extinguishing agent to the new fire. Now there is none left on that wing.

Grigsby knows the next fire could burn through the nacelle fire wall, spread to the wing fuel tanks, and cause an explosion to send the airplane spiraling uncontrollably into the ocean, killing them all. He is determined to keep the plane in the air as long as possible, get it as close to Shemya as he can to increase their chances of survival, but he wants all preparations for a ditching to be complete when the time comes.

Forshay asks Gibbons if they should begin shredding "crypto." Working in the squadron's communications department, he had completed extra training on communication security. "Yeah, let's get started on that," Gibbons says. "I'll take my TACCO bag to the back, and all of your logs, comm, and crypto gear."

Gibbons brings the TACCO bag to Ball and Miller. "Can you start ripping the classified pubs up? I'll have Reynolds install the free-fall chute."

"Roger that. We've got this," says Ball.

It eases Gibbons's mind to keep busy, to have tasks to keep his thoughts off the danger. Gibbons turns to Reynolds and says, "Hey, Dave, I want you to install the free-fall chute so we can dump our classified documents." Reynolds installs the free-fall chute, a hollow cylinder-shaped fiberglass liner that fits into the internal sonobuoy chute, allowing Ball and Miller to drop the shredded classified materials into the waves below.

"Mr. G., no problem. Do you want me to ripple fire all the sonobuoys?"

"Let me check with the flight station and get back to you."

Up in the cockpit Grigsby selects Search Stores Arm, the safety switch that will enable Reynolds to manually jettison the sonobuoys used for tracking submarines into the water as specified in the ditching checklist. The sonobuoy is a disposable aluminum cylinder with a walkie-talkie-style radio on top and an underwater microphone on the bottom. In the ocean, the saltwater battery activates the radio as the microphone descends to a preset depth.

Each buoy is blown out of its tube in the underbelly of the plane by a loud explosive charge—*BAM.BAM.BAM. BAM.BAM.BAM*—in six groups of eight. The rapid-fire noise of it is unforgettable. It sounds like an automatic rifle shooting in an indoor shooting range. Reynolds knows he will remember these sounds as long as he lives. In less than a minute, the aircraft is two thousand pounds lighter and more than $15,000 worth of buoys are hitting the water in a straight line tracing their course.

Grigsby carries on in the cockpit with calm, secure in the knowledge gleaned from his days of flying and landing seaplanes earlier in his career. He is confident that he can bring this plane down safely on the waves—can do it with the help of God. Bible verses memorized as a child flow through his mind—"Come, let us reason together . . ." He has been praying continuously ever since the emergency started. He has never landed a plane on stormy seas, but he knows the practiced techniques will hold true. He is looking forward to going home to his wife and daughters, who are always on his mind, and that thought strengthens his resolve.

They are now flying below the clouds. Grigsby continues a slow descent so he can put the aircraft in the water quickly in case the situation deteriorates further, and all through the descent he keeps an eye on the mountainous waves below. He is looking for the primary swell system, looking for the rhythm of the biggest and most powerful waves.

The published procedure for ditching a P-3 as described in the Naval Air Training and Operating Procedures (NATOPS) manual shows a diagram emphasizing the importance of putting the plane down parallel to those most powerful waves. Grigsby knows that would work well if the crosswinds were below 20 or 30 mph, but today they are gusting upward to 50 mph, with twenty-to-thirty-foot waves. The plane would disintegrate from the force of those crosswinds and waves even before it came to a stop.

His instincts tell him he must fly directly into the wind where the plane will be more stable to maximize control during the final seconds before water impact, but that puts the plane perpendicular to the larger swells. All the while, he relates his thoughts to the cockpit crew, proposing to impact the water with as little forward speed as possible and with a minimum rate of descent in the final hundred feet to minimize structural damage to the airframe. He is open to suggestion, but the crew is in complete agreement with his insights; they understand the importance of working together. They agree that this approach minimizes the chance of the aircraft catching a wingtip into the huge waves and cartwheeling into a spinning, flipping, disintegrating catastrophe. They don't have any idea what will happen after impacting the first wave crest. Nobody has ever tried this in a P-3 before.

Gibbons understands too that it is essential to continue broadcasting their exact position. It is a vast ocean out there, and they could become lost forever if the search and rescue teams can't pinpoint their exact location. Sure, Skyking is keeping an eye on them, but they don't have the means to monitor their precise, exact location, and their exact location is what is needed now. Skyking is out there still broadcasting their encoded rhythmic singsong messages every fifteen minutes—a practiced counterpoint to the dissonant melody playing out in the cockpit.

Mayday! Mayday! Mayday!

Thursday Afternoon

Approaching the Bering Strait

At 1:52 p.m. Gibbons reports they are ditching based on what he can hear from the cockpit:

GIBBONS: "Elmendorf, Elmendorf, Alfa Foxtrot 586, Mayday, Mayday, Mayday! Position 52 degrees 27 minutes north, 166 degrees 00 minutes east. Mayday, Mayday, Mayday! Alfa Foxtrot 586. We are ditching, ditching, ditching. One five souls on board. Three orange life rafts. Three orange life rafts. Over."

ELMENDORF: "Five Eight Six, Elmendorf, Roger, copy. Roger, copy."

GIBBONS: "Elmendorf, Elmendorf, Alfa Foxtrot 586. We are ditching, ditching, ditching. U.H.F.D.F., U.H.F.D.F. three four five decimal five. Three four five decimal five. We have three, I say again, three orange life rafts. We are two niner zero miles west of Shemya."

The aircraft is traveling nearly three miles per minute. Gibbons keeps glancing up at his display, reading the coordinates as they change. Each position difference of a mile could mean the difference between rescue and loss, the difference between life and death.

> **ELMENDORF:** "Roger, copy. Roger, copy."
> **GIBBONS:** "Position 52 degrees 25 minutes north. 166 degrees 8 minutes east. Over."
> **ELMENDORF:** "Roger, copy. Roger, copy."
> **GIBBONS:** "Request you relay nature of our emergency. We had a propeller number one . . . propeller . . . propeller number one overspeed. It would not decouple. Runaway prop. Engine fires . . . Position 52 degrees 26 minutes north. 166 degrees 10 minutes east. Position 52 degrees 26 minutes north. 166 degrees 10 minutes east. Position 52 degrees 26 minutes north. 166 degrees 10 minutes east."
> **ELMENDORF:** "Five Eight Six, Elmendorf, request you say again reason for number one, reason for number one propeller. Over."
> **GIBBONS:** "Roger, Elmendorf. Number one propeller. Runaway propeller on restart of engine. Propeller went overspeed, would not decouple, resulting fire in number one engine. Over."
> **ELMENDORF:** "Five Eight Six, Elmendorf, Roger, copy. Roger, copy."

Gibbons does not understand the exact nature of the propeller overspeed malfunction. The propeller has disconnected from the engine, but that is not important right now. There will certainly be a formal accident investigation later with a focus on the number one prop, and this radio call just set the agenda. In the event they do not survive, the investigators will have a defined starting point. What Elmendorf needs to hear now is that the crew is running out of options and fifteen men will soon enter the waves below.

The time has come to finish dropping the torn scraps of crypto and the classified materials out through the free-fall chute and into the ocean. Gibbons gives the order before continuing to update Elmendorf based on what he can hear from the cockpit over the PA system:

> "Elmendorf, Elmendorf, Alfa Foxtrot 586, revise our intentions. We are still proceeding direct Shemya. Will revise as our status changes, over."

> ELMENDORF: "Roger, copy. Roger, copy."
> GIBBONS: "New position 52 degrees 07 minutes north, 166 degrees 23 minutes east. Over."
> ELMENDORF: "Roger, copy. Roger, copy."

Grigsby continues the gradual descent so he can put the aircraft on top of the waves quickly when the situation becomes unsustainable. He wants to get as far from the Soviet Union as possible.

> GIBBONS: "It appears the number one engine gearbox has total failure. Over."
> ELMENDORF: "Five Eight Six, Elmendorf, Roger, copy."

Gibbons turns the radio over to Forshay so he can review individual ditching station responsibilities with each man in the tube.

> ELMENDORF: "Five Eight Six, Elmendorf. Have ATC request. You ready to copy?"

FORSHAY: "Roger, Roger, Elmendorf. Five Eight Six ready."

ELMENDORF: "ATC requests Alfa Foxtrot 586 verify inbound Shemya and level, over."

FORSHAY ANSWERS: "Roger, Roger. Alfa Foxtrot 586 is estimating Shemya at time 02:00 Zulu, and now at two hundred feet, um, I say, now at five hundred feet, five hundred feet and position 52 degrees 28 minutes north. 166 degrees 30 minutes east, over."

ELMENDORF: "Five Eight Six, Elmendorf, Roger, copy. Roger, copy."

Unlike a civilian airliner, the plane does not have rows of plush seats. Various industrial shades of matte gray dominate the plane's interior and minimize reflections on the various computer displays. The ten crew station seats are designed for both comfort and safety on long flights and are covered in orange mesh fabric with orange vinyl headrests and armrests. These crew station seats contain both lap and shoulder belts. Additional rear-facing ditching stations equipped only with lap belts are located back in the galley and on fold-down stations between the equipment bays.

Gibbons moves systematically from station to station throughout the tube reminding each man what he must do when the plane splashes down. He reminds each of them that Grigsby had been a seaplane pilot and has put planes down on the waves many times. He wants to reinforce an attitude of "together, we can do this." He wants to instill hope, reinforce an expectation, a confidence that this will be a successful ditch and they will get out of it alive. He is responsible for the safety of these men. He will take care of these sailors.

Each ditching station has a sticker with printed ditching duties specific to that position in addition to assigned exit routes. Gibbons reviews the assignments with each man with an emphasis on the roles they will perform when the plane comes to a stop. With their adrenaline- fueled focus riveted on him, he confirms the expected tasks. Gibbons emphasizes that Grigsby will set the plane down and he will get them out and into the three orange rafts. The tube crew is mentally "locked in" to what they need to do as soon as the aircraft stops.

Meanwhile Forshay continues radio updates:

> "Elmendorf, Elmendorf . . . Elmendorf, Elmendorf, Alfa Foxtrot 586. One minute to ditch. Position 52 degrees 28 minutes north, 166 degrees 35 minutes east, over."

> **ELMENDORF:** "Roger, copy. Roger, copy."

Gibbons hears Grigsby say over the PA system that they are going to level out at five hundred feet and continue heading to Shemya. Returning to his seat after completing the crew final check, he takes back control of the radio:

> "Condition has stabilized again. We're now at five hundred feet, position 52 degrees 29 minutes north, 166 degrees 45 minutes east. We're going to try to drag it on in to Shemya at this time. I'll keep you posted on ten-minute advisories or if our situation changes. Request verification that you have alerted SAR, over."

He knows that the Adak Ready Alert is on a one-hour standby, that it is the closest SAR platform, and he wants reassurance that they are getting the aircraft warmed up and on the way.

ELMENDORF: "Charlie, Charlie, Charlie, Charlie."
[affirmative]
GIBBONS: "Roger, Roger. Again, for SAR, we have
sonobuoy U.H.F.D.F. homing on frequency three
four five decimal five . . . Three orange life rafts,
fifteen souls on board, all wearing orange or dark
green anti-exposure suits."

Gibbons repeatedly broadcasts their location and what
the rescuers will be looking for, and then Forshay is back on
the radio:

"Alfa Foxtrot 586, still with you. Position 52 degrees
33 minutes north, 167 degrees 25 minutes east. I
report all electronics, all cipher gear. I say again all
crypto gear has been jettisoned or destroyed, over."

By now, watch personnel must be tracking the slow and
steady eastward progress of the flight as Alfa Foxtrot 586
gradually distances itself from the Soviet Union.

At 2:15 p.m. the Coast Guard command center in Juneau,
Alaska, through the Kodiak Rescue Coordination Center,
directs an HC-130H aircraft, call sign Coast Guard 1500, to
Alfa Foxtrot 586's last known position approximately thirteen
hundred miles to the west. Aircraft Commander Lieutenant
(junior grade) Bill Porter notes they do not have enough fuel
for the rescue event and heads his plane back westbound to
Adak for refueling. It will be several hours before they can
reach the crippled plane.

The P-3 Ready Alert crew at Adak, X-ray Foxtrot 675,
completes their briefing at about the same time and gets ready
to start engines. The search and rescue response accelerates, and
none too soon. Thirty-five minutes have elapsed and the clock

is ticking. Each branch of the military has its own process to initiate a SAR mission, and it takes time to respond.

Gibbons realizes their route to Shemya will take them closer to the ships they saw earlier in the patrol. Then he recalls that when he shredded his classified materials, he had also shredded his RAINFORM Purple mission summary report. That was the last record they had of the position, course, speed, and most importantly, the names of those two ships. Earlier in the flight, while demonstrating the TACCO display functions to Ball, they had deleted the computer radar contacts of the ships from the display because it was already written down in the RAINFORM Purple summary.

They must find those ships again. That is their best hope for a timely rescue. Gibbons remembers that one ship was Soviet and the other was Korean, but he can't remember their names. It really bothers him that he cannot remember; on some patrols, they could routinely photograph eighty or ninety ships, and today he can't even recall the names of only two. When Gibbons goes back to brief Garcia at his radar station, Garcia understands completely and responds, "Don't worry Mr. G., if the ships are out there, I'll find them." He's a good kid, Gibbons thinks. Garcia is a solid young radar operator. He has a bright future ahead of him.

A third fire triggers that damn blaring fire horn again, putting all nerves on edge. As a series of even more violent airframe vibrations shake the aircraft, Garcia is as good as his word. Their low altitude limits the radar horizon and the search radius that Garcia can scan, but he has found a ship hidden in the radar clutter caused by the huge swells. The ship contact is just behind them, less than ten minutes away.

In the cockpit, Grigsby has just taken back the exhausting work of piloting the damaged aircraft from Caylor. He sees the fly-to point on his tactical display indicating the ship's location, course, and speed, and rolls the plane immediately to the left, turning directly toward the ship just as the third fire blows itself out. Moore and Gibbons confirm no visible fire. Forshay provides updates on the wind direction and wind speed over the intercom. Garcia continues to call out the distance to the ship as Caylor spends the next several minutes trying to contact the ship on the VHF Guard emergency frequency and other radio channels, but to no avail. They have no other source for communicating directly with the ship.

Inside the Ready Alert aircraft on Adak, Lieutenant (junior grade) Dennis Mette goes through his final equipment checks at the NAVCOMM station and tunes a high-frequency transmitter to Elmendorf's frequency, calling up for a radio check. Elmendorf tells him to clear the frequency—it is for the Mayday traffic only. He stops transmitting but keeps one receiver tuned to listen in while waiting for his inertial navigation systems to align, a time-consuming essential pre-flight task. If unaligned, the systems cannot give attitude and heading information for the pilots or provide inputs to the computerized navigation system. He has friends on that distressed plane; he is impatient to get going. Time could make the difference between life and death, and the rescue process is unbearably slow in getting off the ground.

> GIBBONS: "Elmendorf, Elmendorf, this is Alfa Foxtrot 586. We are ditching. At this time, we are passing through five hundred feet. Position 52 degrees 30 minutes north, 167 degrees 45 minutes east. How copy? Over."
>
> ELMENDORF: "Five Eight Six, Elmendorf, Roger, copy. Roger, copy."
>
> GIBBONS: Elmendorf, there is a ship in the immediate vicinity within twenty miles of us. We believe

it to be a Soviet trawler. Elmendorf, Elmendorf . . . Request status of SAR aircraft, over."

ELMENDORF: "Five Eight Six, Elmendorf, stand by. Stand by."

THEN METTE TRANSMITS AGAIN: "Alfa Foxtrot 586, Alfa Foxtrot 586, this is X-ray Foxtrot 675, over."

GIBBONS: "Hi guys, this is Alfa Foxtrot Five Eight Six. Lieutenant (jg) Gibbons. Position 52 degrees 37 minutes north, 167 degrees 38 minutes east. We have one five souls on board. Three orange rafts. U.H.F.D.F. three four five point five. Our number one prop has dried up. It's vibrating wildly and we'll be going down in the near future, over."

METTE: "Roger, Matt. This is Denny. We're rolling on takeoff now. We'll be looking for you. How copy? Over."

GIBBONS: "Roger, Roger, Denny. We're two hundred and thirty-five miles west of Shemya. By our best guess, there's a Russian fisher-factory in the immediate vicinity, over."

ELMENDORF CUTS IN AGAIN: "Alfa Foxtrot 586, Elmendorf."

GIBBONS: "Elmendorf, Alfa Foxtrot 586, go ahead, over."

ELMENDORF: "Roger, sir. The intercept, ATC advises it is one zero minutes off Adak. One zero minutes off Adak. How copy?"

The SAR intercept aircraft has not taken off yet and Gibbons knows it, but he also realizes that everyone wants to pass along as much hope as they can.

GIBBONS: "Elmendorf, this is Alfa Foxtrot 586. Roger, Elmendorf. We just talked to them. Thank you so much. Our present position is 52 degrees 39 minutes north, 167 degrees 34 east, and we are ditching momentarily. All classified and crypto materials destroyed. I'll be talking to you as we hit the water, over."

ELMENDORF: "Five Eight Six, Elmendorf. Roger, copy."

Gibbons can see the glowing fire again—a fire that does not blow out. The fire is spreading now, burning farther back within the nacelle. Moore can see the fire from where he sits as well, a fire now combined with stronger, even more powerful airframe vibrations. The propeller is tearing itself apart. He is sitting alone and has no other assigned task beyond that of observer. He has less than a hundred total hours of flight experience in the P-3, and alone with his thoughts, he is scared, expecting the worst. Moore is so visibly agitated that when Reynolds notices, he leans across the aisle and yells, "Howie, it's okay! We'll party when this is over." Moore feels somewhat comforted and calmed by Reynolds's positive attitude and thoughtful effort to boost his morale.

GIBBONS: "And Elmendorf, this is Alfa Foxtrot 586. We are passing through three hundred feet. Position 52 degrees 40 minutes north, 167 degrees 29 minutes east. We've got a ground speed of one three zero knots [150 mph]. Time 0029 Zulu [2:29 p.m. local time]. We are preparing to ditch at this time, this position. We're about ten miles from a ship, over."

ELMENDORF: "Five Eight Six, Elmendorf. Roger, copy. Understand ten miles from a ship, over."

GIBBONS: "Five Eight Six. Twenty seconds to ditch. Position 52 degrees 40 minutes north, 167 degrees 25 minutes east. Position 52 degrees 40 minutes north, 167 degrees 25 minutes east. Position 52 degrees 40 minutes north, 167 degrees 25 minutes east.

Passing through two hundred feet. We have one five souls on board. Three orange rafts. And all personnel in either orange or forest-green anti-exposure suits. We are passing through one hundred fifty feet. Position 52 degrees 39 minutes north, 167 degrees 24 minutes east. This is Five Eight Six. Out."

His deep and resonant voice remains calm, steady, and strong in this final radio transmission. At this exact moment, the navigation and communication activities of the crew's emergency response are complete. It all comes down to trusting the three skilled aviators up in the cockpit to turn into the wind, slow the plane down further, and precisely line up to place it onto the waves below. For nearly ninety minutes, the pilots have wrestled with the excessive drag from the number one propeller as they fought to maintain control. For almost forty of those minutes, the flight officers have provided constant updates of their position and condition to everyone listening. For the rest of the crew, it comes down to taking their survival training, equipment, and hopeful mindset out an emergency exit. In more than sixteen years, and millions of flight hours, no P-3 crew had ever made it this far down the ditching procedure decision tree. Now the question remains: Can they survive the impact and evacuate the sinking aircraft in time?

Spirit in the Sky

Final Seconds of Flight

Moore keeps his eyes on the huge waves just outside his round aft observer window. He doesn't want to miss anything, but he fights against his instinctive reaction to close them in anticipation of the crash landing that he is certain will result in his fiery death. He works to slow his breathing. His mouth is dry, and he feels like he might throw up at any second. He silently prays to God for forgiveness, promising to live a better life if he survives. He knows he's not perfect, but he assures God that he can try to live a better life.

Up in the cockpit, Grigsby suggests that Flow leave the flight engineer's seat and go back to a ditching station in the tube where he might be safer and closer to a raft, but Flow chooses to stay where he is, watching everything. He wants to be available if help is needed. He grips the armrests so hard that he nearly loses feeling in his hands, and he thinks about his safety. He watches as giant waves get closer to the cockpit windows and decides to lower his seat and slide it back in its tracks as far as it will go. His seat is directly below the overhead escape hatch, and as he tightens his shoulder harness, he begins reciting the Lord's Prayer to himself.

Most of the men have no window at their ditching stations, and Wagner is even more isolated from the action, sitting between two large electronic equipment bays. Wearing his helmet, he cannot hear Gibbons or Forshay on the PA system. Reynolds knows the plane is still flying while he looks out his window at a giant dark wave. Moore is practicing opening his seat belt so he can get out as quickly as possible. Brave young men, all experiencing fear beyond any they have ever known.

Grigsby instinctively sets up the ditching as a flat, straight-in descent onto the water—wings-level and slightly nose-high. He flies as slowly as possible with an absolute minimum rate of descent, heading directly into the wind, and perpendicular to the primary swell system. As a team, the cockpit crew back each other up to ensure a wings-level water entry at an air speed slightly less than the published stall speed. In the final seconds of flight, there will be no need to alter course or maneuver, so they can get away with flying slightly below that stall speed.

The plan is for water impact at minimum groundspeed. Caylor continuously calls out altitude from the radar altimeter in a heavy sea state that changes with each wave. Flow calls out airspeed. Meanwhile, Grigsby focuses on maintaining the rate of descent that he manages to hold at fifty feet per minute. Groundspeed is now reduced to around 80 mph. Based on his seaplane experience, he sets up a fifty-feet-per-minute descent even though the textbook P-3 NATOPS ditch procedure is based on two hundred feet per minute. He wants to minimize impact forces on the airframe and to maximize the odds of survival in such an extreme sea state.

He prays ceaselessly for guidance while carrying on with assurance—God is working through him and in him, and he can sense the powerful energy of it. He knows that even a slight misjudgment can kill them all, but he maintains his focus. He is still in control and still flying the plane even as it skims across the top of a wave and then, as engines explode, smacks the next one with more force—a force that sends a searing pain through his arms and shoulders.

Smoke on the Water

After Water Impact

Flow feels his shoulder harnesses cutting into him. He feels as though he has been hoisted up face down into the shoulder harnesses, and thinks there is possibly in excess of two times the force of gravity pulling against him.

Wagner can feel that first slight impact, and then a rebound, and realizes the flight is over. The next impact is more severe as the plane hits tail first at approximately 70 knots (79 mph) groundspeed, slides through massive swells, and comes to a sudden stop against the forces of the sea. The entire cockpit submarines into the face of a wave. For a few seconds, the cockpit windshield is a wall of gray-green ocean; the glass stays intact as the cockpit section absorbs the punishment by crumpling to the left where it joins the cylindrical tube of the main cabin. This crumpling damage causes the observer window at the TACCO station to implode, hitting Gibbons on his left shoulder. Across the aisle at the NAVCOMM station, the observation window has instead exploded into the ocean and the navigation table has slammed into Forshay.

Reynolds sees a bright orange ball of fire outside his window as the starboard wing rips away, and he knows he is dead. Alfa Foxtrot 586 is down, stopped, and floating—for now—impossible! He is alive after all!

The underside of the aircraft ruptures, and cold seawater floods through two huge cracks beneath the fuselage deck. Icy water contacts "hot" energized electrical circuits and the cathode ray tube of the tactical display implodes, sucking the shards of glass inside. The vacuum tube suction is so strong it pulls Gibbons's glasses right off his temples and into the smoking, sparking hole.

Euphoria, adrenaline, and exultant energy fill the entire plane as the men scramble to complete their assigned tasks and exit. Grigsby has done it! He has beaten the odds. The cockpit windows have held, but water is flooding in through the cracked cockpit deck. Water levels are already knee-deep, and rising fast.

Throughout the aircraft, training kicks in; Flow is out of his seat and instinctively opens the overhead hatch before he is conscious of what he is doing. The cabin's air rushes out with a whooshing sound that reminds him of popping the top of a cold beer. He pulls himself to the top of the fuselage and Caylor is behind him, stunned by the impact. Grigsby is stunned as well, and fatigued beyond all measure by the physical and mental exertion of keeping the plane on track during the descent and water landing. The knee-deep, icy water helps clear his mind. He thinks he may have torn a muscle in his shoulder as the plane slammed into the waves, the pain is that great. Grigsby looks back toward the tube and sees men at the exits, and is only a few steps behind Caylor, who yells, "Great job, Mr. Grigsby!"

Gibbons is out of his seat, leaving his glasses behind in his smoldering display as water rises above his seat cushion, and yells, "Let's Go! Let's GO! Let's GO!" He sees Forshay, who had been alert and awake one second, and then dazed, out of it, and wedged under his tight lap belt. Gibbons slaps his buckle open and pulls him from his seat; the NAVCOMM worktable has broken apart, slamming against Forshay on his right side, injuring the full length of his back. Gibbons tells him to hang on his back and guides him to the starboard (right) overwing exit. By the time they get to the exit, the water level has risen from his knees to his waist.

Garcia, seated closest, is the first to arrive at the starboard overwing hatch. He removes the hatch, throws it into the ocean, unclasps the two life rafts stored next to it, and pushes them out the opening as he exits. In the waves, he struggles to open the package with the seven-man raft, and struggles again to get that raft inflated—his fireproof gloves are slippery from the jet fuel he swam through at the exit. Wagner is right behind him trying to find the jug of fresh water he has been told is stored nearby. He cannot see or feel it underneath the incoming torrent of seawater, gives up, dives out through the rising flood, inflates his life vest, and surfaces through a slick of jet fuel. He and Garcia are the first to get into the seven-man raft and begin helping Flow and the others get on board.

Electronic devices are sparking and smoking inside the tube, the emergency cabin lights have gone out, and equipment rack frames have cracked, their doors hanging ajar. Moore, sitting back aft and unable to see in the resulting darkness, runs forward straight into the aircraft's boarding ladder still upright in its storage position. He then continues forward in the direction of the port (left) escape hatch, hoping beyond reasonable hope that he can get out and into his raft.

Reynolds is buried under debris. Loose items that had been hastily stowed in the "head" in preparation for ditching slammed against the wall on impact, causing it to disintegrate. The entire wall hit him with force, and only his helmet has saved him from head injury. His parachute, still strapped into its plastic storage tray, slammed into his helmet. It shattered the clear plastic visor, leaving a jagged snaggle tooth sharp edge over his left eye. The hard outer shell of his helmet is cracked front to back. He clears the debris away just as the fuselage rolls slightly, allowing dim sunlight to reveal his overwing hatch.

Ball, who is even farther back at the galley table, which has collapsed around him, thinks he may have been momentarily knocked out; he calls out for Butch Miller who is seated the farthest back. There is no answer and he senses no one is there. He stumbles forward through the surge of incoming water, then turns back and calls for Miller one last time, getting his left foot caught in the jagged edges of a cracked floor panel, and thinks, *God! Am I going to be trapped in here?* Releasing his foot, he stumbles forward toward the port overwing escape hatch.

Throughout the length of the darkened and smoky fuselage, water floods in with increasing force. Moore reaches the port hatch ahead of the others and throws it into the water to get it out of the way, jumping in after it. Rodriguez works feverishly to release the portside seven-man raft from the tiny buckles that hold it in place near that exit. In the darkness, he is now bending at the waist with his helmeted face underwater trying to find and release the stubborn metal buckle on the lower strap. The flooding water mixed with jet fuel has made his gloves slippery, and he cannot find that tiny buckle. What started out as flooding from the cracked underbelly accelerates as overwing exits and the TACCO and NAVCOMM station observation windows slip underwater.

As the rushing water nears the top of the overwing exits, Gibbons sees that the situation with the rapidly rising water is beyond hope. He grabs Rodriguez by the back of his life vest, saying, "Come on, Randy, let's go," manhandling him across the aisle and shoving him through the starboard side hatch where there should be two rafts attached to the aircraft by their installed sixty-foot tethers.

Forshay experiences the same frustration as he struggles to release the small buckle on the lower nylon strap that holds the emergency sonobuoy in place. His effort is impeded by the slippery, standard-issue, fire-resistant Nomex gloves held firmly in place by the tight wrist cuffs of his survival suit, and by the impossibility of the rising flash flood. Water nearly covers the starboard hatch opening by the time he gives up seconds later. He pushes against the inrushing torrent as Gibbons boosts him from behind, swims through the opening, and pops up to the surface. Gibbons can see out of the corner of his eye someone exiting through the port hatch. Gibbons has been given a clear responsibility, has been assigned a burden of obligation to completely evacuate the tube, and he is determined to live up to that challenge. The ocean is surging in with unrelenting force, covering both overwing exits, as he dives underwater leaving the aircraft thinking he is the last man out of the tube.

He did not see Ball coming forward in the darkness from the galley, swimming through rushing water, barely keeping his head and shoulders up in the dwindling air pocket trapped in the top of the tube. Ball dives down and swims out through the port overwing hatch and into the freezing ocean convinced that everyone else is already out.

Ball surfaces and sees Grigsby on top of the aircraft kneeling, looking toward the back, counting heads, and the two make eye contact. Grigsby doesn't see his assigned raft on the port side and turns his attention to the starboard side.

Everything happens in an instant, and their well-rehearsed actions are instinctive. Ball is buoyed by air trapped in his anti-exposure suit, but he does not see the raft he thought would be there. Seconds earlier, he swam right past it; the raft is now deep underwater, held firmly in place by the stubborn lower strap. He inflates his vest, and all three men swim aft with difficult strokes through streaks of jet fuel. They are slightly protected from the waves by the sinking aircraft, which slowly twists in the swells as they head back past the tail and then around to the other side.

On the starboard side, there is utter chaos — howling winds, driving rain, and monster swells. Gibbons, who has not yet inflated his vest, asks Forshay if he thinks he can make it to the closer raft, and he is already pushing Forshay in that direction when he hears Forshay reply with a "Yes."

Off to his right, the larger twelve-man raft package, still in its storage duffel, is drifting away toward the tail. The raft tether to the aircraft has snapped. *Holy shit*, Gibbons thinks, *we're down to one raft. I have to catch it, or we'll all be gone!*

Adrenaline kicks in again, giving him strength and sharpened focus as he dives into and swims through a wave as tall as his townhouse back in San Jose. A confident swimmer, he heads toward the raft package as fast as he can. The small seven-man raft is already overloaded, and he plans to drag the larger raft back to the smaller one. Upon reaching the raft, he finds the weight of it, the winds, and the waves to be overpowering, way too much to drag it anywhere. He grabs hold of the tether and then inflates his life vest. He hangs on to the raft package hoping to slow it from drifting farther away.

The sinking aircraft itself is being pushed around by the wind and the waves, but it still provides a small degree of shelter to the rafts from the wind. Off to his right, Gibbons sees Ball, Reynolds, and Moore swimming around the damaged tail. Together they unpack and inflate the raft. They know what to do without saying a word. Their prior training kicks in; it is an automatic and instinctive response. Reynolds and Moore find a nylon web foothold, climb in, and then pull

Ball and Gibbons aboard. The fully inflated raft now really takes off, acting like a sail, pushed farther away by the winds.

They can see Grigsby kneeling on top of the sinking plane surveying the scene. It looks as though he is still counting heads before he scrambles aft past the damage and slides into the water. He is the last to leave the rapidly sinking plane.

Grigsby immediately inflates his life vest per his deep-water survival training and then swims toward them. He is swimming purposefully, the huge, inflated life vest lobes interfering with his strokes. Blown away by gale-force winds now that the plane is no longer shielding them, the rafts are skidding across the waves faster than Grigsby can swim. The Mark 12 raft has a light load of only four men, and with its eighteen-inch-high tubes, it blows away more swiftly than the overloaded smaller Mark 7 raft.

Grigsby is already exhausted from the physical and emotional stress of flying the final approach into the ditching. His arms ache and burn, something is wrong with his shoulder, and his progress is slower than it needs to be. Gibbons throws the raft's sea anchor toward him, but it falls far short. "Dear God," Ball cries out, "please save this man!" Gibbons points to the heavier, slower-moving raft and sees Grigsby turn toward it. The last he sees, Grigsby is almost there and men are in the water pulling the raft toward him while Flow throws him a beacon.

"Looks like he's gonna make it; he's in good hands," Gibbons tells Ball before everyone disappears behind a giant swell as the wind and waves drive the rafts farther apart.

Events of the past two minutes have played out in a blur, and in a matter of seconds, life-and-death decisions have been executed. The crumpled plane sinks completely below the waves, leaving only distant steam clouds and smoke where the hot engines had met the cold Pacific.

Meanwhile back at Moffett Field in California, squadron leaders begin planning how to break the news to the rest of the squadron. Commander Powers returned to the squadron spaces from the Tactical Support Center, called in his wife Paula, and held an ad hoc meeting with his department heads. Referring to a binder of how to communicate after an aircraft mishap, a detailed plan of who, what, and how to notify the families of all Adak personnel was quickly prepared and the formal notification of next of kin was initiated.

Cindy's Phone Call

Base Housing, Moffett Field
Evening, October 26

Cindy Mette was waiting for a phone call from Dennis; he had written her in a letter that he would be calling her on the evening of October 26. She had put the kids to bed a bit early and was looking forward to his call. When the phone started ringing, she jumped up off the sofa and ran in the direction of the phone, anxious to hear his voice. This was his second rotation to Adak, Alaska; she was lonely, and she couldn't wait to hear his voice.

When she answered, it wasn't Dennis's voice . . . strange. Who was this man, and why was he calling her? "Hello, this is Lieutenant Commander Dave Loop from the squadron."

She knew Dave, so she said, "Hi, Dave, how are you?" As soon as she said that, her heart started racing because she knew Dave wouldn't call her in an official capacity unless he had bad news. Her stomach started turning flip-flops, and she wondered what was wrong.

Dave immediately said, "VP-9 has a plane down in the Aleutians and we have survivors in rafts."

"Where is Dennis?" Cindy asked, her voice quavering.

Dave started apologizing, "Oh, Cindy, I am so sorry. I did that wrong. Dennis was not on that mission, but he is on the search and rescue flight. He is fine, but very busy now." Dave went on to ask her not to call any other squadron wives.

Cindy had never been told not to call other squadron wives and asked, "What! Why?"

"We don't have a complete list of the survivors yet, and until we know who the survivors are and who didn't make it, out of respect for those families, VP-9 asks you to allow us to contact all wives first. At this time, we are notifying the families of Adak personnel who were not on that flight to reassure them."

Cindy was left to wonder and worry—not for herself, not for Dennis, but for her friends, the other squadron wives who would soon get the dreaded phone call no wife ever wanted to receive.

Riders on the Storm

The men are euphoric, and Matt Gibbons is amazed the ditching has gone as well as it has. He is aware he is the senior officer in this raft, but even so, the raft lends a feeling of closeness and informality, more so even than on the airplane, and he automatically slips into using first names. They are alive and relatively safe, secure in the knowledge that the crew made it and cautiously optimistic that help is on the way.

They are already feeling nauseated from the jet fuel/seawater mix they couldn't avoid swallowing as they left the airplane. Maybe some of it is seasickness. Howie Moore is throwing up over the side. The raft is being driven by the wind up and over one side of a twenty-five-foot wave, and then it slides down on the other side, creating a natural rhythm—up, over, down; up, over, down; up, over, down . . . On the way down, the waves shower the raft with streaks of foaming spindrift.

Matt and the others look around to see what survival gear they have onboard. They locate the homing beacon and want to be sure they activate it correctly because it will aid in the rescue they know is on the way. This is critically important now because they had not been able to release the emergency sonobuoy with its ultrahigh-frequency radio—U.H.F.D.F. three four five decimal five, the one Matt had mentioned repeatedly on the radio with Elmendorf. Matt and John Ball follow the step-by-step instructions on the PRT-5 survival beacon, inflating the donut-shaped flotation collar, putting it in the water, carefully extending the antenna to its full nine-foot height, double-checking everything, and securely attaching it to the side of the raft.

Howie, who must have swallowed more jet fuel than the other three, is so sick that he is unable to help look around to see what else is available to work with. He wants to help, he wants to contribute, but he can't seem to manage it. Dave Reynolds finds the raft cover with a wedge-shaped flap, but the supports to hold it up are missing. They decide to put it up over their heads and zipper it in place for some small measure of protection against the wind and spray, and by then Matt is throwing up, and within minutes they all are.

They continue digging through a side pocket of survival supplies. Each item they find is tethered to the inside of the pocket by lengths of 1/16-inch-thick white nylon braided cord that becomes tangled as the raft rolls up and over the swells. John notes it looks like they are sitting in a giant pile of spaghetti. Matt says, "Yeah, this is out of control. I'm going to use my shroud cutter to cut off anything I think we can use." He uses a short length of cord to attach a signal mirror and flashlight to the straps of his life preserver. Other items such as dye markers, a fishing kit, sunscreen, space blanket, and leak repair kit he stuffs back into the side pocket. It keeps his mind off their situation to stay busy, so he keeps himself entertained for the next several minutes by slicing the cord into small chunks and tossing them overboard. They all wonder the same thing: How much longer will it take for the ship to pick them up?

In Our Hearts

Almaden Valley
Evening, October 26

*T*he continued ringing of the phone brings me back inside the house.

"Hello, Ken Smith here . . . Would it be okay if Sara and I stopped by for a few minutes?" He doesn't say what they want, and I don't ask. Ken is a fellow Lieutenant Commander in the squadron, and he and Sara are friends who live just a couple blocks away, so maybe they want to borrow our tall ladder again.

The sense of foreboding I experienced earlier comes back, and I feel that chill again. I'll build a fire in the fireplace and make a fresh pot of coffee—that should cheer me up.

The doorbell rings and I invite them in, offer them coffee. We sit on the love seats in front of the crackling fire, and after thanking me for the coffee, Ken gets to the point: "There has been a successful ditching in the Bering Strait after a propeller malfunction . . . men in life rafts . . . looks like everyone is accounted for . . . rescue ships on the way . . . don't want you to worry."

Shards of glass pierce my chest and static fills my head as I'm starting to remember random pieces of thoughts from the past, thoughts brought back by Karen's words earlier, thoughts that I had long ago stuffed down to the deepest, darkest recesses of my mind. I am aware that I am miss-ing bits of what Ken is saying. I'm starting to shake but am hanging on to his comforting comments about a successful ditching and rescue ships on the way. I take a deep breath, and then another deeper one, attempting to control my emo-tions. How many times have I done that this evening? Ken said he didn't want me to worry, I remind myself—but what's he saying now? "Sara said she would like to stay with you while we wait for an update."

It's almost time for the girls to come home from their marionette class. Things must seem as normal as possible for them; I can't have Sara here. "No, thank you," I say. "I need to go pick up the girls from their 4-H class. I'll be all right. Just let me know as soon as there's an update. I'd really appreciate that."

I say goodbye. My legs are shaking, giving way, and for the second time this evening, I sink into a chair fighting back tears. I can't stay here alone and I can't have Sara here. I compose my face and head out the front door. Wisps of fog are drifting past, softening the sights and sounds of the eve-ning, and the air has a chill to it. I don't usually pick up the girls because their class is just across the quiet street, but it will be all right. I can have them show me what they are working on. The cold air will give me a reason for the shivering that I haven't yet been able to control.

The Todd home is warm and cheery, just what I need. Everyone is excited about the marionettes, and they want to tell me all about them. They have made two marionettes each and are at the point of attaching strings. Karen shows me how hers works; these marionettes look amazing! They have embroidered faces, yarn hair, and cloth hands and feet. They will soon be putting on a performance, and I tell them I can't wait to see it.

I make hot cocoa when we are back home, and sitting around the kitchen table, I tell my girls in the most matter-of-fact manner that I can muster about the ditching. "Nothing to worry about . . . all are in life rafts . . . rescue ships on the way." Their faces are earnest, and they seem more thoughtful than scared. I want to send them to bed with hope, so I tell them this might mean their dad will come home early, and their faces brighten. They are used to having their dad away, but they do miss him, more than they have words to tell. I remind them of something their dad had said before he left: "When we can't be together, hold me in your heart where I will stay forever."

He is in our hearts; his love and influence will always be a part of us.

Time Is Too Slow for
Those Who Wait

Evening in the Life Rafts
October 26

Time drags on. The wind continues to chill them as the effects of adrenaline wear off. Matt finds the inflatable hood that came with his anti-exposure suit. He puts it on and thinks it helps retain body heat, but every time he vomits, he is concerned he is losing more of that precious heat. The others wear their flight helmets and have not yet found their inflatable hoods. Matt hadn't been able to find his helmet this morning before they left Adak (was it only this morning?), but now he thinks the inflatable hood offers better heat-loss protection from his head and neck than a helmet.

The raft is taking on water from the spray and the waves. Dave takes off his helmet to bail water, and they take turns bailing from the flooded raft, but Howie is still too sick to help much. John and Dave are beginning to feel better as time passes. John starts joking with Howie to get his mind off his nausea: "Howie, I've figured out what you're going to do when you get out of the Navy. You're going to become a great car salesman because you're so good at saying, 'Bu-ick . . . Bu-ick . . . Buick.'"

John gets the laugh he was hoping for; Howie is smiling weakly. Then they start talking about the ship Rich Garcia had found on the radar just before the ditching. Matt is convinced they will be picked up within three or four hours since the ship was within ten miles. They are in good spirits, hopeful, and still cautiously optimistic. The lowering sky is heavy and gray, visibility is limited, and occasionally they catch a glimpse of the other raft as it crests a wave in the distance. They feel relieved knowing everyone is safe. Together they wonder how overcrowded the smaller raft is and how everyone is faring.

The driving rain, peppered with snow and sleet, finds its way under the tarp. The men are sitting in chest-deep water, the adrenaline is wearing off, the anti-exposure suits are starting to leak along the Ziploc seams, and they are exhausted by sustained stress. They can't find the small cans of fresh water they have been told would be in the raft, but in their survival vests they each find packets of coffee-flavored Charms candy, which help rid the taste of vomit. They also locate their pencil signal flares.

The chill deepens, body temperatures plummet, and energy levels sag. They are all still hopeful, but there isn't much else they can do except bail water and wait, and wait, and wait some more. Every once in a while the raft is hit by a stronger swell and they fear it could capsize, so they stretch themselves out full length, bracing one side tube with their backs and the other side with their feet. John and Matt are at one end of the raft, and Dave and Howie at the other. They are quiet and introspective, each alone with his thoughts.

The early Aleutian evening is coming on and they have been in the raft about ninety minutes when they are shocked to hear a giant Air Force jet passing overhead at low altitude, less than five hundred feet above the water. This plane, an RC-135 strategic reconnaissance jet, is designed for high-altitude surveillance where the air is thinner and its jet engines work best. Peering through the cover, it is surreal to see it flying so low. Matt and John shoot each other a knowing look and chant, "Skyking, Skyking." They suspect it is an Air Force PARPRO mission aircraft redirected by Skyking.

Bruce Forshay had done a dynamite job of navigating and pinpointing their accurate position. The homing beacon they had tethered to the side of the raft continues to signal the world that survivors launched a raft, and now the RC-135 can accurately confirm their latest location as they drift along, pushed by the wind and waves.

The toughest job in search and rescue is to locate survivors, and now they have been found more quickly than any of them had reason to expect. The plane flies over several times, and each time Matt or John shoot off a pencil flare. Then within the hour, a P-3 comes racing into the SAR location after establishing a safe transition altitude with the Air Force jet. It is Crew 11, the Adak Ready Alert plane. This is X-ray Foxtrot 675, the same plane Matt had talked to just before ditching. At first, all Crew 11 can see are streaks of jet fuel and they are disheartened to not see the two rafts that the Air Force said were there. Matt is relieved that they have been located so quickly. On a subsequent pass, Crew 11 finds the rafts, and the plane rocks its wings to show the rafts have been spotted. This will certainly speed up their rescue. Now for sure the men in the rafts and in the air have renewed hope that everything will soon work out.

The RC-135 climbs up and away as the P-3 continues to circle over the rafts at low altitude. The sky is becoming darker and the air colder as night comes on. The men in the raft take turns shooting flares toward the plane every thirty minutes or so while they continue bailing water. They suck on the coffee-flavored Charms found in their survival vests. Time drags on. They do not want the plane to lose sight of their location, and though they don't talk about it, they are aware morale is beginning to ebb as they wonder why the rescue ship has not arrived. They have been in the water well over three agonizing hours by now, and Matt knows that Jerry Grigsby put the plane down very close to the ship Rich Garcia had located on the radar.

They begin talking about how they really must pee, trying to wait for rescue, and finally Matt can't wait any longer as he feels the heat of his urine burning along his thighs and is relieved to know he still has feeling in his legs. He is losing the battle to retain precious body heat. He is freezing cold and soaking wet. His hands are almost numb. In response to the cold, their bodies are shutting down the blood circulation to their extremities. Amazingly, the P-3 drops a SAR kit precisely next to their raft. They are exhausted and weak and the SAR kit package is big and heavy. It contains supplies they can use, but they are now weak enough that they can't maneuver it over the side and into the raft, so they tie it to the side and leave it floating in the water.

A mile or more away, the men in the seven-man raft are facing dire conditions. The overcrowded raft means they sit on top of the orange tube perimeter, locking their legs across the center of the raft floor. They have no covering of any kind for their raft and only a single space blanket to share, so they take turns holding it over their heads for some small measure of protection. They alternate trying to use the space blanket to bail the icy water and dye marker mix from the raft with little effect. With temperatures falling and winds steady at 45 mph, gusting to 50, they are experiencing windchill in the low single digits. Their helmet visors cover their foreheads and eyes, leaving their cheeks, noses, and chins totally exposed to the frigid air and spray. This windchill on their exposed faces is excruciating, their soaking wet faces feeling raw. No matter how hard they try, it is difficult to get their hands to work. One chamber in their raft is slowly leaking air, and they have lost the battle of bailing to keep out the seawater.

At the sinking end of the raft, Master Chief Shepard is focused on keeping Gary Hemmer awake and alert. He has been trained that "to sleep is to die," and he won't let that happen to his invited guest. At the other end, Ed Caylor is trying to coax Jim Brooner into staying awake as well.

The cold wind is relentless. They all are fighting to stay awake, to fend off sleep, as their core body temperatures plummet into the hypothermia danger zone. They are drifting in and out of consciousness, exhorting each other to stay awake and stay alive. As their body temperatures continue to decline, they are shivering nonstop; it is now an unrelenting battle against time. As the shivering subsides, they experience the "umbles"—mumbling and fumbling. Their extremities experience reduced blood circulation as their brains attempt to preserve body heat for their hearts, lungs, and brains. They still have hope that rescue will come soon, a hope that is reinvigorated as a Coast Guard HC-130H arrives on scene. It sounds like a P-3, but they know what it is because its lights are different. In the darkness, the C-130 drops a large twenty-five-man SAR package to the men in the MK7 life raft. The nine men in the smaller raft do not see it.

Matt can see the C-130 from his raft as well, through the opening in the cover over his raft, as the P-3 climbs up and away. The HC-130H is a version of the C-130 cargo plane, which has been equipped for search and rescue. John shoots another pencil flare, and the plane rocks its wings and is gone. It becomes ominously quiet on the big dark ocean with no

plane overhead. What the hell is going on? For an extended
period, no aircraft are over the raft. Chilled to the bone and
dehydrated from lack of water, their mental acuity is fading
fast, their legs feel like stumps, and they have only limited use
of their hands.

Matt and John become engaged in a humorous, rambling,
almost incoherent discussion about their predicament in order
to maintain consciousness. Their meandering conversation
leads John to a mental image of the movie *Animal House*, with
John Belushi dressed in a sheet at a fraternity party, when,
from a fog of despair, he starts a feeble chant: "To-ga . . . To-ga
. . . To-ga . . . To-ga." Belushi had used that chant to rally his
dejected fraternity brothers, and now the chant is growing in
strength and rallying the four men in the raft. "Toga, Toga,
Toga" becomes a mantra for the four of them. Somehow, the
absurdity of it and the will to survive revitalize them all a bit
as they wait for rescue.

Howie notices a sparkling luminescence in the water
inside the raft and wonders where it is coming from. The tarp
covers them and no moon or starlight is leaking through, so
he wonders if the others see it. "Look at this," he says as he
wrings water from his flight gloves, which are held firmly in
place by the tight-fitting wristbands of his exposure suit. John,
Dave, and Matt are amazed at the amount of sparkle falling
from the gloves. John thinks it could be bioluminescence. Matt
wonders if it is coming from the dye marker they had stored
in the side pocket, which could be seeping from the package.

It is now Matt's turn to shoot a pencil flare, but his hands
are so numb that he doesn't have the coordination or dexter-
ity to manually screw the flare cartridge into position on the
launcher. This must be loaded one at a time with the firing pin
cocked to the safe position. Out of desperation, he puts the
small cartridge in his mouth and spins the launcher between

his stiff hands onto the screw-in base. He risks firing the round through his mouth and out through the back of his head, but the importance of keeping the HC-130H apprised of their position is so foremost in his thinking that he doesn't have a thought for his personal safety. With his perception of time skewed by adrenaline, he thinks he has been in the icy water for six or more hours and is just trying to hold on until rescue, *which will come soon, won't it?*

The anti-exposure suits they wear have continued to leak around the heavy-duty Ziploc-style slide closures. These suits have been tightly folded and rolled up for space-efficient storage; they have been stored for months like this, and where they have been folded, permanent creases have developed. Those creases have become weak spots that give way to let in the cold water. Now the water level inside the suits reaches chest high and the ice-cold water being held against their skin is excruciatingly painful. An uncontrollable shivering takes over as their bodies attempt to create some warmth.

As the cold continues its assault on their senses, Matt is trying to find a way to put mind over matter and begins to sing the Foreigner song "Hot Blooded":

"Come on, guys, sing it with me," Matt urges.

After a few verses, John is laughing, Howie rallies and shoots a smile, and Dave looks across the raft and says, "Mr. G., you better stick around the Navy awhile, 'cause you can't sing for shit." They all crack up and get a great laugh out of it. For a few moments, it takes their minds off the cold and darkness that surround them.

It's now Howie's turn to watch through the flap. It has been maybe seven or eight hours since the ditch, and he is expecting to see a rescue ship. He thinks a rescue ship is long overdue, in fact. Light appears in the distance and he yells for Dave to come have a look, but the light has disappeared by the time Dave peeks out. "Dunno, guy, you may be seeing things," he says.

As the raft crests the next wave, they both see light in the distance again, and again the light disappears. They all take turns watching over time, but, despite their hopes, the disappearing light doesn't seem to get any closer.

Radio Waves and Time Zones

Thursday Evening
October 26

When Gibbons sent his urgent first plain-voice message to Elmendorf at 1:33 p.m., he had unknowingly triggered waves and ripples of radio traffic on global military channels. Within minutes, search and rescue preparations were beginning in Adak, Juneau, Kodiak, Shemya, Anchorage, and Fairbanks. Across thousands of miles of the "Last Frontier," Navy, Coast Guard, and Air Force operations centers were buzzing with activity and crews were gathering to improvise rescue plans. Now it's a race against time.

At 2:15 p.m. Coast Guard 1500 was setting up its approach, preparing to land at its home base on Kodiak Island, when they were diverted and assigned to this search and rescue case. They immediately turned around and headed back to Adak for more fuel and an updated briefing. It had taken the Coast Guard forty-two minutes of confused communication to assign the case to them.

At 2:25 p.m. the Ready Alert crew of the VP-9 detachment, X-ray Foxtrot 675, had established direct radio communications with Alfa Foxtrot 586 through Elmendorf's frequency.

The aircraft had been on a one-hour standby, and the crew was racing to get everything warmed up for takeoff. That was when Mette told Gibbons they were rolling on takeoff and Gibbons replied with their location and mentioned that he thought a Soviet trawler was in the immediate vicinity. X-ray Foxtrot 675 then departed Adak carrying a hastily loaded SAR kit at 2:32 p.m. Their launch was fifty-nine minutes after the initial radio request.

At 2:30 p.m. Alfa Foxtrot 586 executed a controlled ditching 235 miles west of Shemya, 500 miles from Adak, 1500 miles from Anchorage, 1350 miles from Kodiak, 2500 miles from Juneau, 2241 miles from the North Pole—literally the middle of nowhere. After the ditching, the men had no means of communication other than pencil flares and a homing beacon should a ship or a plane come within range. The emergency sonobuoy and the second seven-man raft with its two-way radio had gone down with the aircraft.

At 2:46 p.m. Scone 92, a Strategic Air Command RC-135, a large Air Force reconnaissance jet, was launched from a Hot Alert Standby on Shemya. The already warmed-up aircraft was unplugged from its support systems and was on the runway within five minutes of the Klaxon sounding. Sixteen minutes after the ditching was confirmed, they were airborne. The crew assumed the alert was for an incoming Soviet ballistic missile test and headed for the Kuna impact area in northern Kamchatka. The Scone 92 pilots, Captains Cliff Carter and Bob Rivas, raced north as they climbed across the Bering Sea toward the Siberian coast where they normally set up their monitoring activities.

A few minutes later, they were briefed in flight about the highly unusual change of plans. They were now assigned to a search and rescue mission, and they turned southwest toward the unknown and unfamiliar open ocean of the North

Pacific. They carried no North Pacific airborne navigational charts; it was not an area where they ever planned to fly. Their navigators, Captains Bruce Savaglio and Gordy Alder, began improvising navigation charts by hand. Scone 92 would not analyze the incoming Soviet missile that afternoon. This missile reentry would be tracked by other very highly classified "National Technical Means."

At 2:55 p.m., twenty-five minutes after the ditching, the TSC at Adak sent an official Operational Report (OPREP) message going to the highest levels of the military that the P-3 aircraft, call sign Alfa Foxtrot 586, had conducted a controlled ditching. This message alerted military commands worldwide, including the Pentagon. It was a Flash Precedence Pinnacle message addressed to the National Military Command Center in the Pentagon. A long day was about to become a longer night for hundreds of personnel beginning the overnight watch around the world.

Back at Moffett Field, the phones were ringing off the hook as the National Military Command Center was on the line seeking confirmation that the plane was down and that a Soviet ship was thought to be nearby. Commander Bud Powers began working the phones with Adak to get the latest ready-alert updates and to request additional help from the Coast Guard. He placed a call to the Naval attaché in Moscow, waking him in the middle of the night. Captain Anthony Bracken agreed to wake up US Ambassador Malcolm Toon, to brief him in advance and to get started with a request for assistance if any survivors were found. Within a few minutes, the ambassador called and had numerous questions about the crew, its mission, and the fact that it carried no weapons that could be used against the Soviet Union. Ambassador Toon reiterated that he wanted to have all the relevant facts before he spoke to the Soviet Minister of Foreign Affairs, Andrei Gromyko.

When Scone 92 reached Alfa Foxtrot 586's last known position at 4:10 p.m., they went into a search pattern of ever-expanding circles; the Air Force crew felt a sense of kinship with the men in the rafts. This type of accident could happen with any military plane, although none of them wanted to think about it. The weather on scene was terrible with huge waves, low clouds, rain, strong winds, and limited visibility. At 4:18 p.m. copilot Rivas reported a flare two miles away, and there was an immediate feeling of exhilaration for every man aboard the plane. They flew over that area and saw no raft. They flew over the area again and saw another flash of orange, and then one raft. A strong beacon signal came from their left side, and they were able to locate a second raft.

As soon as Scone 92 confirmed that there were survivors in two rafts, communications activity accelerated dramatically, expanding well beyond Alaska. Scone 92 was equipped with one of the first airborne satellite communication systems, enabling high-speed communication to the entire US military. Suddenly, the airwaves were spiking with traffic from the Fifth Air Force in Japan, Strategic Air Command in Omaha, Commander in Chief Pacific Fleet in Hawaii, the Pentagon, the National Security Agency, and the National Military Command Center in the Pentagon. Operations center watch personnel around the world had dozens of questions, and the crew of Scone 92 had very few answers. One surprising question from the Chairman of the Joint Chiefs was "Is the aircraft still afloat?"

However, three specific items of key information were passed along: that there were survivors actively signaling in rafts, precisely where the rafts were located, and that there was a Soviet ship in their vicinity. Each branch of the service had a unique set of protocols based on its principal mission, and the tidal wave of questions was overwhelming, confusing, and distracting. This ditching was an unusual event in a highly sensitive area, and nothing in anyone's experience made it clear precisely what rescue step to complete next.

At 4:40 p.m. Scone 92 and X-ray Foxtrot 675 established VHF radio communication with each other and developed a safe transition to avoid a midair collision. Scone 92 climbed to a high altitude where it was designed to fly while X-ray Foxtrot 675 descended, assuming on scene search and rescue command. Lieutenant Pat Conway, Mission Commander of X-ray Foxtrot 675, radioed Scone 92 to search for a surface ship in the nearby area.

Somehow, there was a misunderstanding in their communication. Scone 92's navigation radar had been malfunctioning and a radar search was not possible. All their sensors were designed for very high-altitude search for incoming missiles. The Operational Commander at the TSC in Adak assumed that Scone 92 had gone on to conduct a radar search looking for a possible rescue ship. His Navy-centric P-3 based SAR experience led him to believe that would happen, and confusing communications continued.

Scone 92's crew remained at high altitude in the area, and refueled in-flight. The emergency alert tanker aircraft was launched from Eielson Air Base near Fairbanks, adding another five hours for Scone 92 to provide near-continuous communications updates to the Pentagon, Elmendorf, Omaha, Hawaii, Juneau, and Skyking.

At 4:45 p.m. X-ray Foxtrot 675 overflew the rafts, dropping sonobuoys to help track them later in the approaching darkness.

At 5:13 p.m. Coast Guard 1500, an HC-130H, returned to Adak for an updated briefing, a full load of fuel, and some snacks. They had already flown a daylong fisheries patrol and were looking forward to heading home to Kodiak when they were diverted for the SAR case. They departed Adak, fully refueled, at 6:10 p.m., racing at max power to arrive on scene at 7:38 p.m. in total darkness to assume the position as the low-altitude SAR On-Scene Commander.

X-ray Foxtrot 675 climbed up to begin expanding its radar coverage and started searching for the possible Soviet fishing ship. Earlier they had refused to leave the rafts, even though they had become aware that no one was actively locating the rescue ship. They thought it was vital to monitor raft locations in the ever-changing weather, fearing that if they lost sight of the rafts, they would never be able to find them again on the inky darkness of the ocean.

Back into the Storm

Within an hour post ditching, senior officials in the Departments of Defense and State, as well as staff members of the National Security Council, quickly came to agreement that the Soviets should be asked to help. It was 9:30 p.m. Eastern Daylight Time when Ambassador Marshall Shulman of the State Department sent Ambassador Malcolm Toon at the US Embassy in Moscow a personal Flash Precedence message. It stated simply that he was asking Toon to contact the Soviet Ministry of Defense and seek rescue assistance for downed US aircraft personnel, and added that a Soviet vessel was understood to be in the vicinity. He underscored the urgency by stating that little daylight remained at the ditching site. Shulman got an answer back from Moscow that the Ministries of Foreign Affairs and Defense were contacted at 5:30 a.m., Moscow time, two hours after the ditch. The Soviet Navy was notified as well.

Captain Anthony Bracken, the US Naval attaché, ignoring protocol, called the Soviet Navy's command center directly to seek the duty officer's help. There was reason to doubt that the

Soviet Union would cooperate because the United States had flown PARPRO missions off the coast of the Soviet Union for more than thirty years, and it was likely the Commanding General from the Far Eastern Air Defense District knew what type of mission Alfa Foxtrot 586 had flown. Soviet attempts to shoot down or disrupt these flights in the past were well-known. Patrol Squadron Nine itself had lost a plane, shot up by two MIG-15s in 1955. These PARPRO flights had become less provocative over time, but were still daring and bold. On the other hand, just a few years earlier, the US Navy had rescued Soviet seamen who had been adrift for two months, and perhaps this could be viewed as an exchange of goodwill.

Remarkably, the Soviet ministries coordinated quickly, alerting military air and naval units in the area. The Ministry of Fisheries located ships at sea close to the site, made radio contact with them, and passed on the appropriate orders to start the rescue attempt. The MYS *Synyavin*, a three-hundred-foot-long Russian fishing trawler, among others, was contacted by radio from Vladivostok at 7:00 p.m. Aleutian time. It received an urgent call from the Far Eastern Fisheries Association relaying instructions from the parent ministry in Moscow for all ships in the area to proceed to the ditching site and assist in the rescue effort.

The MYS *Synyavin* was the ship Garcia had found on radar just before the ditch, and the same ship that Gibbons had told Elmendorf about in one of his last radio contacts. The *Synyavin*, however, had not seen the plane go down, had finished fishing in the Bering Sea, and for the past four and a half hours had been heading westerly toward a Soviet port on the southern end of Sakhalin Island to off-load their catch.

The homeward bound ship had only been able to advance twenty-five miles in the stormy weather, but now it had to turn around and head back into the storm it had been trying to outrun. The *Synyavin* was the best chance for the survival of the men in the rafts. It was the only ship close enough to save them from death by hypothermia. It was now an urgent race against time; the closest US ship was over thirty hours away and headed to their position. So, when the men in the rafts wondered what was going on and why they hadn't yet been rescued, this was the reality of their situation.

A Skyking message relayed by Scone 92 came through for search and rescue flights X-ray Foxtrot 675 and Coast Guard 1500 instructing them to light up the exterior of their aircraft so any possible ships could see them. Just before 8:00 p.m., Petty Officer John Hampel, the radar operator aboard X-ray Foxtrot 675, called out a radar surface contact thirty miles west of their position. Coast Guard 1500 continued watch over the rafts while X-ray Foxtrot 675 flew circles over the ship desperately attempting to find a way to communicate. Their P-3 was not equipped with commercial VHF FM radios designed to communicate with merchant, cruise, or fishing vessels. Their VHF AM radios were designed to talk only with other aircraft and military ships.

They were also at "Bingo Fuel" (critically low on fuel), and they would need to head for the closest US air base at Shemya almost immediately. Forced to fly at much lower altitudes than normal to avoid icing and keep an eye on the rafts with all four engines running had dramatically increased fuel consumption. As they flew over the ship, the flight engineer flashed Morse code with the landing lights, flashing C-E-F, which signified "aircraft in water—follow me." They knew the lives of their friends depended on making this basic communication connection and felt a measure of relief when the ship acknowledged their signal with a searchlight.

The ship was already headed in the general direction of the rafts, but it was a dark and vast ocean out there and "general direction" was not sufficient to guarantee rescue. The pilot, Lieutenant Ron Price, flew over the ship at a low altitude repeatedly, pointing directly at the rafts. Well past the prudent limit of endurance, their fuel state critically low, they had no other choice but to head directly to Shemya. Before leaving, X-ray Foxtrot 675 passed information on to Coast Guard 1500 about the ship's location, course, and speed.

Meanwhile, in a dim corner of Naval Station Adak's shared communications center, Coast Guard Petty Officer George Bruhl was standing the evening watch equipped with a government-issued green logbook, a teletype machine, and a Morse code key. A routine shift of broadcasting updated weather reports to fishing vessels in the Bering Sea was about to change. When informed of the ditching, Bruhl called in his supervisor, and together they were able to establish a manual Morse code direct communication link with the MYS *Synyavin*, Morse address UONW. Furious barrages of dots and dashes between the trawler and Adak confirmed that the ship was heading toward the rafts, and further, that the weather on scene was worsening. The *Synyavin* reported that barometric pressure was dropping, winds were increasing in intensity, and swells were building in height.

Around the world, the number of people helping with the rescue attempt was increasing by the hour and everyone involved was hoping for the best outcome for the men in the rafts.

Coast Guard 1500, now alone on scene, dropped marker buoys and flares to mark the position of the rafts, and then flew in an oval racetrack orbit every few minutes between the ship and their markers. They had been trying to make radio contact and finally got through on VHF FM channel 16, a standard commercial shipboard channel. The radioman, however, did not speak English, but a second man had some ability. Bill Porter told him: "Men in the water. Course 090 degrees at twenty-five miles. Please go."

They exchanged names. Manislov was the name of the Russian. "Bill," he said, "we go. Who in water?"

Porter wanted to be careful. He did not know if the Soviet ship would risk its own crew to attempt the hazardous rescue of Americans in the dark and tumultuous ocean. He said, "Manislov, friends in the water. Please go."

"I understand, Bill."

Porter was flying back and forth in a low-altitude oval orbit between the ship and the rafts, renewing the flares in the water and laying out a string of flares to guide the ship.

"Manislov, you speak good English."

"Thank you, Bill. Bill, how far?"

"Course 090 at twelve miles."

"Bill, you speak good English too." Porter laughed. That bit of comic relief heard by the crew was good for everyone; it helped ease the tension they were all feeling in the aircraft.

It was just after midnight when the ship approached the rafts. Porter asked Manislov if the ship could turn on all exterior lights and sound the foghorn. Manislov understood about the lights but not the horn. The lights came on. "Manislov, horn please."

"Bill, Bill, I do not understand. Speak slowly."

Porter's response was a clear "honk, honk, honk," with more laughter in the background.

"Okay, Bill. I understand."

The men in Gibbons's raft had been seeing lights for what seemed like a couple of hours, but the lights never got any closer. They had been in the water perhaps eleven hours and wondered if it was all in their imagination. Maybe they were hallucinating. They took turns looking through a narrow opening between the tarp and the wedge-shaped flap. If they heard an airplane, they would shoot off a pencil flare, and by now they were down to their last two or three. Howie was in such poor condition by this time that he wasn't talking or moving very much. How much longer could they hold on?

It was Matt's turn, and he thought he saw a light, a bright steady light moving toward them. He had John and Dave look, and then they heard the foghorn. This was not their imagination playing tricks anymore! Seeing the ship brought some energy back to them and gave them hope. Matt put the small flare cartridge in his mouth and spun the launcher between his stiff, numb hands onto the screw-in base. It took him an agonizing five minutes or so to make the launch.

The red flare flew up in front of Bill Porter's plane. "Bill, Bill," the *Synyavin* called, "we see."

Captain Arbuzov of the MYS *Synyavin* began to carefully maneuver his ship. The high-powered spotlight swung around, momentarily shining directly on the raft, giving the men a jolt of adrenaline and hope. John, who was dangerously close to unconsciousness, perked up and sang out, "You light up my life!" thinking of the Debby Boone song.

He passed Matt a marker flare, capable of red on one end and smoke from the other. Matt, kneeling by the slit in the tarp, his right arm raised up like the Statue of Liberty, lit the red flare end, intending to throw it in the air at the top of the next wave. He heaved with all his might, thinking it might go up ten or twenty feet above the waves. He was in such a weakened state that it went up only about three feet and was extinguished by the next wave, but the ship had seen it anyway.

Suddenly, it seemed like the ship was right there about a hundred feet from the raft, positioned like a giant windbreak, and at a near stop. Sailors were lowering a motorized lifeboat down the side onto the towering waves.

Matt could hear the men calling out instructions in what sounded like Russian over the deck loudspeaker. "Oh, oh, gents, it sounds like we're going to the Soviet Union!" Deeply ingrained memories from their shared SERE (Survival, Evasion, Resistance, Escape) survival training surfaced in his mind. They had all experienced the type of treatment they could expect if captured by a Communist country. They had experienced it so realistically that no one wanted to go through that training ever again. They knew all about the interrogations they could expect.

Dave spoke slowly and with effort. "Ah doan care. Ah'll nevah say anathin' bad 'bout those guys agin," his deep Carolina drawl coming through in his exhausted state.

Matt wondered to himself if he would ever see home again. The Soviets must certainly know they had been gathering intelligence on a PARPRO mission along their coast . . .

After Midnight

October 27

They watched the motorized lifeboat, illuminated by bright spotlights from the main deck of the huge fishing vessel, bob up and down in the towering waves until it came alongside their raft. A large, burly sailor leaned over the tall side of his craft to the low-slung raft and grabbed John Ball by the harness of his life preserver, lifting him up against the action of the waves and dropping him into the small boat, where he fell over. The sailor then grabbed him again and dragged him to the back of the boat, throwing him onto a slat seat that ran along one side of the lifeboat, taking off his helmet in the process. John wasn't sure what was going on and didn't know what would happen next.

The fisherman took off his own coat and put it around John. It was in that moment that John realized that man was intent on saving his life and there was no way he was an adversary; he was a rescuer.

Another strong-armed man grabbed the listless Howie, who was near death, by his survival vest. Howie couldn't move his arms or legs, couldn't pull or push himself up, and it took the help of a second man to drop him next to John. They repeated this feat twice more, and all four men were aboard, seated along one side of the lifeboat, keeping each other propped up.

A third sailor made a cautious and skillful maneuver with the boat around the tangled mess of their raft and the SAR package, which were left behind, and headed carefully through the enormous waves toward the second raft. Directed by the MYS *Synyavin*'s spotlights, the second raft looked to be about two miles away. A sailor named Vladimir, from what they could gather, gave each of them a lit cigarette. Matt took his oval-shaped Lockheed P-3 1,000-hour lapel pin from his name tag patch and handed it to him as the only way he could think of to show his thanks for this show of concern. Matt, not a smoker, took some puffs and thought the smoke helped warm him; the nicotine gave him a jolt of energy.

The small lifeboat made slow progress through the waves and the pelting rain, guided along by the bright spotlight of the fishing vessel. Matt's shaking hands were still of little use, yet he was able to take out the shroud cutter from his survival vest and slice small drainage slits near the ankles of his survival suit. Ice-cold water began to drain out into the bilge of the lifeboat, but he could not feel it leaving his suit because his legs were still numb and stump-like.

He turned to John and said in a quiet voice that they needed to think up a story about the "routine training mission" they had been flying and get everyone on the same page. They were afraid of their rescuers and what might happen to them if the truth was known. Their core body temperatures were dangerously low, and their minds were not working well. They talked about it during the thirty or forty minutes it took them to get to the other raft—which seemed like forever— their words slow and halting, and their bodies still shaking.

When they came alongside the second raft, Ed Flow was the first lifted on board, and the very first thing he said after he saw who was there was, "Where's Butch? Did he make it to your raft?" At that instant they realized no one had seen Butch leave the airplane. John, who had been momentarily knocked out and trapped by debris, had called out for Butch a couple of times, but when there was no answer, he assumed he was already on his way out in the rapidly rising water and darkness. Butch was Ed Flow's friend and fellow member of the close-knit brotherhood of flight engineers. Matt's heart sank as he realized Butch did not exit the aircraft.

Gary Hemmer and Master Chief Shepard, the two guests, were placed in the lifeboat next, and both looked dazed and out of it. Bruce Forshay was deposited next to Matt, who was relieved to see that Bruce was okay; John Wagner and Ed Caylor were both put on the bench facing him. Ed was so weak that he had to be hauled out of the raft by something like a lasso. He was relieved to hear Russian voices, and not North Korean voices. Matt asked about Jerry Grigsby, but Ed, who was very close to death, said only that he did not make it to their raft.

Matt pieced the story together from what others said that Jerry had been swimming awkwardly toward the raft, got within about six feet, and yelled out for someone to throw him a line. There was no heaving line in the raft, so Flow improvised by throwing the tethered radio beacon, but a wave knocked him off-balance as he threw. The tethered beacon fell short. By the time Flow could kneel and throw the beacon again, the raft was much farther away and the tether couldn't reach Jerry.

Randy Rodriguez, Jim Brooner, Rich Garcia, Ed Caylor, and John Wagner went over the side trying to pull and push the raft to Jerry while others paddled with cupped hands.

Bruce called out steering directions because they could not see where the raft needed to go. They all became so cold and exhausted that they needed to be helped back into the raft. They had made no headway against the strength of the wind and the waves.

The distance between the raft and Jerry steadily increased until they lost sight of him. In his debilitated state, Jerry was no longer swimming and was holding both hands above his head, perhaps to be seen in case they were able to make their way to him, perhaps to relieve the pain in his arms and shoulders.

"Oh my God!" Matt said. "This can't be happening." He was having difficulty processing this new information that not just one man, but now two, were lost.

When three more men, one at a time, landed onto the floorboards between the seats, it flashed through Bruce's hypothermic mind that they had been roughed up and that interrogations were already starting.

Bruce was shocked by the lifeless faces of Randy, Jim, and Rich staring back at him. Less than twelve hours earlier, these same three young men had gone back into the ocean to try to get the raft closer to Jerry. Bruce had not realized that they had died of exposure moments before rescue, so dim was his own awareness, as he was drifting in and out of consciousness. Matt was now totally devastated at the loss of five of his crew.

Ed Caylor was mumbling about something, but Matt could not hear what he was saying over the noise of the diesel engine as the lifeboat turned back toward the mother ship.

The lifeboat motored alongside the MYS *Synyavin* for the dangerous task of being hoisted up to the main deck while lurching about in the turbulent sea. The *Synyavin* provided something of a windbreak, yet with all the jostling about, it seemed the two were bound to collide. Somehow, though, the lifeboat was attached to pulleys, and at the top of the davits, it was locked in place. The men were lifted out of the lifeboat one by one. Matt staggered along the deck on his own, some feeling just starting to return to his legs. Other survivors were assisted or carried into a small dining area. Some of the Russians out on deck cast startled glances in their direction; they must have appeared like alien beings in their survival suits, deflated life preservers, and bits of dangling gear.

Some of the female crew, who were on board to help with cooking and laundry, helped them out of their survival gear, flight suits, and other wet clothing, and wrapped them in warm blankets. They took the survivors' temperatures using Celsius thermometers placed in their armpits. In Fahrenheit, they all had temperatures well below 90 degrees, dangerously close to losing consciousness. Meanwhile, throughout the ship, the male crew members were busy working their shifts processing fish fillets or sleeping in their bunks.

Each survivor received a ceramic mug of hot tea with honey, and after a few minutes, they were taken to a steamy shower area. Bruce was moving stiffly and complaining of soreness from his injuries; Gary Hemmer seemed listless and weak, but after about half an hour in the steam everyone was beginning to feel better. Wrapped in woolen blankets, they were led back to the utilitarian cafeteria area with its rows of metal tables for a second mug of tea and honey and some freshly baked whole wheat bread with butter. To the survivors, it seemed that no bread had ever tasted better!

Manislov, the English speaker from the earlier radio transmission, came in and asked, "Who is senior here?" Ed Caylor hadn't thought about that until asked, and then realized it was him. "Your friends in airplane are leaving. You may send short message." Ed, taking charge as the senior officer present, drafted a quick situation report sent by voice to the departing aircraft:

"Grigsby lost at sea. Miller lost with aircraft.
Brooner, Rodriguez, Garcia bodies recovered.
Gibbons, Ball, Forshay, Wagner, Flow, Reynolds,
Moore, Shepard, Hemmer, Caylor—alive. Caylor."
This message was transmitted to Coast Guard 1500
via VHF radio.

Later that evening, the Morse code message Adak received
from the *Synyavin* read:

"Have thirteen members aboard. Three of these are
dead. Two others lost prior to pick up. Brooner,
Garcia, Rodriguez dead. Miller died with aircraft.
Grigsby lost at sea while trying to board raft."

The *Synyavin* crew rounded up some of their own
clothes for the survivors. They found beds in the large sleeping compartment, with bunks stacked three high, and covered
the crew with more warm blankets. Temperatures taken again
showed improvement. It was apparent that the *Synyavin* crew
knew all about hypothermia recovery. Most of the survivors
crashed and fell asleep as their body temperatures continued
the gradual climb back closer to normal. Bruce, Howard, and
Gary were kept in the ship's sick bay for closer observation.

Sometime in the middle of the night, Gibbons woke up
to pee and was relieved to feel his legs and arms returning
to normal. The bathroom had a ceramic squat toilet fixture,
which caught his attention. Every time the ship plowed into
a big wave, the toilet drain contents would surge up into the
floor pan but not overflow. On the way back to his bunk,
he passed by a porthole. He could tell that the ship was still
moving ahead at a deliberately slow pace, scanning the huge
waves using spotlights; he assumed they were still searching

for Jerry Grigsby and Butch Miller, but how anyone could survive these waves for more than sixteen hours in this cold was beyond him. Matt doubted they could ever be found in these mountainous seas, and his thoughts ran to their families.

After dawn the next day, the survivors were in better shape. Bruce still complained of a sore back, Gary still seemed somewhat out of it, but everyone's extremities were working the way they should, and they all had a chance to talk. The ship was still proceeding at a slow pace, indicating that the daylight search must still be on for Jerry and Butch, and it seemed no one wanted to give up hope.

The crew was served a breakfast of hot tea with honey, more of that delicious whole wheat bread with butter, and a liquid yogurt drink (which some thought was sour cream) that tasted pretty good when a little sugar was stirred in. Then their flight suits and other articles of clothing were returned to them, all freshly laundered, folded, and in good condition. John Ball noticed the pictures in his wallet were out of sequence and wondered who had looked through it and what they were trying to learn.

As they got dressed, they continued to work on the details of their "routine training mission" story. Since they had three pilots, three NFOs, and two guests on board, the story seemed plausible, but since they were planning to tell lies to the Soviets, they knew they had to get every detail worked out. During these conversations, it came out that Gary was on a daily epilepsy medication and needed more of that medicine. The *Synyavin* transmitted out another quick message in Morse code.

Throughout Friday morning, the *Synyavin* continued searching at a slow speed in the area where the rafts had been picked up; the storm continued to worsen, and the seas grew even higher. Then later that afternoon, engine speed increased and the ship departed the search area heading west toward the Soviet Union, and toward an uncertain future for the survivors.

Some of the *Synyavin* crew taught John a friendly card game called "Durak" where the objective was to get rid of cards by somehow outranking the next person. One of the Russian fishermen led him through the rules. The last person holding cards was the Durak, the fool, and that person was John; he had to get under the table to humble himself, which he did. John won at "War," but when he told the fisherman it was his turn to get under the table, he immediately left the room with the others following him. The incident was never mentioned again, but John found it interesting and rather ironic to be playing War with the Russians.

On Saturday morning they could see a Soviet Krivak-class frigate less than a mile away slicing through the waves with ease as the *Synyavin* continued slogging its way toward the Soviet Union. When the *Synyavin*'s engines suddenly slowed about an hour later, Matt, concerned about the frigate, went over to look out the porthole and was surprised to see a Coast Guard HC-130H with the distinctive orange stripe. It was flying in a circle around both ships, making a lot of propeller noise as though to attract attention, and on the next pass it dropped a bright orange container from the ramp at its tail. Matt had never heard of an HC-130H flying this far west, well beyond the Aleutian fisheries patrol area, deep into the PARPRO zone.

A lifeboat was lowered from the *Synyavin* and went quickly to retrieve the floating orange package. Almost as quickly as it had been lowered, the lifeboat was back on board and the *Synyavin* was once again under way at cruise speed. Later, Master Chief Shepard told them the HC-130H had come from Adak with a special delivery of epilepsy medicine for Gary Hemmer. How far west had they traveled, and how had a Coast Guard plane managed to get so close to the Soviet Union?

The survivors were welcomed to eat dinner with the crew on Saturday evening: borscht, baked chicken, bread, and tea. All was friendly and congenial with limited conversational ability but lots of smiles all around as they continued closing in on Soviet waters. "You from California, eh? You been to Hollywood, seen movie star?" And who better then fun-loving John, who had once lived in Pasadena, to tell them he had glimpsed Marlon Brando going into a restaurant once, and from a distance thought he had seen Yul Brynner with his distinctive bald head. They were treated with the upmost in hospitality and no one felt otherwise.

After dinner, they were asked to stay and watch an old Russian black-and-white movie with the crew, *Battleship Potemkin*, as darkness fell. Then an announcement came over the PA system. The only words Matt could make out were "Petropavlovsk Kamchatski." He thought this had huge significance because the MYS *Synyavin* was not based there and Petropavlovsk was the home port of the Soviet Pacific Fleet submarines, and a closed city. He knew the Soviet coast-line well from his hours and hours of looking at navigational charts, so he was aware that this was the closest logical port for drop-off. The *Synyavin* crew, however, listened with only mild detachment as they continued to watch the movie.

The survivors gathered their things after the movie. So far they had been treated well and wondered how it would go when they were handed over to the Soviet military. Matt's nervous system was working on "high alert," and as the ship's engines slowed down, he went to the porthole to see if he could recognize any submarine shapes in the darkness. He was grieving lost crew members and to compensate he wanted to observe everything he possibly could in hopes of reporting it if and when they ever returned home.

Precious and Few

═══════════════════════

Almaden Valley

October 27

I *wake up to the ringing of the phone. I can tell by the faint light of a foggy dawn that it is still early, and after a fitful night of tossing and turning, I have had little sleep. Ken and Sara called me again after the girls were asleep to assure me they were here for me and to tell me to please let them know if I wanted or needed anything, and to also reassure me they would let me know if there were any updates.*

This call is from Ken and he says there are no new updates. He wants to be sure I am still feeling okay. I tell him that I am fine. Sara is available all day to come over at any time if I would like. I have a dull headache and everything seems unreal, has a dreamlike quality, like what is happening has little to do with me or with real life. I feel disconnected from my emotions, but I don't say anything about that. Ken goes on to ask if I have told Jerry's parents about the ditch-ing, which I have not. In fact, I have told no one about what is going on. He says the media has been informed of what is happening, and it will soon be on the radio and television news, and in the newspapers. He thinks the Grigsby family would probably rather hear the news from me personally. I agree, so I call the family home and tell my mother-in-law what I know. I also pass on the bit of hope about the men in the rafts that Ken has given me.

I wake Mary and Lisa for school and explain a little about what is happening. I am careful what I say because I do not want to upset them any more than I have to. I give them a choice about going to school, and eleven-year-old Mary, who loves school, decides to go. Nine-year-old Lisa, who will use any excuse to stay home, decides to stay home, and I decide to stay home from my classes at San Jose State as well. Mary walks the few blocks to school with her friends like any ordinary Friday morning.

A little later Jerry's dad calls to tell me the family has decided to fly to San Jose from Tulsa tomorrow morning, Saturday, and that most of Jerry's siblings will be on the flight. Could someone pick them up at the airport? I am surprised they are all coming because Jerry's family is a big one: he is one of seven. I guess some of them will have to sleep on the floor, and I don't think everyone will fit in my VW squareback. I need help.

I decide to go across the street and tell Frieda Todd what is going on because I know she will be at home. She is all sympathy and concern. She will help me out any way she can. I give her the flight information, and she says she will tell other neighbors because she knows they will also want to help. "Don't worry about any of this," she says, "we'll take care of everything. Won't you stay for coffee?"

"I can't stay," I say, "Lisa is at home. But thank you."

When I go home, reality is starting to sink in; I am beginning to feel frightened even though Ken had given me reassurance. I haven't told my family up in Seattle yet, and I'm not sure how to handle that. I am concerned about my dad. He has had a couple of serious heart attacks recently, and I don't want to upset him. My mother has a high-strung personality, and there is no way of knowing how she will react. My brother Rob is a young dentist still in the process of establishing his practice, but he is the most logical one to call, even though he will be at work today. I tell him what I know—that I think Jerry probably survived—and my voice cracks as I tell him that I don't know what to do. Could he go tell our parents after work? I think someone should be with them when they hear the news. He says he will do that, help me in any way he can. I feel helpless to be living so far away from family, but that is the Navy way, moving us from place to place every couple of years.

I am so tired, exhausted in fact, and my stomach is in knots. I check in with Lisa upstairs in her bedroom, but she seems content putting together a puzzle. I lie down on the sofa hoping for a minute or two of sleep, but sleep doesn't come; memories come instead. Jerry had flown from Adak to Moffett Field several days ago to trade out an airplane for one that had just been updated, and how wonderful it was to have him home, even if just for a day! The girls went off to school the next morning as usual, leaving us for a bit of private time. We listened to the radio while we drank a final cup of coffee, and I remember hearing "precious and few are the moments we two can share . . ." and I thought how right that song by Climax sounded. Then it was time to drive him back to the hangar.

Lisa comes downstairs to show me some pictures of her dad she has drawn in crayon. One shows a stick figure in a raft on the water with a one-word message in a bubble above his head: "Help." I give her a hug, but I can't talk. She says she is hungry. I don't feel like eating, but somehow, I manage to make us some peanut butter and jelly sandwiches along with some apple wedges and carrot sticks to make it a meal. I don't listen to the noon news because I don't want Lisa to hear anything that might upset her.

Frieda calls and says the Grigsby family can stay in the Etessam home; Iraj and Irandokht are in Iran on business and their daughters, Shirin and Lili, are staying with the DeVoys, who have daughters about their same ages. They don't need the house, and the Grigsbys are welcome to stay for as long as they like. A couple of the other neighbors will pick them up at the airport. I am so relieved and grateful for this kindness, and I thank Frieda for her help.

Rob calls me back to tell me he will be on his way to tell our parents soon. He has also called our younger brothers, Doug, who is a student at the University of Washington, and Jon, who is a student at Western Washington University in Bellingham. They are both preparing for midterm exams but will drive down together in a couple of days. Doug's young wife, Becky, can get time off from her job at the Space Needle. She will be catching a flight to San Jose later this evening to be with us, and will call me with her flight arrangements. Rob has canceled patients for Monday and his last couple of patients for this afternoon so he can spend some time with us. He will be flying down this evening as well. Everything is happening in a fog; I did not expect any of this, and I am starting to let go and let others take care of my needs.

In the afternoon, Ken and Sara drive over. Ken has new information: a Russian fishing trawler picked up the men in the rafts and the squadron has received a brief message. Jerry was not among those in the rafts. Ken tells me there is still reason for hope because a Korean ship was also in the vicinity and was asked to help. Perhaps Jerry was picked up by this boat, but communication is vague. This is not going well, but somehow, I am holding on to my emotions and my hope.

Commander Byron "Bud" Powers, Commanding Officer of the squadron, pulls up in front of the house in a Navy sedan. I am feeling even more detached about what is going on, and I am not able to keep a focus on what is being said. He wants to be sure I am doing okay and confirms what Ken has already told me. Frieda sees the cars and realizes there must be news, so she comes over. When she hears what has happened, she offers to pick Mary up after school. Other neighbors begin coming over as well, and when Mary walks in the front door, she looks bewildered at the house so full of people. I can tell she is not sure what is going on. She is accustomed to having her dad away, and that part of it seems normal, but what are all these people doing here?

My parents call me after they have talked to Rob and want to know how I am doing; I tell them I am okay. They want to come, but my mom would like for them to drive down from Seattle to give herself more time to take it all in. They do not yet know Jerry was not in a life raft. They will be leaving soon and plan to be here early on Sunday; they are glad Rob and Becky are coming to be with us. I haven't had the radio on all day and I haven't been listening to the news; I don't know what is being said about the accident. Too much is happening, but I do miss listening to music—miss the soothing effect of music, which touches me on a deep level.

I can tell that Mary and Lisa are beginning to realize things may not be as normal as I have led them to believe. Some kindhearted soul has left us a casserole with chicken, broccoli, and cheese and a salad for dinner; was that Sara? This is a meal the girls like, and as we eat, I tell them Uncle Rob and Aunt Becky are coming for a visit. They look happy about that. They have formed a special bond with Becky, and she is a favorite of theirs. Uncle Rob is fun-loving and playful—they always look forward to his visits. "Go upstairs, take baths, and get ready to pick them up at the airport," I tell them.

Becky spends that night with the girls in Mary's room, tells them it's a sleepover, makes them popcorn and plays a game with them. Rob sleeps in the guest room.

It is a relief for me to be able to be alone in my own room and have a chance to process what I have heard—what I know—and to have a chance to cry. Jerry is the love of my life, my hero, and my rock. He is my comfort and always makes problems go away, but who will make this problem go away? I hang on to Ken's words of hope; he has given me something of an expectation that Jerry will be coming home when this is over. He must be on that Korean ship. He must. It is another night of tossing, turning, and very little sleep. The memories keep flooding in.

When Jerry went back to college after Christmas break of his senior year, we knew we were serious about each other and it was hard to say goodbye. The Vietnam War was heating up and young men were being drafted; our neighbor's only son was drafted into the Army and killed in action almost as soon as he reached Vietnam. His mom came over and broke into tears when she told my mom about it.

I went back to nurse's training, thinking Jerry would be okay because I had heard about college deferments and he only had one semester left. Only a few months before, he had changed his mind about going to medical school, wasn't sure he had the right personality for being a doctor, and instead had applied for a fellowship to pursue graduate studies in something called "radiation biophysics." We had talked about it, and I didn't really understand what that was, but he seemed positive about it even though his major was chemistry. He knew he had the grades.

When he got back to school, he learned that his roommate had been drafted. He would be able to finish his degree, but he would be in the Army after he graduated. They talked, and Jerry realized he needed to make another change in his plans. He did not want to be in the Army, so instead he went to talk to a Navy recruiter. If he signed up to be a Navy pilot, they would allow him to finish his degree and he would start Aviation Officer Candidate School in July. This decision was partly influenced by my uncle Bob who had gone that route during the Korean War. Jerry called me and we talked it over. I did not want him drafted either, so this is where we are now. It turned out he liked the Navy— liked being a pilot.

More Memories

Almaden Valley

October 28

Saturday morning is warm and sunny as it sometimes is in late October; maybe I'll take the solar cover off the pool this afternoon. The last time Rob was here he played "Sharkey" and "Jaws" with the girls in the pool amid laughter and shouts of glee. That's just the sort of thing we need today.

One side of the backyard has a play area for the girls where Jerry had built a playhouse with a Dutch door: they can close the bottom half and leave the top half open. Everything, it seems, brings back a memory of Jerry. Over the summer, the girls had set up an ice cream stand for the neighborhood children. They brought the camping cooler out there and I filled it with chipped ice from the grocery store, a couple flavors of ice cream, and some cones. We propped the backyard safety gate open for easy access, and all the kids had a great time.

The doorbell rings, breaking into my thoughts, and it is Commander Bud Powers again. He has the base Chaplain and the squadron Flight Surgeon with him, and I welcome them into my living room. Rob comes in to join us and introduces himself. They have come to be sure I am doing all right, and they are glad my brother is with me.

"Doc" Espiritu is especially concerned about my well-being and seems surprised about my apparent calm state of mind. He offers me a small bottle of Valium, but I turn him down. I don't like the idea of taking tranquilizers, and I'm not sure what effect they will have on me. I know I need to "be here" for my daughters. Becky comes in from the family room and Doc Espiritu walks over to her and hands her the bottle, telling her the pills are just in case they are needed later. Bud wonders if I have any questions and tells me what he knows, but the information coming in to the squadron is scant, leaving much unknown. He pulls my brother aside for a talk while the Chaplain says a prayer for me.

Squadron wives, friends, and neighbors are soon in and out of the house. The phone has been ringing all day; people have been listening to the news, and everyone wants to know if there are any updates. People are bringing food and asking if there is anything else they can do for me. I spend as much time as I can in the quiet sanctuary of my bedroom while Becky and Rob are entertaining my daughters. I forget about taking the solar cover off the pool, and the evening is too cool for a swim by the time I remember. The season is changing, after all.

The Grigsby family arrives during all this chaos, and I bring dining room chairs into the living room so everyone will have a place to sit. Lisa sits on her Aunt Veda's lap for a cuddle, and they both feel a bit better. She has always been in tune with the emotions of people around her, and she moves from lap to lap. Mary cuddles up against Aunt Dona on the sofa. The Grigsbys are happy about staying in the Etessam home and are ready to eat some of the food that fills the refrigerator. It has been a long couple of days. A neighbor arrives with spaghetti and asks if we would like people to bring more food tomorrow; I thank her but say I think we have enough. I can't even think about eating. My mother-in-law, who normally isn't one to interfere, speaks up and says we will need more food. Eventually, things settle down. Becky washes dishes and Mary helps her tidy the kitchen. The Grigsbys walk three doors down the street to the Etessam home, and I retreat again to the quiet of my bedroom.

I was young when Jerry and I married on December 18, 1964, only nineteen. In the month that Jerry had off between college graduation and the start of Officer Candidate School, we did a lot of soul-searching, and decided to marry during his Christmas break after he became a commissioned officer and had started flight training in Pensacola, Florida. If we didn't marry then, it would be months before we saw each other again, and who knew how the continuing war in Vietnam would affect us. He bought me a diamond solitaire ring with a gold band, and I was thrilled!

We went to tell my parents about our plans and to show them my ring. My mother flipped out and said, "That's horrible!" She grabbed her car keys and started for the front door. This wasn't exactly the reaction I had pictured, but I had seen her act this way before and knew she might be gone for hours. Who knew where she was headed, maybe to the beach where she could walk off her emotions. My dad tried to stop her and said she should listen to our plans, but she would have none of it. She took off driving down the long driveway, and I could see that my dad felt uncomfortable about it. He wanted to hear what we had planned.

I told him I would drop out of nursing school at the end of the term and find a temporary job somewhere, save some money. We could marry the weekend before Christmas and drive cross-country to Florida for our honeymoon, which I was excited about because I had never seen the rest of the country. We could stop for a visit with Jerry's family in

Oklahoma; I had never met them and was looking forward to that. Jerry could find a small place for us to rent before he drove out to Seattle for the wedding, in the new car he was planning to buy after he finished Officer Candidate School.

My dad said he could tell we had put a lot of thought into our plans. He said he and my mom had hoped I would finish nurses' training before I married—just two more years to go—and that was why she was upset. I said that I knew education was important to them, but I was no longer sure about a nursing career. Jerry promised him that he would ensure I completed my education.

I remember that after my mom left in a huff following our engagement announcement, she wouldn't talk to me for months, even though I had moved back home after dropping out of school. I guess she thought that by showing her disapproval in this way, maybe I would change my mind. I didn't have a car but was able to find a job within the walking distance of a mile or so—a job pressing shirts in a laundry. I didn't mind the work because I knew it was temporary and it got me out of the house. I helped at home with cleaning and cooking, as best I could. I spent time with my little brothers playing games or helping them with homework.

My mom would sometimes sit and play the piano for long periods of time, which she had done over the years to calm her nerves and relax. Listening to her play was soothing for me as well. She was talented and I enjoyed her music—and so our days went. My dad was always pleasant to be around, and he would sometimes let me borrow his car so I could go visit my aunt Bev, who was almost like a sister to me. She was closer to my age than to my mother's age. I could talk to her about things and she would listen without judging. Once she spoke to my mom about the wedding, advocating for me. My mom yelled at her, and then they weren't on speaking terms anymore. For some reason, my mom blamed Bev for all the problems because I met Jerry at her house.

Jerry and I wrote almost every day; we had also done that when he was away at college. Some days he didn't have a lot to say, felt tired after a long day, but wanted to be sure I knew he loved me and was thinking about me. After several weeks, I wrote that I thought we would need to plan and pay for our own wedding because I could see my mother wasn't going to change her outlook. I thought perhaps we could get married in my aunt and uncle's small Baptist church and have a simple afternoon wedding and reception. We made plans over the next several days. We would invite a small group of friends and relatives. I would get a short wedding dress and veil—appropriate for an informal afternoon wedding— and Jerry could wear his dress blue uniform. By now he was a commissioned officer and had started flight school, but money was still somewhat tight for us, and weddings could be expensive.

We were also trying to decide what kind of car we wanted and decided on the sporty new Ford Mustang; we could swing the monthly payments. It was all going to work out; things were coming together.

Then, out of the blue, one Monday evening after dinner, my mother said we should go shopping in downtown Seattle for a wedding dress. It was such a surprise to me, but we still weren't really talking much and my feelings were so badly hurt by that time that I didn't have a lot to say to her. She wasn't aware that Jerry and I had started making plans on our own, so when the sales clerk asked me what type of dress I wanted and I told her something short and informal because we would be having a small afternoon wedding in a tiny church that was more the size of a chapel, Mom cut in with a cranky voice and angry face, her eyes blazing, saying *that wouldn't do at all. She proposed a more formal floor-length dress on a certain budget. The wedding would take place in the beautiful new Des Moines Methodist Church.*

She had obviously given it a lot of thought. She knew the small church I had mentioned was my aunt's Baptist church. I remembered her telling me once that she didn't think I would be happy with Jerry because he was a Southern Baptist from Oklahoma and those people didn't believe in dancing. She also pointed out that he had a strong jaw and was probably stubborn, hard to get along with. I thought he was kind and pleasant as well as intelligent, so although I'm sure she wanted the best for me, I could not see it her way.

In the end, we had a lovely wedding in the Des Moines Methodist Church, which was decorated with evergreen boughs and ivory ribbon for Christmas. Jerry wore his dress blue uniform, as did my uncle Bob—who was a pilot in the Naval Reserves and Jerry's best man. We drove across the country for our honeymoon, had a second reception at Jerry's parents' place, and set up house in a rented trailer home just outside the training base in Milton, Florida. Other young officers had married over the break and were renting trailer homes there as well. It was all friendly and cozy, and I had instant new friends. Lots of fond memories . . .

But now I was taking classes at San Jose State University and hoped I would still be able to complete my degree despite everything.

The Closed City

The *Synyavin* tied up to a pier lit only by a couple of spotlights, and the survivors were escorted by crew members down the gangway to a paved pier-side parking lot. They were walked about a hundred yards over to a low-slung, elongated concrete block building with a metal roof for what appeared to be some form of custody transfer. Armed guards were everywhere, and a group of men got out of unlit sedans and boarded the ship.

Their "welcoming committee" was composed of uniformed guards in dark green uniforms with pistols in brown leather hip holsters, accompanied by civilians in suits with long black overcoats. Two additional guards, with AK-47s pointed to the ground, stood off to the side. Inside the stark, drab building, men in dark green uniforms stood on the far side of two long tables highlighted by the faint light of a couple of bare bulbs. The rest of the building's interior was shrouded in darkness. A representative from the ship, who might have been Captain Arbuzov—though no one had met him while they were on board—turned them over to the Border Guards in exchange for signed receipts. The survivors had limited knowledge of the Russian language, and all they could do was watch, wait, and wonder what would happen next.

A darkened diesel-powered bus, with the engine running, was waiting out front. The larger pier area and the port city beyond were all hidden by the darkness.

An English-speaking civilian directed the survivors to board the waiting bus for a brief ride up the hill to the Petropavlovsk Naval Hospital where they were greeted formally by the medical staff and a few "doctors" wearing new white lab coats over fine quality suits. The survivors were given blue cotton hospital pajamas, assigned to rooms on what appeared to be the top floor, and then they were all told to go to their rooms and sleep. It had been a long and uncertain day—probably well after midnight by now—and they were grateful for the chance to rest.

The next morning, they were served a hot breakfast in a spacious common room with windows overlooking the rear of the large military complex. The buildings, including the hospital, were older and industrial looking, made of concrete block and steel, built to withstand the harsh Siberian winters. After eating eggs, bread and butter, apples, and tea, they were individually sent off for physical exams including lab work and chest X-rays using equipment that seemed quite old and dated by Western standards.

John Ball, being John, refused to get into a dilapidated 1940s-era machine that looked like a broken-down phone booth. The technician and a doctor huddled to discuss it and relented, giving John his way. *Take my temperature, take my blood*, he thought, *but I'm not being "zapped" by some out-dated machine that may do me more harm than good.*

The doctors spent extra time with Bruce Forshay who had deep bruising along the length of his back from his neck down to his knees. His bruising hadn't shown up when his body temperature was so dangerously low, but now they treated him with aspirin and some type of electric massage device to promote healing. Gary Hemmer looked to be doing much better, his medication taking full effect. He and Master Chief Shepard were already discussing Gary's first ever P-3 flight and the "sea stories" they could tell back in Adak someday.

Sometime later, the Soviet doctors approached Ed Caylor and Matt Gibbons about the three deceased crew members. The doctors needed to perform autopsies to determine the cause of death, and although it seemed obvious to both Ed and Matt that hypothermia was the cause, the doctors had reports to file. Matt told Ed that he would accompany them to ensure proper identification since the Soviets wanted a witness to sign off on the reports and confirm identities.

———————

These men were part of Matt's tactical crew, and he wanted to be sure they were properly identified for the sake of their families. It would be difficult for him to watch, he knew, but he wanted to do what he could.

He followed two of the doctors down to the morgue in the basement and watched the process. He had never witnessed an autopsy before and was shocked to see the entire torso opened, the organs lifted out one by one and inspected and then put back inside the cold, gray lifeless bodies. Matt's lack of knowledge of the Russian language and their limited English proficiency slowed down the entire process until he was able to explain in halting Russian—"*Nyet pah Ruski, pah Espanol*"—that he also spoke Spanish. In less than an hour, they found a Cuban "teacher," and they spent a few hours going over autopsy questions and personal effects in Spanish. There was a sincere concern on everyone's part that nothing be mixed up.

On the wide staircase leading back upstairs to the rooms,

they happened to pass by two men in dress suits with audio headsets draped around their necks. It was clear to Matt that the crew was being monitored by agents on the floor immediately below where they were staying. Prickles of fear shot through him as he remembered the danger they might be in as captives in a Communist country. He quickly spread word in a whispered voice, and soon the crew got an idea to adopt a deep southern drawl and some down-home southern vocabulary to confuse the agents.

They still had no clear idea of what the Soviets had in mind for them. They were aware that Petropavlovsk was a "closed city" and that no foreigners and very few Russians were allowed in, yet here they were. Oddly enough, there were English-language magazines to read, as well as that Cuban "teacher"; it was obvious the hospital had been prepared in advance for their arrival. One of their "hosts" who spoke some English asked if they wanted anything added to their meals. John, still being John, requested beer and pizza. Beer was served with their next dinner, but no pizza was available.

Later that afternoon, and generally feeling better, they asked their doctors if they could arrange for them to go for a walk to get some fresh air and exercise. Later that evening, after darkness fell, they were issued long black Russian flight jackets and big black leather and fur hats. They were allowed to go on an escorted walk around the block that held the hospital grounds.

The night air was cold, and it felt good to be out of the stuffy rooms. It looked like they had been turned loose in a 1950s vintage movie set; the architecture was all about function and utility, and most of the buildings looked similar. In the corner of each building was a large white rectangle with a black building number painted on it. They were escorted back upstairs for bed still wondering what their futures held.

The men endured another long day of waiting around, and then they found out they would soon be moved to another city. The crew thought perhaps that the other city might be Moscow, but it turned out they were going to fly to Khabarovsk, a larger Siberian city near the Chinese border. There was an impromptu farewell ceremony, and each man received a blue plastic Petropavlovsk pin with a picture of the volcano and a package of postcards before being loaded onto a bus and driven through the dark streets of Petropavlovsk to the nearby Yelizovo Airport.

The bus pulled right up alongside an Aeroflot airplane with blue-and-white logos. They boarded under bright lights and walked down the center aisle wearing the baggy flight suits and the clunky lace-up boots they had been wearing all along. They were also wearing the Russian flight jackets and fur hats from the hospital. They carried the rolled-up MK7 raft and their deflated life vests past a mostly full passenger load to the back rows of the plane where four burly KGB agents dressed in suits and dark overcoats sat in the very last row.

They were told to stow the raft and vests in the open overhead shelf that looked like something you might see on an old US passenger bus. None of the Russian passengers made eye contact or even looked their way. They all stared straight ahead. Matt assumed they had been told to ignore the American captives. After all, as the crewmen learned from their Navy SERE school training, they were the dreaded "Yankee Air Pirates."

The outside of the plane had looked clean and well maintained, but the inside was something altogether different: it was shabby and worn looking and in need of maintenance and TLC. Some seats had missing seat belts and there were tears in the fabric. Armrests and tray tables rattled as they began to taxi.

The periphery of the taxiway and runway was littered with the mangled remnants of crashed airplanes. Matt saw at least a dozen wrecked planes that looked like they had been bulldozed off to the side. These were the remains of Aeroflot Tupolev and Ilyushin Soviet national airlines planes with the distinctive white-over-gray paint, blue horizontal stripe, red Soviet flag on the tail, and the Cyrillic Aeroflot logo along the fuselage. Having just survived a ditching, it was disconcerting to see that marketing safe air travel was not a priority here.

Despite the shocking differences, the two-hour-plus flight was uneventful. Matt understood almost nothing of the announcements, and noted the absence of flight attendants and in-flight snack service. Their flight headed mostly west over the Sea of Okhotsk and the lights of Sakhalin Island, which Matt could make out from his window seat. He could see many fishing boats and wondered if any of them might be the MYS *Synyavin*.

The Telegram

Almaden Valley

October 29

My parents arrive after their long trip down from Seattle, and it is good to see them. My dad looks tired, and I'm sure he has been the one driving the entire way because that is the way my family travels. We are all seated in the living room along with the Grigsby family. People have been eating lunch from the food in the refrigerator, and Becky is making a fresh pot of coffee. Lisa is still sitting on laps, and Mary, who is sitting between two of her aunts on the sofa, is listening to the adults talk. I am explaining that we still have reason for hope, that Koreans may have rescued Jerry; I don't want to give up hope while there is still some hope to be had.

I am sitting in an armchair looking out the front picture window when I see black official Navy sedans drive down the cul-de-sac and circle back around to park in front of the house. Men in Navy dress blue uniforms get out, and I know what they have come to say; somehow, I have experienced this scene before. My brother Rob lets the men into the house. Jerry's sister Veda begins to cry, and Lisa pats her back as a show of comfort. An officer says the search for Jerry has been suspended; there is no way he could have survived given the frigid conditions, and there is an official declaration of death. I see my father-in-law's head drop as though this information is too heavy to bear.

Now there is more crying from across the room. I am gone, lost in a fog of sorrow and grief with a tight suffocating pressure rising within my chest. I don't know how long I have been sitting there staring out the window when I become aware that everyone is staring at me. I can hardly breathe, but I know something is expected of me. I say, "Now I know that love never dies." All eternity lies before me.

I hear someone ask, "What did she say?"

Mary says, "You can't tell me my father is dead!" She sounds angry, and I know how she feels.

Doc Espiritu, the squadron Flight Surgeon, says there are tranquilizers if anyone would like one. My mother is the first to say she would, and Becky goes to get the bottle she has set aside, and then she brings a glass of water. Then there's more crying, and more people taking tranquilizers while I continue to sit isolated in my own private mist, detached from the reality of it all. Doc Espiritu comes over to me and looks deeply into my eyes. "How can you remain so calm?"

I don't know how I can be so at peace, but I am experiencing the warmth of love, a feeling all through my chest, as though Jerry is here with me. I am also remembering our first date way back when I wasn't quite seventeen. It seems that I have known since then that this would be happening to us, and that realization is somehow a comfort. Things are the way they were meant to be, even with all this crushing sadness. I am grateful that the reality of Jerry's death has unfolded slowly over the past few days. It has given me a chance to gradually accept what I now must face.

Doc Espiritu is asking more questions and now I feel my own anger rising, a rising scale of fury. This isn't the time or place for these personal questions. I don't want to think about these other things; I just want to be left alone. I lash out at him, letting go of some of my bitterness. His questions seem to imply that perhaps Jerry was experiencing some kind of personal emotional issue that impeded his ability to deal with the emergency at hand. I am blunt and straightforward: the men have been pushed too hard. They have been under a lot of pressure working long hours without enough downtime, and that is what may have contributed to the accident. He claims that when pilots are kept to a busy schedule the accident rates go down. I just want to be left alone. Enough of this!

Commander Peter Cressy, the squadron Executive Officer, is telling us about Jerry's last moments, about his heroism. Ditching that type of aircraft in heavy, stormy seas was some-thing never before accomplished. Jerry waited until he could be sure he was the last one out of the cockpit, and then he paused to count the men in the life rafts before diving into the water himself. Cressy is near tears as he tells us this, and my sweet mother-in-law has something to say.

She has just lost a son, but somehow manages to tell us a story about when Jerry drowned in the lake at summer camp. When it came time to do a buddy check, twelve-year-old Jerry couldn't be found. Everyone got out of the water and there was Jerry lying on the bottom; who knew how long he had been there? They pulled him out and started CPR, but he was not responsive. A camp counselor, who would not give up hope, kept working with him even after others were sure nothing more would help. Jerry was cool to the touch, blue around the lips, and still not breathing when the camp director called the hospital.

A hearse was sent for him, and the camp director called

Mr. and Mrs. Grigsby to give them the sad news. Still, the counselor did not give up hope and kept working with Jerry until the hearse arrived to take him back to town. Somehow, during that trip, Jerry revived and was taken to the emergency room instead of the morgue. Mrs. Grigsby tells us she always wondered why Jerry's life was spared at that time, but now she understands. It was so he could save the lives of others on this flight.

I had heard the story of the drowning before, of course. Jerry had told me about it when we were dating, when we were trying to get to know each other better. A few months ago, I learned even more about that time. I had been telling him about a book I was reading called Life After Life. It told of experiences people had had as they faced death, many who had already been pronounced dead but somehow had been able to come back. There seemed to be a common theme among them that they had traveled through a tunnel or some other type of enclosed space, saw bright lights ahead, and heard singing.

Jerry looked amazed and said he had never heard anything about that before, but had experienced something like it when he drowned at summer camp. He thought maybe he was dreaming and was a little confused at the time; it seemed like he was traveling in a bus and his friends were singing. He saw bright lights ahead and then woke up in the hospital, but he'd never talked about it. He seemed excited to know other people had experienced something similar. We talked about it a little and wondered what it might really mean. Now I have a strong feeling about what it means: that there really is life after life.

There's another knock on the door. This time it is a telegram for me. On yellow paper with a Western Union logo, it reads:

I DEEPLY REGRET TO CONFIRM ON BEHALF OF THE UNITED STATES NAVY THAT YOUR HUSBAND, LCDR JERRY CARSON GRIGSBY, USN, PREVIOUSLY REPORTED MISSING, DIED ON 26 OCTOBER 1978 AT SEA AS A RESULT OF AN AIRCRAFT ACCIDENT WHICH OCCURRED 200 MILES FROM THE ALEUTIAN ISLAND OF SHEMYA. IT IS WITH FURTHER REGRET I MUST CONFIRM THAT SEARCHES FAILED TO RECOVER YOUR HUSBAND'S REMAINS. A LETTER FROM HIS COMMANDING OFFICER SETTING FORTH THE CIRCUMSTANCES OF DEATH WILL FOLLOW. YOUR HUSBAND-DIED WHILE SERVING HIS COUNTRY. MY SINCEREST SYMPATHY IS EXTENDED TO YOU IN YOUR GREAT LOSS. IF I CAN ASSIST YOU, PLEASE WRITE OR TELEGRAPH THE CHIEF OF NAVAL PERSONNEL, NAVY DEPARTMENT, WASHINGTON, D.C. 20370. MY PERSONAL REPRESENTATIVE CAN BE REACHED BY TELEPHONE AT 202–433–4823 DURING WORKING HOURS AND 202–694–2768 AFTER WORKING HOURS.

VICE ADMIRAL ROBERT B. BALDWIN,
CHIEF OF NAVAL PERSONNEL

The Letter

October 30
Almaden Valley

DEPARTMENT OF THE NAVY
PATROL SQUADRON NINE
FPO SAN FRANCISCO, 96601

IN REPLY REFER TO:
FF 12/VP9/10:fs
1700
OCT 3 0 1978

Mrs. Loreen Grigsby
1420 Calle De La Paz
San Jose, California 95120

Dear Loreen,

On behalf of all the Officers and men of Patrol Squadron Nine, I extend to you, Mary, and Lisa, our sincerest and deepest heartfelt sympathy. Truly a professional in every sense, Jerry served his country proudly and with distinction.

The mission Jerry and his crew were conducting was a routine patrol in the North Pacific Ocean. Approximately five and one-half hours into the patrol the aircraft developed mechanical problems and while declaring an emergency Jerry set course for Shemya Air Force Base at the western end of the Aleutian chain. Enroute to Shemya the malfunction became so critical that ditching the aircraft was unavoidable. Considering the high winds and high seas, Jerry did an extraordinary job in landing the aircraft on the water. Search and rescue operations were set in motion immediately; however the nearest surface unit to the scene, a Russian vessel, did not arrive until twelve hours later due to the high winds and seas.

Communications between US search and rescue aircraft and the Russian vessel and subsequent communications between Russian and US officials at the State Department level indicated that of the fifteen crewmen aboard the aircraft, thirteen had been taken aboard the Russian vessel from the life rafts and that ten of the thirteen were reported alive. It was with the deepest sorrow that we learned that Jerry was not among those taken aboard and that an extensive search of the area by US Navy and Coast Guard units as well as aircraft and ships from the USSR was unsuccessful.

Both as a professional Naval Officer and Aviator and as a personal friend, Jerry always gave completely of himself. A man of impeccable character, honor, and integrity, Jerry's inspired leadership and genuine concern for his shipmates earned him the distinction of being one of the most highly respected Officers in the command. May you find comfort in knowing that by putting his unsurpassed skill as an exceptional aviator to the supreme test, Jerry literally gave new life to his crew. Jerry was a compassionate and magnificent person who will be greatly missed and always revered as a true hero by all of us.

Jerry's shipmates join me in extending our deepest concern to you and your daughters. Your strength has been an example to all of us, but I wish to assure you that we are most anxious to extend any assistance which you may desire. Loreen, please do not hesitate to call either Paula or myself at any time.

Very sincerely,

B. L. POWERS
Commander, U. S. Navy
Commanding Officer

Lingering Concerns

Khabarovsk, Siberia

October 31

The landing in Khabarovsk was smooth despite all the rattling in the cabin. Matt Gibbons could tell the other passengers must have been instructed to wait in their seats as the Americans made their way forward. He did not know what they been told, but once again they were obedient; there was no eye contact or any other type of interaction—it was just another strange moment in a strange journey. The crew went down the stairs and were handed over to another set of KGB agents in suits and then loaded onto a waiting bus for the drive to an undisclosed location. This airport seemed larger and busier than the last, even though it was the middle of the night.

The long drive across the dark and mostly deserted downtown revealed a much larger city that looked to be stuck in the past with large functional buildings all with a similar design that made Matt think of the old *Batman* TV show set in Gotham City. The buildings were gray and utilitarian, and the mood somber. They arrived at a Border Guards base before dawn and once again were escorted upstairs to the top floor of an empty wing of the hospital. They were all exhausted and sleep came easily.

Later that morning it was back to business: another physical exam after breakfast, another visit to a vintage chest X-ray machine, then more prodding and poking. The common area they shared had a bank of windows with a view out toward the edge of the city. From this vantage point they could see a steady flow of Army green jeep-like vehicles delivering patients for the floors below. A large military communications facility, nicknamed an "elephant cage" because of its vast antenna array for long-range communication, stood out in the distance; it stood about forty or fifty feet tall and was probably about half a mile in circumference.

The crew ate lunch and then learned that they would soon be receiving visitors from the US Embassy. They had no idea if the visitors would be from Moscow or from across town, but hoped to learn what the plan was for them. A few "doctors" were wearing freshly starched lab coats with shiny new stethoscopes, none of whom were present during the crew's physicals yet were carefully observing them. Listening to bits and pieces of conversation, they gathered that the nurses and staff were shocked to see how young the crew looked.

Ed Carter from the US Embassy in Moscow's State Department staff joined them in the common room. He was an energetic young Black man from Chicago, and he brought with him a Sunday *Chicago Tribune* and a copy of the *New York Times*. There were small articles about the ditching and rescue. Although their prior POW training had conditioned them to be skeptical, the newspapers, plus his impressive demeanor, convinced them all that he was the "real deal."

While the crew read the newspapers, the nurses were mesmerized by the full-page ads from department stores—especially the high-fashion models promoting perfume, fall fashions, and jewelry. They looked at each other and at them-selves, and by their animated exclamations, the men could see they were surprised at how slender and tiny the models were.

Captain Anthony Bracken, the US Naval attaché in Moscow, Dr. Nydell, and Hospital Corpsman Briggs arrived at the room an hour later, after their bags were inspected by the Soviets. Dr. Nydell and Corpsman Briggs gave Gary Hemmer and Bruce Forshay brief physical examinations to be sure they were fit to travel. Captain Bracken handed out some souvenir Zippo lighters engraved with the US Embassy Moscow crest to the survivors. His first order of business was to ask about the destruction of the communication crypto gear and the other classified materials. When he was satisfied with their answers, he said arrangements were being negotiated back and forth to return the crew to the United States via Japan within a few days. The survivors all felt a strong sense of relief that they would head for home soon. They were not going to be forgotten in Siberia.

Later that afternoon, the Soviet doctors requested a photo of the ten survivors in front of the hospital. The press photographers gave the original proposal. They wanted to take some candid shots of them inside the hospital, and again outside kicking around a soccer ball in the front courtyard. None of the survivors were interested in posing for propa-ganda purposes, and Master Chief Shepard was vehemently opposed. He flatly refused to participate in any photo op.

Ed Caylor and Matt Gibbons had a diplomatic discussion with him and found out that he had grave concerns about his reputation as a senior enlisted man back on Adak. He did not want to be perceived as cooperating for any propaganda effort. He had left his family behind in Missouri for this unaccompa-nied tour of duty—he was a "geographical bachelor" back in Adak, with a tight-knit group of fellow Chiefs that were like family to him, and he did not want anything to come between him and the other Chiefs. After a bit of back and forth discussion, they agreed to pose on the hospital steps for one group photo. The ground rules were simple: no obscene gestures, no big smiles, just look straight at the cameras and let them click away. The photographers were hoping for more, but the hospital staff was pleased to get the publicity, and after a few minutes the crew was back inside.

The crew had lingering concerns later in the day because they had heard nothing back from the embassy or the hospital staff about a possible release. Could they really trust the Soviets? Had they figured out what the crew's mission was all about? The nurses continued to be fascinated by the full-page ads in the Chicago newspaper; they also continued to remark about how young the men were and how far from home they had been sent. The crew's limited understanding of the Russian language and the nurses' limited understanding of English led to a few humorous interactions as they tried to make the survivors feel comfortable on their assigned floor of the hospital.

The doctors who were watching over them seemed disinterested at best. That night at dinner, Captain Bracken joined them and said that the diplomatic arrangements to fly to Japan were in place and that they would be leaving Khabarovsk and flying to Japan late tomorrow afternoon on a commercial charter. Sleep came easier that night. Six days after the ditching, they would finally be one step closer to home.

The next morning, November 2, they awoke to a hearty breakfast of tea, cheese blintzes, and fruit. They were told that a farewell celebration was planned for noon. Captain Bracken and his staff were there, and he informed them that there would be some ceremonial toasting of their hosts in Russian as well as in English. He advised that it would be a major diplomatic faux pas and an insult to their hosts if the crew did not drink vodka with them. Having a senior Navy Captain encourage young aviators to drink up was a little out of the ordinary, but the survivors were up to that challenge after all they had experienced.

The farewell ceremony began with the presentation of Khabarovsk picture postcards and orange plastic tourist pins to the crew. Captain Bracken and Ed Caylor presented US Embassy Moscow engraved Zippo lighters and chocolates to the doctors, Border Guard Colonel Dmitri, and the nurses. The table was set with bowls of apples, chocolates, carafes of apple cider, and multiple bottles of vodka. Captain Bracken toasted the hospital staff, Ed Caylor toasted the MYS *Synyavin*, and they continued to toast and slam back vodka until all the bottles were empty. The Russians learned to say "Cheers," and the Americans learned to say (phonetic) "*Nah-stroh-vee-yah.*" The combination of vodka shots with apple cider chasers was surprisingly good, but not too many of the crew bit into the apples. After all the vodka was consumed, the doctors suggested that they switch over to something stronger to continue the celebration. Captain Bracken said, with the wisdom of experience, that it was time to leave for the airport. Everyone was literally in good spirits as they shook hands with the hospital staff, gathered their things, and were loaded onto a bus to be driven across the city to the airport.

In the daylight, they could see a very large city where the buildings were drab, utilitarian, gray, and similar to each other. At major intersections they saw patriotic banners or stone monuments of the comrade workers holding flags. At the airport they were surprised to see a shiny Japan Airlines DC-9 waiting for them. They boarded quickly, along with the embassy team, and were greeted by very welcoming English-speaking flight attendants. The short flight across the

Sea of Japan took about an hour, and they landed at a regional airport in the city of Niigata in central Japan. The JAL DC-9 taxied up directly next to a waiting USAF C-141.

On the tarmac in Niigata the ten survivors, the three wooden caskets, and the Embassy Moscow team transferred onto the waiting USAF C-141 medical evacuation plane for the short flight south to Yokota Air Base near Tokyo. The hosts from Commander Naval Forces Japan and Seventh Fleet briefed the crew during the flight on what to expect next. The public affairs team briefed Ed Caylor on the prepared remarks he would deliver after they deplaned. The surviving officers and the Master Chief were provided with khaki Navy hats. The enlisted crew got blue Navy ball caps with their rank insignia. They all received black-and-white standard-issue name tags. They were informed that over the next day or two their "routine medical evaluation" would also include a deep intelligence debrief while the recent events were still fresh in their minds.

After the C-141 aircraft stopped at a receiving area on the tarmac at Yokota Air Base, the large cargo hatch at the rear opened to reveal the flag-draped caskets. A Marine Corps Honor Guard rendered full military honors while the caskets were transferred to waiting hearses. When that transfer was complete, the ten surviving crew members appeared at the ramp and the small crowd of Air Force and Navy personnel assembled there burst into cheers. Deplaning in single file based on descending rank order, the crew was led down the ramp by Ed Caylor, the senior survivor. Their welcoming party included Lieutenant General George Loving Jr., Commander US Forces, Japan, and Rear Admiral Lando Zech Jr., Commander US Naval Forces, Japan.

After brief welcoming remarks, Ed Caylor spoke a few words of praise for Lieutenant Commander Jerry Grigsby:

"He was an exceptional pilot, and without his experience and expertise, there would be none of us here to talk to you today."

The crew boarded a large US Air Force step van for a quick ride to the Yokota base hospital. The base was large and sprawling with extensive modern facilities; most of the buildings were painted beige, featured lots of glass, and were well maintained. It was a shared base, built up over a decades-long partnership with the Japanese Air Self-Defense Forces. The base featured a stunning view of Mount Fuji from just about everywhere.

Emotions on Edge

Almaden Valley

October 31

Mary reminds me that I had promised them a Halloween party, and she wants to know if they can still have it. They have their costumes ready, and Becky says she can help. It will be a little get-together with friends out in the backyard, some games, and something to eat before they head out trick-or-treating. I ask them to talk to their friends and find out how many will be coming. Parents are surprised and ask me if I am sure I want to do this, and I tell them it will be fine, the kids still need to be kids.

Rob needs to fly back to Seattle because he has patients scheduled for tomorrow. It has been good to have him here and I am grateful for how supportive he has been, but I still have support all around me. My parents drive him to the airport. I have given them my bedroom, but that is what I always do when they come for a visit; I will miss the privacy and sanctuary of my own room, but the guest room will be okay.

Ken Smith calls to find out how things are going and to let me know that a memorial service is being planned for Thursday, November 2. This will be a joint service for all five men who lost their lives in the accident, and it will be held in the Moffett Field Chapel. I haven't even gotten that far in my thinking, which is still foggy, and it is a huge relief to me that someone else is coordinating this. The families will still be here, and I know Jerry's family will be pleased when they hear about it.

I don't think any of my dresses will be appropriate, and when I tell Becky, she says she will take me shopping. Almaden Fashion Plaza is only a couple miles away, and Becky and I decide to shop today since the girls have their Halloween party tomorrow—and there are still pumpkins to be carved.

Mrs. Grigsby says she will need something new also because she had only brought her everyday comfortable housedresses. My mom says she will help her with the shopping and get herself something new at the same time, maybe tomorrow. My dad calls my younger brothers to ask them to bring his suit when they drive down. They will be able to be here in time for the service; everything seems to be taking shape. My parents and Jerry's parents are calling friends and relatives to let them know what is going on . . .

I try on several dresses and realize I don't like black. Becky says I can choose a different color, perhaps something neutral and relatively plain. I'm not really in a frame of mind for shopping, but then I see a dress in a warm beige color made of a soft knit fabric and I know right away that's the one—that will work just fine. I'm ready to head back home, and when we get there, I head upstairs for another sleepless nap.

The next day, my mom takes my mother-in-law shopping. My dad drives them to the mall, and my mom tells Mrs. Grigsby what to buy. My mom, despite whatever good intentions she may have, can be dictatorial in the extreme. My dad tends to go along with her because, after years of experience, he has found that is what works best. My mom has her own *ideas about the way things should be, and she has limited capacity to change her views.*

I don't know what happened during that shopping trip until Jerry's sister, Veda, pulls me aside and gives me a stern talking-to about it. I feel terrible and I apologize, saying that I hadn't known anything about what had transpired with my mom. Veda is not ready to let it drop, and I feel overwhelmed with everything. Apparently, my mom believes every woman of a certain age should wear a corset when dressed up; Mrs. Grigsby has never worn a corset in her life and is in tears by the time they get back to my place. My mom thinks it is because she has lost her son; I am sure that is the biggest part of it because emotions are running at a fever pitch all the way around, but still.

Mary goes outside, finds her aunt Dona sitting on the back steps with her head buried in her hands, and sits down beside her. My mom makes beauty shop appointments for herself and my mother-in-law, and the Grigsbys escape to the privacy of the Etessam home. I go upstairs for some quiet time while Becky and Lisa start setting up for the Halloween party. I don't know what I would do without Becky.

A Folded Flag

NAS Moffett Field
November 2

My younger brothers drive down from Seattle and arrive the night before the memorial service, bringing my dad's suit. The day of the service dawns sunny and pleasant, a counterpoint to the way I am feeling. My mother-in-law looks lovely in her new dress and hairdo. We are all ready to go, and my dad drives my mom, my daughters, and me to Moffett Field. The chapel is full to overflowing. I feel all eyes on me as we are ushered to the front pew. Above all else, I know I must not cry, though that is such a burden. I was brought up to keep my strong emotions private, and I know Jerry had been brought up that way as well. He would expect me to keep a stiff upper lip. It is so much work to maintain my poise that I am not completely tuned in to the service. The songs and readings hold my attention:

"O Lord, my God! When I in awesome wonder consider all the worlds thy hands have made, I see the stars; I hear the rolling thunder thy power throughout the universe displayed.

Then sings my soul, my savior God to thee; how great though art. . . . When Christ shall come with shout of acclamation and take me home, what joy shall fill my heart!"

I take in the scripture lesson.

John 11:25: "Jesus said unto her, I am the resurrection, and the life: he that believeth in me, though he were dead, yet shall he live. . . ."

Jerry believed this, heart and soul. He believed Heaven was his true home, and although I know he didn't want to leave us, had fought as hard as he could to come back to us, he was now in a state of perpetual joy in his eternal home. Then I am in a fog of sorrow again. I am aware I am missing some of the pieces as my mind wanders.

Commander Cressy is speaking: "We are bound together—all of us in this squadron, our departed, and their families—in the service of our great nation. Our loss has been great, but our gain has been greater. Because of the effort of the five deceased, ten others live, but more than that is the legacy of heroism, courage, dedication, and service, which they have left for us to follow.

"Lieutenant Commander Jerry Grigsby, a man of faith, a man devoted to his family, and a man dedicated to the service of his country. We will remember him as a gentle person, who was compassionate and concerned for those who worked for him and with him. Jerry was a superb, professional aviator who shared his skills as an instructor with many. He was dedicated and solid and good. . . . We have been brought together, then, more closely in the face of this loss—of this challenge given by God. We who fly His skies and

search His oceans have learned again that God alone rules them. And, in His wisdom, He has once again displayed His might. But more importantly, He has turned this challenge into an example of heroism, courage, dedication, and service. . . . And we are thankful, God, that in Your mercy You allowed their unselfish actions to save ten others.

"We realize also that in Your divine plan, You have used them to show us that in the face of the world's danger we are dependent one nation upon another, and You have shown us that sometimes an enemy can be a friend. We have been humbled by the size of the seas and the fragileness of life, but we have also gained confidence in our calling. We know now that with God's help, we are adequate to the task, and that as a squadron and as families we are closer and stronger than ever. In war or peace, we who fly in patrol aviation are always on the front line. We have spoken those words before, but now we understand them. In understanding them, we are now more ready than ever to honor the memory of those we have lost by rededicating ourselves to the love and service of our great nation. . . ."

We stand for the Navy Hymn and Benediction:

"Eternal Father, strong to save, whose arm hath bound the restless wave, who bid'st the mighty ocean deep its own appointed limits keep. O hear us when we cry to thee for those who peril on the sea!

Lord, guard and guide the men who fly through the great spaces in the sky. Be with them always in the air, in darkening storms or sunlight fair. O hear us when we lift our prayer for those in peril in the air!"

A folded flag is presented to me, and to each family of the deceased. Now the ceremony is over and my father leads us toward the car. I am living in a world suddenly without Jerry—without his kindness, without his comfort, without his touch. I still don't cry, though cold waves of disbelief and sadness keep hitting me. It all seems highly unreal, and I am struck again and again by the absence of him. Somehow, I believe he may still be alive, picked up by another ship and taken to another country. Hadn't someone told me a Korean ship was in the area and had been asked to help?

Yokota Air Base, Japan

November 3

The crew was again sequestered in their own wing on the top floor of a hospital, the Yokota Hospital, just like they had been in the Soviet Union. They were checked into private rooms, and the first order of business the Air Force asked of them was that they order their dinners. It seemed the survivors could order anything they wanted, and the crew was hungry for a big, juicy steak-and-baked-potato dinner. As they ate together, they were all pleasantly surprised at how the Air Force dining facility operated, quite confident the Navy would never splurge like that. It was a fabulous meal.

Next came the cryptographic security debrief. Two civilian specialists from the National Security Agency paid them a visit and wanted a detailed line-by-line accounting of every classified document and piece of encryption material that the crew had on board; they were extremely thorough. They even asked if anyone had physically destroyed any hardware with the crash axe. When they were finished with Matt Gibbons, they cross-checked the information with Bruce Forshay and then with John Ball to corroborate the status of each piece. Later that evening, they delivered a case of beer to the nurses' station for the crew, and it was the last they ever heard from them.

Intelligence questions came after that and lasted late into the night. Matt was amazed by the oversized high-resolution satellite photos of Petropavlovsk and Khabarovsk—the detail and clarity of them—laid out in front of him on the tray table in his hospital room. The intelligence analysts wanted a detailed overview of where the crew had stayed, how they had traveled, and whatever details he could recall. They were the first Americans on the ground in Petropavlovsk since 1948, and there was a lot of interest in whatever "human intelligence" he could provide. Finally, in the early morning hours, Matt was allowed to sleep. It had been a very long day.

The next morning started with another physical exam and the third chest X-ray that week. Matt was beginning to wonder if he would soon glow in the dark. After breakfast, he was able to make a phone call to his parents. It was relayed by way of the Defense Department: from Yokota Air Base in Japan the operator dialed Griffiss Air Base in upstate New York, and then a local operator dialed his parents' home. Due to a thirteen-hour time difference to the US East Coast, his family was awakened in the middle of the night. They were very happy to take the call, and it was a great relief for him to talk to them and let them know he was okay. When he got back up to the ward, he learned that men from a squadron based nearby in Atsugi, Japan, had stopped by with a box of brown leather Navy flight jackets, but by the time he got there, they were all gone. Ed Caylor hadn't gotten one either. Oh well, that's life.

Commander Bud Powers came to join them from Moffett Field. Admiral Prindle supported his trip by issuing travel orders, and Powers flew on an Air Force transport from Travis AFB direct to Yokota. It was important to him to go there to support the survivors, and it was great for the crew to see him.

Commodore Jerry McKay, the Commander of Seventh Fleet Patrol and Reconnaissance Forces, stopped by as well. Technically, Alfa Foxtrot 586 was working for him in the Navy operational chain of command, as well as for Fifth Air Force on their Skyking flight monitoring chain of command when they ditched. To complicate matters further, they were homeported from a US Navy Third Fleet area, paid for by Third Fleet budgets. They had taken off from a Third Fleet detachment site, and once airborne, became attached to both Seventh Fleet and Fifth Air Force.

The flurry of communications between all these different commands must have been a watch officer's nightmare as multiple admirals and generals thought they were in charge and wanted to be kept updated on a frequent basis.

McKay was a highly regarded leader in the western Pacific. He carried a lot of influence in his dealings with the Air Force and Allied military leaders. He informed the survivors that arrangements were in progress with the Air Force and that they would be leaving for Moffett Field the following day.

Later that evening, Lieutenant Commander Mike Jamison from Task Force 72 in nearby Kamiseya paid Matt an unexpected visit. He was directly involved in PARPRO program coordination with his counterparts at Fifth Air Force. Jamison was surprised and disappointed that the crew were getting ready to leave Yokota the next day because watch officers were planning to "liberate" the crew from the watchful eyes of the Yokota nurses and go off base for some beers and sushi the next evening. He relayed that the blizzard of official message traffic had finally subsided. He was on the PARPRO watch team the day of the accident, and had been actively listening to Matt's and Bruce's Mayday radio calls; the watch officers thought the crew were something akin to minor rock stars because of their calm and steady handling of the emergency situation.

Jamison was deeply interested in any "gouge," or relevant information, Matt was willing to share. Matt told him some of his first impressions: that they had survived because of the skills of the pilots and that the airframe was basically strong. When he said that the wing had ripped off and the emergency lights failed, Jamison was shocked. Matt went on to explain how quickly the aircraft sank and that the tiny buckles on retaining straps meant that many survival items did not make it out of the tube during evacuation. After Jamison left, thinking about the plan to go into Tokyo, Matt was wondering what they would have worn—flight suits with clunky boots, hospital pajamas and slippers, Russian flight jackets?

Matt still had no idea how things would go with the official accident investigation. He knew they had made mistakes and every aspect of their lives would soon be put under the microscope. However, they were the first crew to survive a P-3 ditching and had a ton of firsthand knowledge to share. Matt finally got some sleep Friday night, still uncertain about what would happen back at Moffett. He wondered if they would fault him for not wearing a helmet, not launching all three rafts, losing five crew members, or for any other shortcomings in carrying out his duties. In the hurried scramble to evacuate the sinking aircraft, the emergency sonobuoy and the second seven-man life raft were left to sink inside the aircraft. The second small raft had a two-way survival radio instead of a homing beacon. In an ideal scenario, the Patrol Plane Commander and the TACCO would be in that raft communicating with search and rescue. October 26 was about as far from ideal as you could get. Nobody had ever trained for a ditching evacuation with more than 10,000 gallons per minute of cold ocean flooding in. He knew he was overthinking it, but he could not let it go. Growing up as the oldest of seven children, Matt had learned to take his responsibilities seriously.

The survivors woke up early Saturday morning and had a group breakfast in a corner of the hospital cafeteria downstairs. At the breakfast meeting, Commander, Naval Forces, Japan (COMNAVFORJAPAN) Public Affairs Officers (PAO), a husband-wife team, were introduced. The couple worked for Admiral Zech, representing the administrative side of the US Navy in Japan. They explained the proper way to interact with the media because it was certain the men would receive media requests to talk about the events of the past ten days. Their advice was detailed, specific, and on-target. The guidelines given ensured that the reporters got their stories without becoming too demanding, too invasive, or too abusive with them in their quest for the next headline.

Commander Bud Powers, who had put hours into accommodating the survivors' desire to return with the deceased, balanced the joyfulness of the survivors' return with the respect and solemnity of returning the deceased crewmen to their families. He informed them that the plan was to land at Moffett Field at 10:30 a.m. on Saturday morning for a brief homecoming ceremony, followed by a press conference, and that the accident investigation would begin on Monday. He shared that they would be transported nonstop by an Air Force C-141 Starlifter. Thanks to the magic of the international date line, Yokota was ten hours ahead of Moffett, and in local time they would be "gaining a day," technically landing in California before they took off from Japan.

Back upstairs, they thanked the doctors and nurses, packed up their "souvenir" hospital pajamas into little gym bags, and waited for the bus to take them to the ramp. Once again, the Air Force did not disappoint: the bus was a newer diesel bus with comfortable upholstered seats, painted Air Force blue. It took them directly out to the ramp and parked right next to the plane, and unlike most international travel, there were no passports, no formal check-ins; their names were on a flight manifest, and they were set to go.

The Lockheed C-141 from the 63rd Military Airlift wing based in Southern California was already pre-flighted, fully fueled, and ready for taxi as they entered through the forward passenger door. The flag-draped silver metal caskets of Brooner, Rodriguez, and Garcia were already loaded near the rear cargo ramp. The deceased had been transferred from the plain wooden caskets of the Soviet Union to metal Defense Department–style caskets, and in the Yokota Hospital they had been dressed in dress blue uniforms for the trip home. The survivors insisted that the deceased crew members accompany them home to Moffett. The crew had taken off from Adak together, and they wanted to return together. This point was nonnegotiable.

The survivors were seated in a small section of backward-facing seats upholstered in Air Force blue, which were supposedly safer than forward-facing airline seats, and they were in favor of anything safer. The plane interior was cavernous, almost twice the size of the P-3. It had a wide body with a windowless, utilitarian, military industrial look that fit its role as either a troop or a cargo carrier. There was a metal floor with tracks and rollers. Along the edges were fold-up web benches. The interior could be reconfigured to suit many possible missions. The senior enlisted loadmaster gave them a quick pre-takeoff safety briefing and showed them where coffee, lunches, and lavatories were located, and then they were ready to go.

After the plane climbed away from the greater Tokyo area, the pilots invited them to come forward and tour the cockpit. They were proud of their airplane and eager to show it off. The survivors felt welcomed by the Air Force crew on this, their fourth flight since the ditching. They were able to climb up a short ladder from the cargo bay to the huge cockpit, which held seats for three pilots, two flight engineers, a navigator, a loadmaster, and bunks for crew rest. They had never seen a cockpit that big. Many of the gauges had red, yellow, or green dials, and Matt checked quickly to be sure nothing was red. The cockpit was remarkably quiet compared to the cargo bay; despite the noise in the cargo bay, they were able to sleep in their seats for most of the transpacific flight back to California.

A few hours later, they awoke to the sound of engines winding down, the Air Force crew slowing the plane in order to land at the right time. Just like the PARPRO flights, the Air Force was going to land within the appointed time window — not too early and not too late. They were still out over the ocean and could barely make out the California coast in the distance.

In the Quiet of the Evening

Almaden Valley

November 3

*F*riends and relatives are still stopping by, some with food, but the pace is much less hectic. I'm beginning to enjoy visiting with those I haven't seen for some time. Becky and my brothers need to get back to their lives—to work and to school. They will drive back with Jon in his car. Doug tells me their old Ford Pinto is on its last legs and they may need to get another car soon, hard to do on their limited college income. He's looking forward to graduating from the University of Washington in the spring, getting a job, and then it will be Becky's turn to go back and finish school. I look out the front window and see our VW squareback in the driveway. I picture Jerry driving home from work and turning into the driveway; the memory is painful. I won't need two cars and I feel inspired to sell it to them. We talk about it for a while, decide on a fair price, and I tell them they can pay for it in installments. They will leave tomorrow. Becky has already been away from work for over a week.

My mom tells me she will stay with me until I am back on my feet, and I am relieved because I'm not ready to be left on my own. My dad will drive back to Seattle in a couple of days, and my mom will fly home when it is time for her to go. The girls and I will go back to school on Monday. Things are starting to settle down to a new normal. The Grigsbys need to return to Oklahoma and plan to fly out tomorrow, but for now, I am still enjoying their company. It will feel lonely when everyone is gone.

Aunt Miriam, my dad's sister, comes by with her son and daughter-in-law. We don't see her often because she lives in Magalia, up in Northern California, but through the weekend she is staying with her son in Fremont. Mom fixes them some tea, and we sit around the kitchen table visiting. Aunt Miriam tells us she had had a premonition a few days ago that someone in the family would die, though the image was vague and she couldn't tell who the person was. I feel a chill. Her oldest son had drowned in a rafting accident on the Colorado River. She had a feeling about that trip and asked him not to go, so now she takes these things more seriously. I tell her about my own premonition, and now I take these things seriously too.

Mary and Lisa have been sleeping on the love seats in the family room because their beds have been taken over by guests. I am helping them get the love seats ready for the night and am feeling particularly lonesome in the quiet of the evening. Lisa asks me if Mr. Gibbons was a survivor of the accident. I know both girls like him because he is fun-loving and playful like my brothers, but I am wondering what made her think of him now. They have only met him once when Jerry hosted a barbeque and pool party during the summer for his crew. I haven't really been thinking about who else was in the accident, and I know the survivors are not even back in California yet, but she shocks me with what she says next. She wonders if I could marry him. I take *in a deep breath. Unbelievable . . . hard to understand the thought processes of a nine-year-old child. Perhaps she says this because she misses her dad and understands he won't be coming back.*

Anchors Aweigh

NAS Moffett Field, California
Saturday, November 4

Exactly on time, the C-141 landed at Moffett Field on Runway 32L, and taxied back to the ramp in front of the control tower and base operations building. Much to the survivors' surprise, a hundred or more of their squadron mates were standing in formation in their dress blue uniforms along with hundreds of friends, family members, and reporters.

Commander Powers led them out onto the tarmac as the Navy band from the San Francisco Naval District played "Anchors Aweigh." The ten survivors filed out and stood behind him near a podium. Admiral Charles O. Prindle, the Commander Patrol Wings Pacific, spoke first as he welcomed the crew back home and delivered remarks honoring those who had died during a vital mission for the nation's defense:

> "Reflecting back on the past ten days, this is clearly a time of mixed emotions. For even as we rejoice in the return of ten of our friends and loved ones, we are mindful of the five courageous members of Crew 6 whose heroic actions contributed so much to make this reunion possible."

Commander Powers followed with a few remarks of his own. He praised Lieutenant Commander Jerry Grigsby's airmanship in executing a controlled ditching into a raging North Pacific storm with waves of unimaginable size.

Then it was Ed Caylor's turn:

"Without the expertise of our senior pilot, there would not be even one of us here to talk to you today. We had a catastrophic propeller failure that caused several fires, the last of which we could not extinguish. In the end, Lieutenant Commander Grigsby had thirty seconds to ditch the plane or it would have exploded in midair. He rewrote the book on ditching an aircraft into water. While it's great to be back, at the same time we have a lot of sorrow and regret about those who were lost."

The Moffett Field Navy Chaplain, Captain Richard McCue, delivered a short prayer while the rear ramp doors of the C-141 were lowered. As he finished, a Marine Honor Guard delivered a twenty-one-gun salute and the flag bearers formed up to lead the three caskets through two long lines of saluting shipmates. The three teams of pallbearers were composed of friends from the squadron and Marines from Base Security. As the Navy band played the Navy Hymn, "Eternal Father, Strong to Save," the caskets were loaded into three black hearses waiting to the left of the base tower. The official ceremony concluded and spouses, relatives, and friends rushed the survivors.

Standing on the ramp in front of hundreds of people, a random thought flashed through Matt's mind: Would the Navy make him pay to replace the aircraft? Thoughts about the investigation and its consequences continued to dominate his thoughts. He worked to push them out of his mind as being unlikely. Matt was surprised to see his sister Clare, who came running up, gave him a big hug, and told him she was proud of his courage in the face of impossible odds. She had flown in from New York to represent their family. Lost for words, and working to hold back tears, he told her that he had only been doing his job. Squadron mates and flight training friends from sister squadrons came up to shake his hand and welcome him back.

He was experiencing many mixed feelings including gladness to be home, grief for those lost, and concerns about how the accident investigation would play out. When he saw Jerry Kimble, a very senior Lieutenant and fellow NFO who was going to law school in the evenings, Matt thought he would be a perfect candidate for the Accident Investigation Board, and in his unfathomably naive outlook, asked him to take part in the board—as if he, Matt, had any choice in the matter.

The survivors stopped to express their condolences to the relatives of their lost shipmates as they were being ushered into the conference room of base operations for a press conference with the Bay Area media. They exchanged quick handshakes, expressed feelings of sorrow and sadness, and Bruce and Matt said they would be in touch, planning to be with them for the services.

Ed Caylor, introduced to the media as the copilot and senior survivor, did a great job of providing basic answers. He said: "We had a crucial propeller failure and then multiple engine fires. We knew that if we did not set the plane down on the water it would have exploded in the air. I can't believe it, but Grigsby put us down safely even against the force of strong winds and monstrous waves." He went on to explain that the Navy would conduct a full accident investigation and those results would be made public at the conclusion.

Matt handled a question about the deceased saying that they would prefer to meet with the families directly so that they would hear from them in person before they read about it in the media. He then went on to answer a question about the aircraft evacuation: "In any hazardous profession you do a lot of training for emergencies. You never think it will happen to you, but you train nonetheless. Our training and procedures paid off in the first successful ditching under these circumstances. Our own squadron, the Air Force, and the Coast Guard had aircraft circling above us, and even though it was dark, we could see their lights. When they flew over us, we would set off survival flares to let them know we were still alive, and they would blink their lights to let us know they saw us."

Ed Caylor answered a question about the Soviet ship: "We could not have had better care, not even in our own country. The Russian fishermen knew exactly what to do, and they were marvelous. They risked their lives to save ours. The medical care we received on the ship was outstanding. They treated us as well as our own people would have."

"One of the first things they said to us," Matt added, "was that they were astounded that ten of us were alive. They expected to recover more deceased bodies. As for the crew on the ship, they were friendly, and given the limited English they knew, we got along very well."

A few reporters were angling to get any juicy details that they could once they made it to the conference room. Some of the questions were insensitive about how people had died, and other questions were premature about an accident investigation that had not yet taken place. There were many questions about why they were flying so close to the Soviet Union, and it was a good thing they had been coached by Public Affairs Officers in Japan or they would have been caught off guard and stumbled over their answers.

After about thirty minutes of questions, they were free to go. Matt reminded the crew to be at the hangar at 8:00 a.m. Monday morning in dress blue uniforms when they would learn about the plan of the day. They wished Master Chief Shepard and Gary Hemmer safe travels back to Adak. Another Moffett squadron would fly them back to their home base later that afternoon.

Matt was amazed that his sister Clare had his car, and they drove around the field to the VP-9 hangar to pick up his personal belongings from Adak. Lieutenant (junior grade) Ray Enzenauer had packed out his BOQ room in Adak, and when Clare arrived at SFO, she was met by squadron escorts—including Ensign Martha "Marty" Eggert—who drove her down to Moffett Field and gave her Matt's car and townhouse keys. It seemed the squadron had thought of everything.

Matt was busy with phone calls to family and friends all afternoon. In the evening, they went to Lieutenant Mike Carrig's house for a get-together with a few other junior officers who were interested in the whole story. As it turned out, that Friday morning after quarters, Commander Cressy had gathered the squadron around the podium to hear the audiotape of the Mayday radio communications between the plane and Elmendorf radio. Matt wondered what impact the tapes would have on the accident investigation, and he was tired of all the questions and too preoccupied to relax and enjoy the party.

The next day, Matt, Clare, and Marty played tourist in San Francisco, visiting the usual sites of Fisherman's Wharf, the Golden Gate Bridge, and Ghirardelli Square. They had dinner in Chinatown at Sam Wo's—a narrow three-story restaurant with the kitchen on the first floor—and were served by a legendary waiter named Edsel Ford Fung who had been featured in numerous newspaper articles. Edsel loved to tease his guests, seating his favorites on the second floor, and sending the others up to the third floor with a different waiter. Edsel would make fun of his guests, frequently putting them to work taking orders or busing dishes into the dumbwaiter for the dishwashers below. Edsel was an entertaining diversion, but Matt couldn't quite let go of his preoccupation about the investigation; he played along anyway because he wanted his sister to have a good visit.

He felt that finding fault was going to be the priority of the investigation, and that after being put under the microscope, he could potentially shoulder blame for many things.

In the late 1970s, the Navy culture reflected a curious blend of high-tech advancement and a two-hundred-year heritage of honor, courage, and commitment. Rapid technological advances in digital computing, new software, and improved solid state electronic hardware were being introduced into a fleet where long-standing norms of "this is how we always do it" prevailed.

Change came slowly, and one long-held value was that an officer was always responsible for everything that happened under his command. The concept was deeply ingrained into every level of the organization so that fear of failure, combined with a zero-defects mentality, meant that if you messed up, you could expect to be held accountable. It was a culture where errors were never acceptable and mistakes were neither tolerated nor forgiven.

However, there exists a fine line between being responsible and being blamed when things go wrong. Throughout Naval aviation, mistakes were always analyzed and any lessons learned were widely shared. At the onset of the investigation, Matt knew that areas he was responsible for—namely the safe and complete evacuation of the tube with the full complement of survival equipment—would be studied in detail. He owned the fact that he was responsible for it all.

The key question for him was how much he would be blamed. Would he be blamed for "failure to communicate" for leaving the emergency sonobuoy and the second seven-man life raft behind? Weighing heavily on his mind was the reality that the unavailability of communication equipment could be considered a major contributing factor in as many as four deaths. His key lesson learned was to use a parachute shroud cutter to cut through straps and quickly remove needed equipment.

Throughout his training, emergency drills had been practiced repeatedly. So much so that they were habitually performed on every flight. These ditching drill rehearsals rarely occurred in complete darkness. They never occurred in simulated environments with thousands of gallons per minute of inrushing seawater. By contrast, the Navy's submarine and surface personnel did simulate flooding during emergency simulations. The combination of the darkness and the depth of the flooding seawater called for instant on-the-spot reactions and judgments.

During his basic and advanced flight training, the syllabus emphasized that emergency procedures had evolved over time and that they had been "written in blood." That said, it was also pointed out that rigid adherence to following step-by-step procedures was no guarantee of success, and that aviators were trained to exercise their best judgment under stress to pursue a successful outcome.

Matt's concern was that his snap decisions in a dark, flooded, and rapidly sinking tube would be nitpicked within the warm and comfortable confines of a California conference room. Had any of the investigators ever envisioned five feet of water in the tube while still trying to get gear out? He was not looking forward to the process. What if he was faulted for failing to launch the third raft and for pulling Randy across to the starboard overwing exit instead? The one positive thought he had in his mind, at least, was he was alive and could defend his thought process, a luxury Jerry and Butch no longer had.

Back to School

Almaden Valley
November 6

I leave my mother behind at home, drop my daughters off at Los Alamitos School, and then I head to my classes at San Jose State, traveling north up the Almaden Expressway. My mom has been a big help, cleaning house and cooking meals she knows the girls will like; they have gotten a little tired of the casseroles from the refrigerator. I am wondering how hard it will be to get caught up with my studies when I realize I am heading the wrong way on a one-way street. I have traveled this route so many times that I thought I could do it in my sleep, so how did this happen? I am more than a little shaken, but manage to find my way to the parking garage without further incident. It feels good to be back, a little more like the way my life used to be.

I work hard to keep my focus on the lectures and to take notes. My mind wants to wander. I can always borrow notes from someone if I think I have missed too much, but I am determined to take control of myself. At the end of each class, I ask the professors what I need to do to get caught up. They are all understanding and kind, and they tell me to *take whatever time I need. Out in the hallway after class, a friend asks me how I'm doing. Up until now, I have held it together, but I break down in tears and my friend gives me a hug. I notice the professor watching from the doorway, but when he sees me look up, he goes back into the classroom.*

When I drive up to the house after classes, I notice that the living room windows are open. Then when I get out of the car, I can hear piano music, and as I walk toward the front door, I smell lemon Pledge. Mom stops playing and tells me about her day when I walk in. She has been busy cleaning and cooking. She shows me the sparkling clean crystals from the dining room chandelier and tells me how she cleaned them with a toothbrush and ammonia. I have lived here almost two years now, and never noticed that the crystals needed special cleaning beyond dusting. She also washed the living room windows on the inside and polished the furniture. She has a meatball stew simmering—meatballs instead of stew meat because she has noticed that Lisa doesn't like to chew chunks of meat. The girls aren't home yet. They will be walking home with friends and should be here soon; I have timed my class schedule so that I am always here by the time their school is out.

The phone rings and it is Ken Smith. He has Jerry's things from his BOQ room at Adak and asks if he can bring them over this evening. He would like to bring the Casualty Assistance Calls Officer (CACO) with him to introduce him to us because he can help me with paperwork. I think that is a good idea.

Mary and Lisa come home with friends and ask if they can play outside for a while. Mom tells them we will be having dinner at five o'clock, so stay close enough for us to call them. That's no problem because we live on a small cul-de-sac and the kids all like to play out front, probably because most of the houses have backyard pools. Most of the kids are in upper-elementary school and seem to get along with each other quite well. Right now, they are drawing a town on the street with large pieces of chalk, and it looks quite elaborate with lots of detail. Mary draws a floor plan with a swimming pool in the back. These are creative kids and this project will keep them busy for days; a couple of the younger teenagers have gotten involved as well.

Mom starts cleaning out the refrigerator and washing casserole dishes, many of which are not marked with names, and she doesn't know what to do with them. I tell her to leave them on the kitchen counter and we'll figure that out later—will ask friends and neighbors as they drop by if they know who owns these unmarked dishes. At five o'clock she stops washing, starts setting the table, and asks me to call the girls in for dinner. Mary is happy to be called in because some of the kids are arguing about who was taking up too much space with their drawings.

Lisa is excited about the bite-size meatballs and cleans her plate. It is Mary's turn to clear the table and Lisa's turn to load the dishwasher. They have it all marked out on the calendar, and Mary likes to keep track of how long it takes them to clean up. They have a bit of competition going between them and like to get the work done as fast as possible. They have become motivated to get these chores out of the way, and I rarely need to remind them, which is amazing for kids their ages. I can't quite remember how all of this got started. When these chores are done, I tell them it's homework time. Mary gets right on it, but I always need to prod Lisa along. Her favorite part of school is recess and Friday pizza made by Jo in the cafeteria. I have her work at the kitchen table so I can keep an eye on her. Meanwhile Mom is washing casserole dishes again.

Ken Smith arrives with Lieutenant (junior grade) Bob Masoero, the CACO, and introduces us. They ask where they *should put the boxes of belongings, and I ask if they would mind carrying them upstairs and putting them in the master bedroom. When that is done, I invite them to sit in the living room while Mom makes tea. Ken tells me that Jerry left a dollhouse he was working on for the girls, but he didn't bring it with him today because it is unfinished. A small group of officers and their wives would like to finish the project if that is okay with me. I tell him I would like that very much. Bob goes on to tell me I will receive monthly Social Security and Veteran's benefit payments and he will help me fill out the paperwork when I am up to it. I will be eligible to receive additional Veteran's tuition benefits until I am finished at San Jose State University. I am relieved to hear this because I would like very much to be able to stay here in this house until I finish my degree, and with that money, I'm hoping to be able to make the house payments and have enough left over to cover our basic expenses. Mom brings in tea and cookies, and Bob and I set up an appointment for next week. He asks if I would be able to gather certain paperwork together before that meeting, and I tell him that I can do that—I know exactly where everything is. Jerry has everything organized.*

After they leave, Mom comments on how nice these young men are and how helpful everyone in the squadron has been. I know that is true; I have many good memories from over the years. Navy life can be hard on families, but the people are wonderful and supportive. At every duty station, there has been a strong wives' club ready to get me involved in their activities. They have a monthly luncheon at the Officers' Club, and various other activities, including volunteer work. Frequent parties and "happy hours" make it easy to get to know other couples. Medical care is free at small base dispensaries and at larger regional Naval hospitals. On most bases there is a hobby shop, which offers a variety of classes. There is usually a swimming pool and a movie theater, a commissary with discounted groceries, a Navy Exchange with clothing and many other necessities. Base housing is typically offered in lieu of the off-base housing allowance, but we usually prefer to buy our own home, which we can afford to do because we got into the California housing market early on with a VA no-down-payment loan.

Dual Investigations

Moffett Field

November 6

Monday, November 6, was much like any other day in Hanger Three at Moffett, except that it wasn't. The mood was a mix of awkwardness and tension as the survivors tried to return to normal. At an All Officers Meeting the Friday before, plans were shared for their Saturday homecoming event and the squadron was instructed to give the survivors some space.

The eight survivors were all there before 8:00 a.m. wearing their dress blue uniforms while the rest of the squadron wore their brown leather flight jackets over khakis or flight suits. A conference room upstairs on the second deck had been set up for the investigations that would begin at 9:00 a.m. The first order of business would be to define the purpose and scope of the investigations and to start interviewing survivors to establish the facts.

Lieutenant Commander Jim Dvorak had returned from Adak and was appointed to lead the Judge Advocate General (JAG) Manual Command Investigation; he was the Maintenance Department Head. Lieutenant Eddie Angel was the squadron Legal Officer who would act as the investigation secretary to ensure compliance with the JAG investigation guidelines. The JAG Manual Report had a thirty-day deadline so superiors in the squadron's chain of command could route it for review and approval.

In parallel with the legal investigation, the Accident Investigation Board was chaired by Lieutenant Andy Pease and assisted by Lieutenant Larry Carr. Both had attended the six-week Aviation Safety School training program in Monterey, California. Both were well-versed in the proper conduct of an aircraft accident investigation. Andy was the Aviation Safety Officer and would guide the accident investigation process and produce the report for the Navy Safety Center. He and Larry both had ground jobs in the safety department, recently headed by Jerry Grigsby.

The two investigation teams had distinctly separate roles, but equal scope and power to request documents and interview witnesses. By design, they were completely independent of each other.

The JAG Manual Command Investigation was tasked with producing a report summarizing the legal facts of the accident. After all witnesses were advised of their rights, privacy, and the right to have a lawyer present, their interviews could begin. Their report would read like an old-school history lesson. It would focus on events, names, times, and dates. The final report would consist of three major sections: Findings of Fact, Opinions, and Recommendations. The goal was to quickly provide Navy leadership with a factual overview of what happened—with an emphasis on any legal repercussions that might arise. Commander Powers would provide the first level of approval before the report was circulated further.

The Accident Investigation Board had a completely different goal and timeline. The Naval Safety Center was more concerned with the "why" behind the root causes of the accident. Their focus was less on dates and times and more on analyzing all contributing factors, developing and finalizing conclusions, and then documenting specific corrective actions that could be implemented in order to prevent future accidents.

In 1978, a Class "A" mishap was defined by the Navy as damage to an aircraft exceeding one million dollars, or an accident resulting in severe injury or death. Clearly, losing a $23 million aircraft and five lives ensured that this was serious business that would be investigated with a fine-tooth comb.

For the legal record: The incident aircraft Navy Bureau Number 159892, P-3C Update 1, Lockheed Model 285A, Lockheed Serial Number 5643 delivered to the Navy on 22 September 1976. The preliminary finding was classified as a Strike Loss (removing it from the Navy's active aircraft inventory), effective 26 October 1978. Preliminary cause of loss was classified as ditched and sunk in North Pacific Ocean, 200 miles southwest of Attu, Aleutian Islands, Alaska. Deaths 05.

The five deceased crew members were each identified by name, rank, Social Security number, and crew position. Their service records were submitted for review. They were all quickly deemed to be fully qualified for their in-flight roles on 26 October aboard Alfa Foxtrot 586. Investigation into their state of mind or other human factors would happen in follow-up sessions.

During a break from the morning's JAG Manual preliminaries, a fellow NFO asked Matt if he was planning to request to have an attorney present. Despite the formal nature of the JAG investigation, the thought of legal representation had never really crossed his mind. His thought process was that after what he had just been through, and all that he learned firsthand, what else could the Navy possibly do to him—send him back to the Aleutians? Just as naive as ever . . .

The JAG Manual team decided to play the entire forty-minute audiotape of the Mayday communications between Alfa Foxtrot 586 and Elmendorf during the morning's second session. The survivors were instructed to listen and write down any recollections triggered by the audio to help establish an approximate timeline to firm up the flight's ninety-minute sequence of events. The audio was surprisingly clear inside the conference room, without the noise and vibration inside the aircraft, and despite being quite dramatic and emotional to listen to, it served to jog the individual memories of the survivors. Black Skilcraft ballpoint pens were busy on yellow legal pads as the crew made their notes. With this step accomplished, the investigators were able to develop an accurate timeline that aligned with the time stamps on the recording. The next step was to stitch together individual observations into the "big picture" of what happened and when.

After lunch, the focus of the investigation was almost entirely about the restart of the number one engine, the propeller overspeed, the fluid leakage observations, and the confusing and conflicting annunciator light behavior. The emphasis focused on the emergency shutdown procedure and the timing of the oil tank shut-off valve circuit breaker reset.

All squadron maintenance records were safeguarded and introduced into evidence. The recent propeller replacement records were requested as well.

In parallel, the Accident Investigation Board emphasized again that this was not going to be a rush to judgment, and their focus would be on root cause analysis and lessons learned. Day one ended with a sense that the crew was in for hours of fact-finding. The engineers and technical reps from Lockheed California, GM Allison (the engine manufacturer), and Hamilton Standard (the propeller manufacturer) would be questioned in the days ahead. The surviving crew had dodged any major criticism on day one and wondered what day two would bring.

Monday evening, Matt dropped his sister Clare off at SFO for a late-night flight back to New York and then fought the Silicon Valley traffic back to his home in San Jose. He needed to catch up on his Adak laundry, so later that night, he went to a neighborhood Laundromat and to Renato's Pizza next door to grab some dinner. He was still preoccupied about what tomorrow would bring. He didn't realize until he got home that he had left a load of laundry in the dryer. By the time he got back to the Laundromat, his clothes were long gone and he had a clear feeling this was going to be "one of those weeks."

On Tuesday morning, November 7, Ed Caylor, John Wagner, and Ed Flow met with Hamilton Standard technical reps Robert Madsden and George Nesky to review in detail their observations, the timing, and the series of steps they had taken in the cockpit. Andy Pease and others would spend many weeks with them trying to precisely pinpoint the exact cause of the propeller overspeed and develop new procedures to prevent future overspeeds.

John Ball, Bruce, Matt, and Dave met with the Lockheed engineers, led by John Christensen, to share their observations from the tube as well. Lieutenant Eddie Angel moderated these sessions because, as an NFO, he was very interested in how the tube performed. The session got off to a rocky start as the Lockheed team was in total disbelief that the starboard wing ripped off. They were shocked that the emergency lights that had been manually switched on before water impact failed after water impact, and that the small two-inch metal buckles on the lower straps of multiple survival equipment items were difficult, if not impossible, to release in the dark under three or four feet of inrushing North Pacific water.

The Lockheed engineers challenged these observations saying that you could fly this airplane into a mountain and the wings would still stay attached. The Navy-Lockheed conversion from the Electra airliner added a stronger wing spar and redesigned engine mounts. They were proud of their design improvements, as well as defensive and dismayed. Their strongly held point of view was that when impacting the waves at 80 mph—even with approach flaps selected—the wings would have stayed attached. Dave provided his eyewitness account of the starboard wing passing his observation window in a giant fireball.

They also said there was no way those emergency exit lights could have failed. John Ball said he remembered that the lights were turned on and gave a detailed description of how the lights went out. The engineers said that was impossible and that they had engineering data showing that couldn't have happened. At a fifty-foot-per-minute descent into the water, the fuselage structure should have performed well—it was designed to withstand the ditching forces as described to them. Gradually their denial turned to acceptance as more people confirmed in their own words what they had observed. These were professional engineers who needed time to process new and totally unanticipated information.

The survivors described the extensive damage to the fuselage and were surprised to learn that the engineers thought it had performed exactly as designed. The forward end of the fuselage had bent to the left where the curved cockpit met the cylindrical tube. This caused the observation windows at the TACCO station to implode, and to explode at the NAVCOMM station. From the starboard side of the aircraft where the two life rafts were launched it looked like a bomb had gone off. It was possible that propeller blade fragments or entire blades impacted the fuselage there. As the ocean flooded into the tube, these two gaping holes acted as large vents allowing air to escape until the point where they too were submerged. At that point, the ocean flooded in even faster.

The structural failures at the aft end of the fuselage, called the empennage, were a focus of the investigation, especially because that was most likely where Butch Miller had died. The engineers were not surprised as the failures happened where the fuselage tapered into the rounded tail and pointy magnetic anomaly detector (MAD) boom. They explained in detail to the survivors that aircraft are designed to dissipate energy by crumpling back there. The sizable crack in the vertical stabilizer was completely expected above the aft pressure bulkhead. Matt wondered to himself why there were ditching stations in the back galley.

The atmosphere was more cordial after lunch because the Lockheed team had had a chance to digest the survivor observations, though they were still somewhat in denial about the emergency light failure; they had requested more engineering data from the factory. Overall, the crew was feeling listened to and that Eddie Angel was dutifully recording their insights.

Reconvening after a coffee break, Matt was stunned by a question addressed to him: "With only fifteen men on board, why did you assign Butch Miller into Ditching Station Twenty-One?" It hit him like a gut punch as he realized that this might be an attempt to hold him responsible for Butch's death, and his face showed the shock he felt. John Ball, who had been seated across the aisle in Ditching Station Twenty-Three, jumped to Matt's defense, and said that they had been allowed to pick their own seats. He and Butch were in the back where they had been shredding classified materials by hand on the two galley tables. That seemed to be enough for the time being, but it reignited Matt's paranoia, and he wondered if a Lockheed lawyer had posed that question during the break.

He and John were reasonably confident that Lockheed lawyers were actively involved behind the scenes proposing questions even though they never saw any face-to-face meetings with them. Multiple accidents in the past had yielded a ton of negative press for Lockheed and had placed them on the defensive. Matt knew that Lockheed had way more money than he did, since a Navy salary of $12,800 a year would not go very far. He was young, idealistic, and naive enough to think that if he told the truth, everything would work out. After all, he kept repeating to himself, they were the first survivors who were able to provide any information at all.

On the second day of the accident investigation, the pilots continued with discussions and research requests about the "new and improved" cold weather propeller fluid, the recently rebuilt prop, and the version and dimensions of the O-ring seal. The interviews continued with the off-speed increase then decrease, the final runaway prop overspeed, and the delay in restoring oil flow to the reduction gearbox. There were lengthy discussions about the annunciator lights, how and when they were tested, and what they indicated at various times.

The non-pilots were broken out into individual sessions for one-on-one interviews. Matt felt lucky that Eddie Angel conducted his interview. They had been next-door neighbors on the Kadena, Okinawa, deployment the year before. Eddie was curious about Matt's missing helmet since it had not turned up in Adak and was going to be replaced anyway; it would be "surveyed" or deemed damaged beyond repair. Eddie asked Matt about the performance of the inflatable hood that came in the QD-1 survival dry suit and how well it worked.

During the review of Matt's training records, it came out that he was overdue for his annual instrument rating recertification. Navy policy was to complete the exam in your birth month. Matt was thirteen weeks past due. This could have been a big deal, labeling him technically not qualified to fly that day. It would have been critically essential if he had been flying a smaller Navy tactical jet with a traditional instrument panel.

The P-3 TACCO station was centered around a large circular tactical display with dozens of rows of touch-sensitive switches. It had none of the typical black-and-white cockpit flight instruments to monitor. Nevertheless, he was still required to be instrument certified. As an NFO, he was fully aware that it was his responsibility to recertify and he acknowledged the fact that he was overdue. Every time he had been scheduled to take the proctored exam, he was added to an event on the flight schedule. He was aware of how the crews had been overextended to fill the flight schedule, and copies of the past three months of schedules were available and quickly cross-checked, confirming that he was flying on the days the test was offered.

Within the hour, arrangements were made for him to take the exam on Thursday. Eddie had used every bit of southern charm he had to push this through.

That afternoon, the squadron received word that funeral arrangements were scheduled for Rich Garcia and Randy Rodriquez for Wednesday. Ed Caylor, Bruce, and Matt expressed interest in representing the squadron if they could. Doc Espiritu medically cleared them to return to flight status, encouraging them to get back in the air as soon as possible, and travel orders were issued.

Seaplanes and Paradise

Memories

Almaden Valley

I'm getting used to being back in school; it's a good distrac-tion for me, although I'm still having trouble keeping my attention on the lectures. My heart is heavy with sadness, like a cold stone resting in my chest, keeping me down. Mom is busy cleaning my house like it's never been cleaned before: kitchen cupboards, closets, and bathrooms. I always con-sidered myself to be a good housekeeper, although recently there have been a lot of people in and out of the house and I haven't exactly been on top of things.

She has questions for me every day when I get home, wanting to know where things should go. I tell her I wish she wouldn't work so hard; she says she is here to help me and doesn't have anything else to do while I'm away at San Jose State most of the day, and I can see her point. I decide to have a couple of the neighbors drop in on her for a visit, or maybe take her to the grocery store to get things she would like to have on hand. I still tire easily—my mind in a fog of grief—and I try to take a little nap before the girls get home from school, especially on Tuesdays and Thursdays, which are shorter school days for me.

I answer all Mom's questions and then head upstairs for a nap. As frequently happens, I can't fall asleep, and I find myself thinking about when Jerry and I first moved to California. He had finished all his advanced flight training in early 1966, had earned his Wings of Gold, and had been assigned to his first duty station—the Marlin Warriors of VP-50 at NAS North Island on Coronado, across the bay from San Diego. He was assigned to fly P-5M seaplanes, not his first choice, but an okay assignment considering that the following year the squadron would be transitioning into the newer P-3 airplanes, which was his first choice.

When we arrived in Coronado, I thought we had moved to paradise. The town was quaint with unique shops and restaurants, and cute little houses. The weather was perfect—not a cloud in the sky—the white sandy beach sloped gently toward the bright blue ocean, and the rhythm of the crashing waves was almost hypnotic. The main access to the town was by ferry, although to the south there was a long, narrow strand of land connecting Coronado to Imperial Beach down by the Mexican border. Housing in Coronado was expensive, exceeding the housing allowance, and no base housing was available for students. A few squadron couples decided to live in Imperial Beach where they could get more house for their money, an idea I liked quite well. Jerry wanted to live in Coronado, which was convenient to the base. It would cut down on commute time and make it easier when he had to stand duty.

We were able to find a little two-bedroom house—after much searching—with affordable rent, but it needed a little TLC. The owner agreed to pay for paint if we would do the work ourselves. The new paint and a new area rug in the living room gave the little house a cozy feel, and it was within

walking distance to the beach and shopping, a huge conve-
nience since we owned only one car. A few friends that we
knew from Jerry's flight training days were also stationed at
North Island NAS, and they had all been assigned to additional training.

The seaplanes would land in San Diego Bay and taxi
toward North Island NAS. They had boat-shaped hulls—not
pontoons—and had the right-of-way over small pleasure
boats and the ferries. It was exciting to ride the ferry, feel
it slow down and watch as a seaplane cruised by. It was a
happy and comfortable time for us. The Vietnam War seemed
a million miles away . . .

I started feeling a little restless after Jerry began seaplane
training, and I wanted something more to do. I still enjoyed
wives' club luncheons, took bridge lessons, and worked in the
base thrift shop once a week, but something was missing.
We bought a television set, but that wasn't it either. I was
spending a lot of time reading and going for walks; officers'
wives didn't have careers during those years. We wouldn't be
there long enough for me to go to school—the current semester was already well under way—and the whole squadron
would be moving to Moffett Field to transition into the new
planes in a few months. After spending time with friends who
had young children, I realized what was missing in my life. I
talked to Jerry about it, and we both got excited about the
idea of starting a family and proceeded in that direction. My
life was about to change in ways I couldn't have imagined.

That was when the Navy changed its schedule, and the
Vietnam War suddenly became a lot closer. VP-50 would be
deploying the whole squadron to Southeast Asia soon to a
base in the Philippines where they would fly patrols off the
coast of Vietnam. Jerry would be joining the squadron over
there after he completed training. The Navy could change

schedules, but Mother Nature already had me on a schedule that was fixed firmly in place. I was excited about having a baby, but now I was also apprehensive.

Jerry was not officially part of VP-50 yet—not until he completed training—and I wasn't part of that wives' group. We knew two or three other young officers and their wives from the training squadron who would be joining VP-50 in the weeks ahead. We were friendly with a couple who were also expecting their first child in the middle of that rescheduled deployment, but Jan quickly started making plans to stay with her parents on the East Coast until Drew came back from the Philippines. I didn't want to stay with my parents in Seattle because I was still hurt by my mother's behavior toward me during the months before Jerry and I married, and I didn't know how she would react to this new predicament of mine. She could easily become angry, say, "I told you so," and go off on me again. I started imagining going into labor while waiting for the ferry to take me across the bay to Balboa Naval Hospital. How would that work? I had recently heard about a police officer delivering a baby in a car because the baby wouldn't wait to get to the hospital. Would that be me?

Meanwhile, we continued to enjoy our life in Coronado. Summer was even more pleasant than spring; neither one of us had ever experienced such glorious weather. We adopted a cute little mixed breed puppy that was great company for me, and I enjoyed our walks along the bay together. My parents decided to drive down for a visit, and I was looking forward to seeing my dad and little brothers. I didn't realize how much I had been missing them, but I was still uncomfortable about seeing my mother.

Our reunion went well. Mom was excited about becoming a grandmother. She encouraged me to come stay with them while Jerry was away, to have the baby in Seattle where she and Dad could help, but I was still stubbornly holding on to my independence, wanting to prove myself strong. As the time for Jerry to leave came closer, though, I started reevaluating my situation. I knew I would be lonely with no family nearby and few friends. Jerry encouraged me to go to my family, said he would feel better if I did. He said we could drive up to Seattle together, the car would stay with me, and he could fly to the Philippines from Sea-Tac. I was talked into it.

It all went better than I could have imagined. My parents gave me their master bedroom and bathroom so I would be comfortable. I bought a bassinet so the baby could stay in the bedroom with me, and my mom and I went shopping for essential baby clothes, diapers, and bottles. I visited with longtime friends from my childhood and drove up to Whidbey Island for several days to be with my grandmother and cousins.

Word came that Jan had her baby, a boy; I was excited for her and sent a gift with a card and cheery note right away. A few days later, I learned that her baby was born with a serious heart defect and had to have open-heart surgery. His future was uncertain. I felt sad; my first note had been so happy and optimistic, so I wrote a new letter to her expressing my sorrow and saying she and the baby were in my thoughts and prayers. This was no time to have husbands away on the edge of war, and I was thankful to be with my parents, hoping nothing like that would happen to me and my baby.

In the middle of one cold December night, when the baby decided to come, my dad drove me through the snow to the hospital in downtown Seattle and stayed with me until Mary was born. He drove home to get my mother so she could see Mary. Mom was excited and kept talking about Mary's full head of dark hair, her one dimple, and her smile . . . such a beautiful girl! The next day, my dad passed out cigars to everyone at work—cigars with little pink bands.

I sent a telegram to Jerry in the Philippines. It was a standard format Navy message stating that I'd given birth to a healthy baby girl on December 7 with few other real details. Even though we wrote back and forth every day, my letters were slow to get to him, and sometimes out of sequence. The Fleet Post Office would sometimes use ships, or occasionally aircraft, to move the mail on a space-available basis. My letter telling Jerry all about Mary and how smoothly everything had gone was delayed, but a later letter had gotten to him first. He wrote back asking the baby's name. He was frustrated that he didn't know her name, wondered why I hadn't told him, and was embarrassed when people kept asking. We had it narrowed down to two names before he left on deployment, and I hadn't made up my mind which one it would be until I saw her. I would be so happy when he came home—marriage by mail was a challenge.

Funeral Flights

Moffett Field

November 8

With the initial round of investigation interviews mostly behind them, Matt and Bruce wanted to attend the graveside services for Rich Garcia and Randy Rodriguez, wishing to represent the squadron as well as to speak personally with the families. Wednesday morning began early with a "dawn patrol" to the Denver area. With Bud Powers at the controls, they were able to justify this flight as a pilot training flight for new pilots.

Randy's midmorning graveside service was near Denver. He had a large extended family who deserved to hear what happened and to get their questions answered. Local TV stations were there, and the public relations coaching the survivors received in Japan helped them give the reporters the storyline they needed while graciously declining on-air interviews. It was difficult enough for them to be there under these sad and emotional conditions, and none of them wanted to be surprised by an on-air curveball question. The reporters understood their reluctance, given that they were in Siberia only a week earlier.

After that, it was on to Little Rock for Rich Garcia's late afternoon graveside service. Rich also had a large extended family, and again, local TV stations had reporters there. Two services in one day were a bit of a blur for them, but they felt it was the least they could do. The flight back to Moffett Field was a quiet, reflective return home after a long day that was more mentally exhausting than physically draining. At the squadron duty office, they learned Jim Brooner's funeral was scheduled for Friday in Oregon.

Investigations—Day Four

Moffett Field

November 9

On Thursday morning, Matt received a call that his prescription glasses had come in and he went to pick them up after his instrument exam. Once again, he could look the part of a Naval Flight Officer, wearing Navy issue aviator-style glasses instead of an old civilian pair from his college days. There was a running joke that you should never trust a Naval aviator with glasses or an NFO without them.

He sensed that everyone at the base medical dispensary was staring at him. They knew he was one of the survivors because the eyeglasses were expedited. There were numerous glances, whispers, and side conversations while he was waiting, and he felt more than a little self-conscious. He was not accustomed to having people treat him that way. He had not sought any attention and felt strongly that throughout the ditching he had been just doing his job. He was still very uncertain about the investigation process and how his decision-making inside the sinking tube would be evaluated. It was a great relief to get back into his car wearing the new glasses and to drive to the hangar knowing he had passed the instrument exam and that Eddie was able to steer the investigation in a different direction.

In the afternoon, he had a follow-on JAG human factors interview regarding the crew's state of mind leading up to the accident. He was one of the squadron members with more than a hundred days in Adak, and the board had questions about the environment, logistics, scheduling, or any other factors that might have contributed to the accident. He was quite outspoken and candid that the squadron was undermanned and many individuals had been overscheduled.

A series of questions led directly into Jerry Grigsby's state of mind. Matt had flown with him for ten months. They got to know each other quite well during that time, and Matt found him to be a skilled pilot, a respected mentor, a dedicated Naval Officer, and a devoted family man.

Jerry was openly positive about his experience as a Catapult Officer on the USS *Hancock*, where he had performed very well, and he encouraged young P-3 pilots to consider a carrier-based "Shooter" tour as a viable option for a career path. He said it was a great place for a P-3 officer to stand out. He felt that any average P-3 aviator would be a standout performer as part of the carrier's complement of officers.

Jerry was also a big advocate for a tour at the Naval Postgraduate School in Monterey, California, which was open to any qualified Naval Officer. He had majored in operations research there, a major that dealt with large-scale data modeling, lots of computer programming, and many real-world problem-solving class projects. He talked about his class projects, one of which involved designing a computer program to help AT&T size the hardware to effectively support starting up the 911 system in a new city. These class projects led to civilian employment connections and unsolicited verbal job offers that he could not act upon until after he completed his Naval service.

His time in Monterey was a great shore duty assignment for him and his family. He developed a lot of confidence there as he realized that while other officers with big-name university degrees struggled, his chemistry degree from a small state university in Oklahoma had prepared him very well. He enjoyed computer programming, found he had a talent for it, and his thesis adviser suggested he consider changing into that career track.

As this interview session went on, it became clear that the accident board was probing for possible distracting human factors in Jerry's life and his mindset during his final days. He had, three weeks before the accident, found out that he missed his first opportunity for promotion to the rank of Commander—been "passed over," as they call it. Initially, this was a disappointment to him. He had always thought if he did his best that this promotion was within his reach. There were some officers in the squadron who thought that some form of preoccupation with being passed over could have been a human factor in the accident, but Matt doubted that was true.

Not widely known, Jerry had already applied for redesignation as an Aviation Engineering Duty Officer specializing in computer programming. This career path would take him off the track toward squadron command and place him into more research-oriented work, which better suited his personality. This was not a typical career path, but it had the benefit of fewer and shorter trips away from home, something his wife favored. He was looking forward to more time with his family after four deployments in Vietnam, one in Okinawa, and now this tour in Adak. In 1978, the new digital Navy needed all the computer programming and software engineering talent it could find, and with his master's degree he felt he had a strong chance of making major contributions in that field.

The legal team was looking deeply into his personal life, and from Matt's point of view, they were looking in the wrong direction. Jerry was a devoted husband and father. Even on this detachment, he was thinking of his young daughters and building a dollhouse to take home to them. He lived in a nice suburban neighborhood in Almaden Valley and had a back-yard swimming pool and a new VW camper van. His family life seemed drama-free—better than many of the other officers in the squadron, some of whom believed in "open marriage" as a solution to the loneliness of long family separations. Matt had seen how that frequently didn't work out and unfortunately often ended in divorce. There was never any hint of marital or family discord for Jerry.

Later that afternoon, the survivors met and discussed whether anyone was considering turning in their wings to stop flying after what they had experienced in the accident. To a man, the answer was "no"; only the specifics varied. Some were very eager to get back in the airplane, while others wanted to take a few weeks before jumping back in. None of them wanted to be considered a quitter, and nobody was talking about taking extended PTSD recovery time in those days. They all wanted to "hack it," or to "suck it up," and return to flying. It was time for them to move on.

Matt remembered discussing the ditch experience and comparing it to having a car accident as a teenager and deciding to never drive again. He shared with the group his decision to continue flying. Ever since his first P-3 flight in 1972, he still thought being a P-3 TACCO was the best job in the Navy. Ultimately, all eight VP-9 survivors were back flying again within weeks.

Ironically, two NFOs who knew Matt from their flight training days together decided to turn in their wings. Both had prior enlisted service and, similar to John Ball, were a few years older. They had wives and young children to consider. They were seeking safety at their families' urging. Their decision followed the old Navy adage, "There are more aircraft at the bottom of the ocean than ships up in the sky." Matt's friends were quietly transferred to ships in San Diego to retrain as Surface Warfare Officers, forgoing their monthly flight pay of $165.

After the questions were answered, the survivors were pleased to learn that the Lockheed team was heading home to Burbank and Palmdale. Lockheed's part of the investigation was almost over, and the survivors were invited to come down to the factory to meet the people who built their airplanes; each was given a scale model of a P-3. After manufacturing hundreds of P-3s, the Lockheed team felt these were their airplanes as well. Now that they had had time to process these new observations, there were no hard feelings. Instead, they were committed to figuring out how to make the plane safer with additional engineering changes in the future.

To Bend, Oregon

Moffett Field

November 10

Jim Brooner had been in the squadron nearly two years and was well-known, so there was a full flight going to Eugene, Oregon, for his funeral. Ed Caylor was now ready to take the controls as copilot, so, along with Lieutenant John Healey as Patrol Plane Commander (PPC), they took off at 8:00 a.m. for the two-hour flight up to Eugene.

Jim had grown up in the small town of Creswell, a few miles south of Eugene, so that was where the memorial services were held. He had joined Crew 6 in August as the lead acoustic operator, so Matt had gotten to know him over the past six or eight weeks, and as a result, he was asked to say a few words during the service. Matt wasn't prepared for this, so he kept it brief, explaining what Jim did on the crew, how important these missions were, and how valiantly he had tried to make it home alive. Jim was a hard worker and a quick study. He was awaiting his promotion to AW2 in December. The Eugene TV reporters were outside to get the story, and Matt provided them with the basics while declining to go on tape for the evening news.

After the memorial service, the funeral procession formed and began the ninety-mile drive eastward to Deschutes Memorial Gardens in Bend, Oregon. Some of Jim's friends from the squadron rode with family members, and the rest went back to the airport for the quick flight to Bend. On the flight, lost in thought and still in possession of a package of Brooner's personal effects, Matt could see the funeral procession winding its way through the Willamette National Forest from the bubble observation window at his TACCO Station: Jim's last ride was through some spectacular countryside.

They arrived in Bend with plenty of time to spare, which was a good thing because the airport was small and without a control tower. There was a little confusion about where they should park the aircraft, but after they parked and locked the P-3, they were met by the funeral home staff and driven to the cemetery. The crew was already waiting graveside as the funeral procession arrived. The ceremony was brief, the Navy bugler played "Taps," Ed Caylor and Matt folded the flag, and Ed presented it to Jim's mother, saying:

"On behalf of the President of the United States, and the Chief of Naval Operations, please accept this flag as a symbol of our appreciation for your son's dedicated service to this country and to a grateful Navy." This was a bittersweet moment for Ed because, as a four-year-old, he had witnessed his mother receive her folded flag; his father had died while serving aboard a Navy submarine.

Ed, Matt, and Bruce stayed to answer any questions the family might have, and to provide a small degree of closure. Matt spoke with a local reporter and delivered Jim's package to a relative. They all headed back to the airport. By the time they got back to Moffett that evening, they were exhausted and emotionally drained.

Matt's Visit

Grigsby Home
November 11

On Saturday morning, Matt called over to the Grigsby home and Jerry's daughter Mary answered the phone. He introduced himself and asked to speak to her mom. He had learned how important it was to provide closure after meeting with the Garcia, Rodriguez, and Brooner families, in order to answer questions and to reassure the families that their loved ones did not suffer. It was also important to him to thank the Grigsby family for the simple fact that Jerry had saved his life.

Matt had first met Loreen at a backyard barbeque and pool party in June at the Grigsby home. Jerry wanted to bid farewell to several of his crew members who would be rotating out of the squadron shortly, though none of their replacements had yet arrived. Throughout the summer, Matt had bumped into Loreen at squadron social gatherings where they had had a chance to visit and get to know each other, and he found her easy to talk to, which would make today a bit easier for him. They arranged to meet at the Grigsby home later that same afternoon. That gave Matt some time to figure out what to say about the accident and how heroically Jerry had performed.

On one hand, Jerry was about to become a legend in the maritime patrol community as the first pilot to successfully perform a controlled ditching of a P-3. In sixteen years, and millions of flight hours, it had never been successfully accomplished. Now they had learned many lessons. On the other hand, there was a long-standing Naval tradition of holding the officer in command responsible, if not at fault, and with that fine line the Navy might blame him to some degree for the accident.

You hear about a "water landing" when you fly on an airliner, but that is something of a misnomer. There is no such thing unless you are in a seaplane. Airline pilots don't usually practice for this, and knowing the sea state, winds, and controllability of the airplane will determine if it is even feasible. A "controlled ditching" is where the airplane is controllable and the ocean conditions are at least somewhat favorable. Given the variables of winds and waves, there is no practical way to simulate the final hundred-foot descent into the ocean during the aircraft's last minute in flight.

Matt felt fortunate that Jerry was the Mission Commander on this flight as he was the only pilot in the squadron with prior seaplane experience. Because of that background, Jerry was perhaps a better judge of the primary and secondary ocean swells as they descended through the last hundred feet of altitude. His prior experience landing a P-5M seaplane on the waters of San Diego Bay and in the South China Sea had given him an understanding of the forces impacting an airframe on contact with the water.

As a result, Matt could relay how Jerry had conferred with Ed Caylor and Ed Flow to set up a wings-level, slow-speed, and gradual descent leading to the water impact to minimize airframe damage. It might sound easy to discuss in theory, but this required a lot of real-time fine-tuning because the waves were running at twenty or more feet tall. Slamming into the face of one of those waves would be like driving a car into a concrete wall at nearly 80 mph. These thoughts were on Matt's mind as he drove across town to meet with the Grigsby family. On that drive across San Jose, Matt decided to share only the positives and wait for the JAG report to see how the Navy would officially play the "blame game."

Loreen, her daughters, and Loreen's mom, Mrs. Walker, greeted him. They sat together in the living room, and he asked where they would like him to start. He began with the events leading up to the accident and how amazing it was that Jerry was able to precisely position the aircraft wings-level at a very slow speed and make a gradual descent to bring the plane down on such huge waves. He explained how Jerry skillfully read the ocean wave patterns and essentially "skipped" the aircraft across three wave tops before it finally shuddered to a stop. Jerry maintained precise control to successfully conduct that landing before the plane quickly sank. His skilled landing bought precious seconds for the crew to exit the rapidly sinking aircraft.

Matt emphasized that Jerry deliberately waited on top of the aircraft above the cockpit escape hatch counting heads to make sure that all the crew had left the aircraft. He was the last to leave the plane; he crawled back past the damaged navigator station and then dove down into the huge waves. By this time the plane was almost totally submerged. He immediately inflated his life preserver based on his training, and the two large lobes in front of his chest were so big that they interfered with his swimming strokes. He swam purposefully, trying at first to head toward Matt's raft, which was rapidly being blown farther and farther away from him. Matt then directed Jerry to his left, pointing toward the smaller raft that was closer to Jerry and moving more slowly.

"From our position and from what we could see, we were confident that he had made it to the other raft," he said. "I want to be abundantly clear that he was desperately trying to swim with all his might to get home to his family and be with you here today. The man I knew was a very devoted husband and father, and I am sincerely sorry for what has happened." Matt's eyes had teared up as he spoke. It was clearly difficult for him to tell this story.

Loreen asked him if he thought Jerry had suffered much. To the best of his knowledge and from what he had experienced, he told her that the chilling effects of hypothermia were numbing and not painful, and Jerry had likely lost consciousness not long after his immersion in the water. He went on to say that Jerry was last seen by the men in the other raft drifting away until he quickly became a tiny dot in the fog, and then invisible among the huge waves. It was unfortunate that his body was not recovered, even after two more days of continued searching with the Russian ship, several more aircraft, and a Coast Guard cutter.

Loreen also wanted to know what had caused the engine fires. Matt told her that no one knew conclusively what had gone wrong with the propeller control. The accident board was investigating various possibilities, and if they were able to determine what had gone wrong, he would let her know.

He went on to say that the Navy learned a lot from this ditching and there was an ongoing safety investigation to learn more in order to prevent this type of situation from ever happening again. He also told her that she might be asked questions as part of the investigation, some of which might seem personal and unpleasant. None of these questions would be directed at Jerry or anybody else personally, but it was all based on a culture of really digging in to understand what went right and what could be improved upon.

Loreen said Doc Espiritu had already asked some probing and hurtful questions, and Matt told her that Doc was just
doing his job to ascertain Jerry's state of mind and his fitness
for flight on the day of the accident. The timing may not have
been the best, but the overarching goal of all this was for future
crews to learn from these lessons and never lose sight of the
simple fact that, but for the grace of God, it could have been
any of us.

It was time for Matt to leave; he had said what he had
come to say, and he could tell he had given the family a small
measure of peace. Loreen was a strong and resilient woman,
he thought, and she had held herself together for the telling.
As he was saying his goodbyes, Mrs. Walker thanked him
for coming by and telling them what had happened. Then
she leaned forward and asked for a favor. When you are in
the home of a man who saved your life less than two weeks
earlier, it's hard to say no to his grieving mother-in-law. She
said Jerry had promised to take the girls to the Great America
Amusement Park when he got home from Adak. Was that
something Matt could do for them?

"Of course," he said. "They can count on it. We can make
a full day of it in the spring when the weather is better, and
we can have some fun together." He thought Jerry's girls were
well-behaved and welcoming to him—and at the same time
fun-loving, and he was sure they would have a good time. He
was impressed at how well Loreen was handling her grief and
how strong she was throughout the entire conversation. He
had expected more emotion and drama, and once again, he
found her easy to talk to.

Jerry's Closet

Almaden Valley

November 13

Mary goes upstairs to her room after school and finds her grandma working there. She has cleared out Mary's closet and has things spread all over her bed. She is wiping down a set of shelves in the closet, a set of shelves her dad had made for her. Mary watches in stunned silence as Grandma pulls a sticker off the edge of a shelf, a sticker her dad had given to her. It is not anything important, Mary knows it, and she knows she had stuck it to the edge of her shelf in a lopsided way, but this is her closet and she feels Grandma had no right to get into it. Grandma tells her to put things away neatly in her closet now. Mary is angry and yells that she is going out to play and flounces out of her bedroom. Grandma is stunned to be treated that way after she has been so helpful and worked so hard.

I come upstairs to see what is going on, and my mother gives me a lecture about Mary's bad behavior, about how I should teach Mary to respect her elders and keep her room clean. I tell her I will deal with it later in my own way. Mary is on the verge of puberty, and I wonder if that is part of the problem, or if it is all about losing her dad. Mom goes downstairs to make dinner, and I go down to help. I turn on the radio to listen to music; I haven't had the radio on much since before the accident, and I'm enjoying it until my mom says to turn down "that racket." That's what she used to tell me when I was a teenager. I didn't like it then, and in my own house I like it even less now, but I turn the volume down before I start setting the table.

When dinner is ready, Mom goes outside to call the girls in. Mary comes running in, slams the door shut, and locks it. Mom rings the doorbell a couple of times, and when I open the door, she tells me I really need to have a talk with that girl. We eat our dinner in strained silence. Lisa doesn't understand what is going on and tells us all about the little town they are drawing with chalk on the street.

After dinner, the girls get up from the table to do their chores as usual. Mom goes upstairs, and I explain to the girls that Grandma is here to help us and she doesn't mean to upset us. She won't be here much longer; she means well and has been a big help. We just need to be patient for now. I get the girls started on their homework and go upstairs to see what Mom is up to. I find her in my bedroom going through Jerry's closet. She tells me that it is best for me to get rid of his things, that I don't need these reminders around. I tell her that I'm not ready for that. Now I understand better what Mary is feeling . . . The grief comes over me in waves, waves as endless and cold as the vast gray ocean, and I ask Mom to go downstairs. Maybe we can find something to watch on the television to distract us.

Appreciation

Checking in Monday morning, Matt asked Pat Conway and Eddie Angel if there were plans for any more interview sessions. Fortunately, there were not any more on the horizon. The legal department was swamped collating all the interviews and supporting documentation into a draft "Findings of Fact" document to be reviewed and published before the extended JAG Manual report deadline of December 26.

For Matt, it had been a crazy three-week whirlwind, which had taken its toll. It was now time for him to think about taking some well-deserved time off, heading back to New York to catch up with his own family. He needed some time alone to process all his thoughts and feelings, and the idea of a cross-country road trip felt right. As Matt walked down the hall to check about taking some leave, he bumped into the Executive Officer, Commander Peter Cressy. In a surprisingly casual and informal manner, he said, "Come on into my office, let's talk for a bit."

When Cressy asked what he was up to, he said that he was checking into taking some convalescent leave. After the accident, leave had been discussed earlier, typically up to thirty days, at the discretion of the command. So far, the squadron had been incredibly supportive. Cressy asked Matt if he could be back by December 6, as the squadron had a major exercise coming up and there was a training opportunity he wanted to discuss. Matt agreed, and then Cressy asked what his leave plans were, so he told him he planned to drive back East to see his Marquette friends in Milwaukee, his family in upstate New York, some cousins in Washington, DC, and to attend the Army–Navy game in Philly with his former TACCO, Lieutenant Vince Nigro. Cressy remembered Vince had rotated from the squadron shortly after he became XO. When he recalled that Vince was the assistant baseball coach at Navy, he thought that joining him for the Army–Navy game was "splendid."

With that, Matt thought the little chat was over, but as he stood up to leave, Cressy stopped him and said, "By the way, all things considered, your crew performed admirably. You all did what you could with what you had. Go see Chief Johnson and get those leave papers. Come see me on December 6. We'll have some more things to discuss when you get back."

After getting leave papers typed up through December 6, Matt had one more stop to make later that afternoon.

Per a long-standing tradition, mostly from Naval Aviation's aircraft carrier squadrons, when an emergency forced you to use your survival equipment it was customary to recognize the persons who maintained that gear with a bottle. During his lunch hour he went to the "package store," an on-base store selling beer, wine, and liquor at discounted prices that were exempted from California sales taxes.

He purchased a bottle of Jack Daniel's for the PR shop—the "Parachute Riggers" who inspected and serviced the helmets, life vests, and life rafts. On an impulse, he bought two bottles of Crown Royal, mainly for the trademark purple velvet bag, for Commander Powers and Commander Cressy. He appreciated how many miles they had flown from California to Adak, and to Japan and back in such a short time span, rallying the squadron, coordinating funerals, keeping families informed, and juggling crew rotations. They both had been working nearly nonstop for more than three weeks.

Returning to the hangar, Matt walked into the Parachute Rigger's shop and placed the bottle of Jack Daniel's on the counter just inside the doorway. He personally thanked PR1 Harvey Puckett and his team and said that more would be following from the rest of the crew. Going upstairs, he dropped off the Crown Royal boxes with Chief Johnson who placed them in the offices of the Commanding Officer and the Executive Officer.

Later that afternoon, he let the other survivors in on what he had already started in following that old tradition. Over the next few days, the displayed bottle collection grew, and word of it spread like wildfire across the hangar as a steady stream of curious sailors stopped by to check it out. Hangars were always an alcohol-free workplace. For the young men who supported the flight crews, the healing process after the accident had begun with a simple gesture of grateful appreciation from the survivors.

Aunt Bev to the Rescue

Almaden Valley
November 19

When I get home, I find Mom going through Jerry's closet again. She has been washing and sorting his clothes, and I'm out of patience. I tell her I don't want her doing this; I'm not ready for it. She tells me it must be done and she wants to finish the task before she goes back to Seattle. I tell her I want her to go back now, that I have had enough. She says she can tell I'm not ready to be left alone, and I tell her I have had enough of her meddling in my affairs. She keeps working with the clothes.

Exasperated, I tell her again to stop. Why do things always end up this way with her? I go downstairs and call my dad. He is sympathetic and says he understands. I ask if he would talk to Mom, get her to back off, and he says he will. I yell up the stairs to Mom and say Dad wants to speak to her. Afterward, she still refuses to leave, says I'm not ready to be left alone. I know she's right about that, and I decide to call my aunt Bev, Mom's younger sister, who understands my plight. She says she will come stay with me for a few days so that Mom will go home, and so we make the flight arrangements.

I go to the airport to pick Bev up in the same trip that I drop Mom off to send her home. When she sees Bev get off the plane she starts laughing, points to her boots, and says she is wearing those funny-looking boots just like Loreen does! Bev and I look at each other and roll our eyes. To smooth things over, I tell Mom that I am looking forward to coming to Seattle for Christmas, and I mean it.

I like having Aunt Bev stay with us; she is helpful without being intrusive. She is still with us for Thanksgiving and we have a low-key celebration, which suits all of us just fine. It is nice to have her there when I get home from school, and we visit while making dinner together. I'm not ready to come home to an empty house that holds so much of Jerry.

I'm starting to sleep a little better at night, am no longer taking naps in the afternoon. While getting ready for bed one night, my mind is drawn to the jade tree on the dresser and I pick it up. It is a pretty piece made with several different colors of jade. We picked it out together when we were in Hong Kong while Jerry was a Catapult Officer on the USS Hancock.

He was in the middle of a nine-month deployment off the coast of Vietnam and the ship would be anchoring in Victoria Harbour, Hong Kong, for a week of R&R. The airlines were offering deeply discounted fares for spouses of military members stationed in the war zone, and Jerry encouraged me to come over so we could be together.

My mom at first hesitated when I asked her if she would watch the girls so I could go, but after talking it over, my parents decided they would enjoy having the girls for a long visit. The girls and I could fly to Seattle together, and then I could fly direct from Sea-Tac to Kai Tak Airport. Mom told me later that while I was gone, Lisa would go around saying, "Mawma's in Hawng Kon" in her throaty three-year-old voice.

It was a wonderful, relaxing trip and I was so glad that Jerry had encouraged it; it was good for both of us. We stayed at the Hong Kong Hilton. When we first arrived in a taxi, a handsome Indian attendant wearing a white turban and immaculate white livery opened the door to let me out— the first sign that Hong Kong was a delightful blend of Asian and British culture. Our days were filled with visiting exotic sights and eating in world-class restaurants. I soon learned that the shopping area along Nathan Road in the center of Kowloon was amazing with imports from all over the world. Hong Kong was a free port and collected no import taxes. We could buy Waterford crystal, jewelry, and custom clothing for about one-third the cost we would pay at home. Jerry could bring everything back with him on the ship. I left feeling refreshed, and the separation clock had been reset.

Nine months is a long separation. Three-year-old Lisa had been sick with one ear infection after another, often awake and crying during the night. Five-year-old Mary kept getting strep throat, and the doctors at the base dispensary knew us by sight—Dr. Znyder kept threatening to take out Lisa's adenoids (which eventually happened) and Mary's tonsils (which never happened). I had needed my own R&R by that point, just as much as Jerry did. Jerry was loving and thoughtful to the end. During his three years and two deployments on the Hancock he encouraged me to meet him for other R&R visits as well.

I set the jade tree back down.

It helps me to have the routine of my class schedule and I am enjoying my classes, enjoying visiting with classmates, even enjoying eating veggie sandwiches in the student union. I had changed majors—from nursing to English—and the books I have been assigned to read provide something of an escape for me. Books seem to transport me to another time and place, and when I get to the end of a book, I feel I have said goodbye to a good friend.

Keeping everything as normal and routine as possible seems to help the girls as well, although Lisa still has days when she doesn't feel like going to school. I let her stay at home perhaps more often than I should. We all go to church on Sunday mornings just like we have always done, and Aunt Bev goes with us. The girls continue with their 4-H activities. Another father has taken over teaching the electricity course that Jerry had been teaching on those Thursday evenings when he was home. Both girls continue taking the electricity course even though they say it's not the same. They also continue taking ballet lessons.

Mary wants new books from the library; the old ones are way overdue and I hadn't even been thinking about it. As Mary and Lisa look for new books, I apologize to the librarian for returning the books so late. I say I'm not usually so irresponsible, but my husband has just died in an airplane accident. She looks surprised and says, "Oh," before telling me how much the late penalty is. Oh, well. I guess life goes on.

Lisa's teacher calls me in for a conference and tells me Lisa isn't completing her assignments like she should. I explain that her dad has recently died in an airplane accident and she's still trying to get past that. The teacher says that Lisa has had enough time for that and now she should settle down and get back to work. What? My professors at San Jose State are far more understanding than this fourth-grade teacher . . . Guess I need to spend more time working with Lisa.

Christmas

Seattle, Washington

*A*unt Bev goes home to Seattle, and the girls are looking *forward to Christmas. I tell them that we are going to Grandma and Grandpa's house and they are putting up a tree; we don't need a tree at home this year. The truth is, I don't have the energy or the desire to decorate for Christmas; just keeping up with everyday routines and with school assignments is all I can manage. They like telling me what they want for Christmas. Lisa wants a Barbie Doll Camper and a Barbie Dream House. Mary wants French jeans and Famolare Earth Shoes with thick, wavy soles.*

I can spend a bit of time shopping on my way home from school, and I find out that these are expensive things the girls want. My monthly benefits haven't started coming in yet, so I'm concerned about finances. I want to do my best for them; I guess I'm trying to be both mom and dad. I can use my Wells Fargo credit card for now, and I will get Lisa the camper and Mary the jeans. I can get them the other things when the benefits start coming in, but I decide to call Bob Masoero, my CACO, and see if he knows what's going on with the benefits. He puts me in contact with a Naval Reserve lawyer who will be at Moffett Field for his weekend duty.

I bring all my paperwork to the legal office, and the lawyer tells me this case is a little complicated because no body was recovered. He will obtain a death certificate for me and we will proceed from there. He reminds me to always check the box as an "Unremarried Widow" to ensure my claim is processed correctly, explaining that any benefits will be reevaluated and discontinued should I decide to remarry at a future date.

I remember talking with my parents on one occasion years ago about whether we wanted to be cremated or have a burial. My parents both wanted cremation, and that seemed like the right choice to me. Jerry, however, said he wanted to be buried at sea; he thought that would be fitting given his Navy career. In a way, he was buried at sea, just not with the ceremony, nor the time or place he had imagined.

Christmas vacation with my family is nice. My brothers play with Mary and Lisa, roughhousing around in my parents' living room and getting them all wound up like they usually do, until my mother tells them to "simmer down" (one of her favorite phrases) and to cut out all that "racket." One day my brothers take us all skiing; they want to be sure we are having a good time. Doug and Becky help the girls with their ski technique. After a while, I get tired and head to the lodge for hot chocolate and to give my aching legs a rest . . . I'm out of shape.

A few evenings later, my brothers and Becky take me to a disco—my first ever. I enjoy it in a low-key way, even though it is only my brothers who ask me to dance. I can still feel a cloud hanging over me, and I suppose I wouldn't be much fun as a dance partner; the vibes just aren't there.

Mary has that cloud hanging over her too. She has lost some of her spunk; she was always more of a daddy's girl than Lisa. When we get back home, I should let her get that *puppy she has been asking for. It is the granddaughter of a dog we used to have, and she has asked about it several times. Her friend Katie Hughes has the puppies and hasn't started giving them away yet. They say there's nothing better than a puppy for what ails you. When the benefits come in, I'll get Mary the shoes she wants, and Lisa the Barbie Dream House.*

Jerry Grigsby Aviation Officer Candidate School Photo.
Photo Credit Naval Aviation Schools Command.

Loreen Student Nurse Photo.
Photo Credit Saint Joseph's Hospital School of Nursing.

Jerry and Loreen's Wedding.
Courtesy of Walker Family.

P5M flying boat seaplane flown by Jerry on his first Vietnam deployment.
Courtesy US Navy.

PD-2 Bureau Number 159892 on approach to Naval Air Station Willow Grove, PA in February 1978. Courtesy of the Ron Picciani Collection.

Jerry preparing to launch aircraft as Catapult Officer, USS Hancock, CVA-19. Courtesy of Grigsby family.

Jerry in between launch cycles on USS Hancock.
Courtesy of Grigsby family.

Jerry on crew rest day in Diego Garcia, British Indian Ocean Territory,
Summer 1977. Courtesy of Grigsby family.

Grigsby Family Photo 1977.
Courtesy Olan Mills.

Lcdr. Grigsby's Official US Navy photo checking into
Patrol Squadron Nine 1977. Courtesy of US Navy.

P-3 Cockpit view showing striped Emergency Handles just
below the windshield and the small rpm indicator below the
larger horsepower and turbine inlet temperature gauges.

Mark 7 life raft in heavy seas. Designed for a seven person capacity.
Nine men boarded this raft. Within a minute of boarding the raft, five of
them returned to the water attempting to drag it closer to Jerry Grisgby.
Three of the five would later succumb to hypothermia before rescue.

Captain Aleksandr Arbuzov, master of the
Soviet Fishing Vessel MYS Synyavin. Courtesy of Arbuzov family.

The crewmen who manned the lifeboat that rescued the ten survivors and
recovered the three deceased crewmen. Courtesy of Arbuzov family.

Survivors waiting for an update on their return to the US
after meeting with US Embassy Moscow personnel. Left to Right,
Matt Gibbons, Gary Hemmer, Howard Moore, Dave Reynolds,
Garland Shepard, Ed Caylor. Photo Courtesy of US Embassy Moscow.

Deplaning at Yokota Air Base Japan. Left to Right, Ed Caylor,
Matt Gibbons, John Ball, Bruce Forshay, John Wagner,
Garland Shepard, Gary Hemmer. Courtesy of US Navy.

21 Gun Salute for Jim Brooner, Rich Garcia, and Randy Rodriguez.
Courtesy of US Navy PH2 Rodney Wright.

Saluting the three deceased Anti Submarine Warfare operators
as they passed through an honor Guard of their shipmates. RADM Charles
Prindle and his Flag Lieutenant Perry Martini salute far left.
Courtesy of US Navy PH2 Rodney Wright.

The Doll House Jerry Grigsby was building for his girls to occupy his time in Adak. The Doll House was completed by the Loop, Smith, and other families. Courtesy of Grigsby family.

April 30, 1979 Awards Ceremony in Hangar Three at NAS Moffett Field. Loreen Grigsby received Jerry's posthumous Distinguished Flying Cross in a private ceremony. Crew Six Survivors and Crew Eleven rescuers received Air Medals with Bronze Star devices. Left to Right Kneeling Bruce Forshay, Gene Cummings, Howard Moore, John Wagner, Dave Reynolds. Middle Row, Len Northrup, Pat Conway, Matt Gibbons, Ed Caylor, Rear Admiral Charles Prindle, John Hampel, Bill Rattenni, John Ball. Back Row, Dennis Mette, Randy Luecker, Pete Geldard, Van Gamble, Hugh Littlejohn, Ed Flow. Missing Ron Price.

July 1980 Wedding, Seattle. Courtesy of Gibbons family.

October 1983 Dedication Ceremony for the Jerry Grigsby
Survival Training Center. Courtesy of NAS Pensacola Public Affairs.

Mr. and Mrs. Grigsby were joined by his brother George,
sister Dona, and Mary and Lisa to witness the dedication and
unveil the Plaque. Courtesy of NAS Pensacola Public Affairs.

2004 Las Vegas Reunion Remembrance Table for those lost, Still On Station,
still wearing their Wings of Gold. Photo Courtesy of Bill Porter.

2004 Las Vegas Reunion Survivor and Rescuer group photo before things got out of hand. Left to Right kneeling Bruce Savaglio, Bill Porter, Ed Caylor, Matt Gibbons, Dave Reynolds, Howard Moore holding MYS Synyavin model, John Ball, Captain Arbuzov, Ed Flow, John Wagner, Alan Feldkamp, Bruce Forshay, Gordy Alder with bagpipes. Missing from Photo Barry Philippy and Dan Malott.

Part Two
October 2004

They shall grow not old,
as we that are left grow old;
Age shall not weary them,
Nor the years condemn.
At the going down of the sun
And in the morning.
We will remember them.
—ROBERT LAURENCE BINYON

Accept the things
To which fate binds you and
Love the people with whom fate
Brings you together
But do so with all your heart.
—MARCUS AURELIUS

Reunion

They could hear the chatter even before they rounded the corner at the end of the hallway and knew they were in the right place. It had been twenty-six years, and there was much catching up to do. Some had married, some had divorced and remarried, and many had changed careers. Even Captain Arbuzov, skipper of the MYS *Synyavin*, was here with his wife Tamara and granddaughter Olga. The survivors had collected the money to cover the cost of bringing them here. They could not imagine what it must be like for them, coming from a remote fishing village on the Siberian coast of the Soviet Union for their first time in America. Not just anywhere in America, but Las Vegas of all places. Could a fairy tale seem more unreal for them? Matt quivered with anticipation and excitement. They had never met the Captain during their voyage to the Soviet Union, and now he would not only meet this man for the first time but also be able to thank him in person for saving his life.

Once the idea for this reunion had materialized, Cindy and Dennis Mette had pulled the many detailed plans together—coordinated it all—working tirelessly to make sure every detail was in place. They lived in Las Vegas, hence the venue, and there they were, just around the corner, sitting at an official-looking table decked out with name tags and event packets.

Dennis said, "Hey, Matt, great to see you!" Cindy, looking up, saw Loreen was with Matt.

"Hi there, Dennis, Cindy! You guys have done an awesome job here. It means so much . . . Is Captain Arbuzov here yet?" Matt located their name tags, and Cindy handed him a packet.

"He's not back from sightseeing." Cindy had found a Russian-speaking real estate agent who was happy to take the family around the sights of Las Vegas. "I expect they'll be here soon. We've reserved this suite for happy hour for the next three nights so everyone can reconnect and visit, and tonight it's dinner on your own. They have a good buffet here in the hotel if you guys are hungry."

"Thanks," Matt said. "You know, two days on the ship and we never met the Captain."

"We heard that from Bruce Forshay as well. Seems strange, doesn't it? Well, go on in and get something to drink. We'll be trading off here, and there'll be plenty of time to talk later."

The hospitality room seemed already filled and was alive with laughter, hugs, and tears of joy. Tonight they would keep it light, but later there would be a lot of questions to help put some remaining puzzle pieces together. The vibe was very casual as retired Colonels and Captains mingled with old officer and enlisted friends on a first-name basis. There, across the room, was Ed Caylor, the copilot during the emergency, and his new wife, Janet. Not so new, actually—they had already been married for many years and had an adult daughter. They were in deep conversation with Ron Price, the pilot from X-ray Foxtrot 675 who had circled above the rafts for hours at three hundred feet, keeping them in sight until relieved by

Coast Guard 1500. The survivors and their families were here not just to reconnect but also to thank everyone involved in their rescue.

Ed and his daughter had helped make the contacts in the Soviet Union that eventually led to connecting directly with Captain Arbuzov. Ed's daughter, Rachel, spoke Russian—had minored in it and spent a semester abroad in St. Petersburg. Locating Arbuzov had been no easy feat. Rachel was in Scotland for graduate studies while Ed was at home in New Hampshire. At the same time, telephone service was rationed on Sakhalin Island. The Arbuzov share was only two hours in the morning and another two hours in the evening. Siberia is a hard place to reach, but survivors of the accident wanted to officially thank him for saving their lives. Organizing their phone conversations in three widely distant time zones was a challenge. Ed and Rachel also arranged for the Arbuzov family to obtain the money collected by the survivors so they could fly to Las Vegas.

It was Bruce Forshay and his wife Pattie who traveled to Moscow over Labor Day weekend of 2004 to hold a thank-you ceremony with some of the Russian officials who had been involved in the rescue effort.

Matt spotted Bruce and Pattie coming into the room. Matt, Loreen, and their daughter Erin had been honored to witness Bruce and Pattie's wedding at Lovers Point on Monterey Bay years earlier. Matt walked toward them saying, "Bruce, Pattie, how're you doing? You're looking well, both of you!" He wanted to hear about the trip to Moscow. "It was wonderful that you were able to make arrangements with Captain Arbuzov—a miracle, actually."

"You two are looking good as well," Bruce replied. "Tracking down Arbuzov with the help of Ed and his daughter was more of a miracle than you probably realize. I think you remember that I work as a contractor for the Department of State now and I have a clearance. I had to send emails through SECSTATE Diplomatic Security. It took six months to work through everything, and I had to keep our embassy in Moscow informed. I didn't know if I would be able to renew my clearance with a thick stack of Russian communication emails and a visa stamp to Moscow on my passport, and that was just the beginning."

Matt glanced up and saw Ed Caylor looking their way. He waved him over to join them. Bruce continued with his story: "We arranged for a Mercedes limousine after landing at the Sheremetyevo Airport because we had heard that taxis would be stopped on the highway and "fined" by the local gendarmerie. When we arrived at our hotel, we saw several Land Rovers with two or more armed men escorting fur-hatted occupants to the entrance. We had to go around the block because there were too many bodyguards with machine guns protecting their VIPs for us to try and enter the hotel at that time."

"Ed, what you and Bruce have done to get Arbuzov here for this reunion is beyond amazing," said Matt.

"There's more to this story, Ed, and I may not have told you all of it," Bruce added. "Pattie and I had agreed to take part in a press conference on the evening we arrived. After we changed clothes, we decided to walk to the headquarters of the *Trud* newspaper. It was impossible to get a taxi, and the traffic in central Moscow is the heaviest and most chaotic that I have ever seen. The news event turned out to be quite an affair with five other news agencies in attendance. There were cameras and reporters everywhere along with Russian Naval Officers and US Embassy liaison members.

"Captain Kramtzov, who was the senior Naval Officer of the 1978 Soviet rescue operation and the skipper of a Krivak destroyer, was there in his dress uniform," Bruce continued.

"He received our praise and thanks; we learned later that he was not involved in the actual rescue. His job had been to ensure Soviet control as we passed from the *Synyavin* to the custody of the pier-side Border Guards. The Border Guards signed for our custody and took the crew on a short bus ride up the hill to the Naval hospital overlooking the port of Petropavlovsk. He was, however, more than happy to receive the credit for our rescue.

"The real heroes, of course, were Captain Arbuzov and his crew. At the end of the news conference, I was allowed to speak to Arbuzov on the phone. Up until that time, he was only allowed to listen in on the conversation, and in frustration had heard Kramtzov accept credit for the rescue. Other than that, the press conference went well with respectful praise recorded for the evening news. It was followed by a lengthy reception, and then a second interview at a major radio station.

"Since we were there to show our gratitude for the rescue, the evening was all we had hoped it would be. There were some people over there who thought we Americans showed no thankfulness for the rescue effort, so this helped set the record right."

"The Soviet Union is an interesting place," Matt put in. "You remember how the *Synyavin* docked after dark? Looking back on it, I think the ship's progress was purposely held back to arrive just when it did. Forty-six hours after our rescue we walked down a gangplank at midnight and set foot in the closed port city of Petropavlovsk—closed to all Westerners as well as most Russians. It was a completely dark night, not a light on anywhere except for a few by the pier-side. A darkened bus idled to stay heated at the head of a line of barely visible sedans. Armed guards stood around the ship and the bus, and others stood in shadows everywhere along the pier. The Soviets apparently did not want us to see much of anything.

"We were led beyond the bus toward what looked like a one-story warehouse," Matt continued, "and immediately a group of men got out of the sedans and boarded the *Synyavin*. Men in dark green uniforms stood on the far side of two long tables inside the warehouse, which was dimly lit by bare bulbs. A representative from the ship turned us over to the Border Guards in exchange for signed receipts. None of us spoke Russian; it seemed we had just been handed over to the KGB. I expected to be handcuffed at any minute."

Bruce said, "Yeah, I remember thinking, *We've gotta follow the rules we rehearsed in SERE school: Say little, agree to less, sign nothing, resist everything . . .*"

Bud and Paula Powers made their way over to them; Bud had been the Commanding Officer of VP-9 at the time of the ditching. He shook hands with everyone in the group while Paula gave big hugs to the wives. Bud had worked hard to get the survivors back to Moffett Field as quickly as possible, and had earned the respect of everyone in the group. Not only was he allowed to stay in the Navy after the accident—he had thought it doubtful at the time—but he got a promotion as well, and eventually retired as a Captain.

Paula Powers worked tirelessly after the accident, organizing wives to sit and wait with the crew spouses. She put hours into coordinating a meal train for the Miller and Grigsby families throughout the first few days.

When the plane went down in the stormy North Pacific, Bud was convinced that was the end of his Navy career, as there was that long-standing Navy tradition that the skipper was held accountable for everything, and even something not his fault was still his responsibility. It was great to catch up and give their "thanks," showing their gratitude to Bud.

About a month after the homecoming, the squadron received another aircraft back from a major overhaul at NARF

Alameda with a similar number one propeller replacement. The standard procedure was to perform a full maintenance test flight to check out all systems. During that flight, with Bud and his crew flying around the Moffett Field traffic pattern, the number one propeller went overspeed. Everyone on the ramp heard the propeller tips go supersonic; Bud declared an emergency and conducted an immediate three-engine landing. It was a good thing they were over the airfield. His aft observer was none other than Howard Moore, on his first flight back from leave after the ditching. Howie now had the dubious distinction of having experienced two propeller overspeeds in his first ninety flight hours.

Powers taxied back to the hangar, where the squadron maintenance crew immediately disassembled the prop to identify the issue. Bud then took the cracked and shattered parts over to Admiral Prindle's desk and showed him that this was the smoking gun—the root cause of the accident. The parts Bud put on Prindle's desk caused the Admiral to redirect his endorsement of a finding of "pilot error in judgment" to include the part defect as well. Bud advocated that the Admiral should consider grounding all aircraft with that particular version of the new propeller seal. Instead, a new inspection policy went into immediate effect, the rebuild procedure at NARF went back to the older version part, and the planes continued to fly. At the time, many people thought Bud came across as too strong and that there was friction between him and Prindle. In fact, years later they worked together in the Pentagon and got along very well.

Dennis and Cindy Mette joined the group. Paula mentioned that her 1979 Christmas cards were filled with news of Loreen's engagement. She looked at Matt and said, "Right then and there, I knew she was going to be all right." As often happens at events like this, some of the others drifted away, then Cindy added new energy into the conversation when she said that she had always wondered how Matt and Loreen met, how they decided to get married.

"I was on Jerry's crew for ten months," Matt said. "Jerry hosted a backyard barbecue and pool party during the summer to say goodbye to the crew who were rotating out of the squadron—even though new crew hadn't yet been assigned. Jerry was always generous with his appreciation for the men who worked for him.

"I had a good time playing Sharkey and Jaws with Jerry's daughters in the pool that day, everyone splashing and laughing until it was time to grill the meat. After eating, I had a chance to talk to Loreen for the first time, and found her easy to talk to. From time to time after that, we would bump into each other at squadron social functions, and each time I enjoyed chatting with her."

Matt continued his telling, "In February, after the accident, Dave Loop and Ken Smith and their families delivered the dollhouse that Jerry had started to build in Adak—and that they had helped to finish—to the Grigsby home. They wanted to make it a special occasion with the girls, so everyone went out for pizza together to the very first Chuck E. Cheese pizza parlor located just off Blossom Hill Road, which was a very big deal for the children.

"Somehow, I was invited to tag along and I brought with me a few rolls of quarters and my playful, rambunctious personality. I suddenly became the favorite 'Uncle Matt' to all the kids as they fed quarters into the various games and machines. I mean, none of these kids lived near relatives, and I was having fun getting them wound-up and excited. I had a chance to sit and visit and have some pizza and salad with the adults while the kids continued to go crazy playing games and collecting those little paper prize tickets.

"I rode back to Loreen's house in the back seat of the Loops' Volvo station wagon. The kids were teasing each other about whose Uncle Matt I really was: 'He's my Uncle Matt.' 'No, he's MY Uncle Matt!' Just as we pulled into the driveway, Mary said with emphasis, 'He's MY Uncle Matt, and he sleeps in our extra bedroom.' I never got out of a car so fast in all my life, said my goodbyes, went straight to my own car parked in front of the house, and drove away down the short street at breakneck speed. It was much later that night before I recovered."

"Mary was quite innocent in her remark and didn't realize the embarrassment she had caused," Loreen added. "My brothers did sleep in the extra bedroom when they came for a visit, and she was too young to understand the implications of what she said. I thought I probably would never see Matt again."

"That was in February," Matt said, "and then in late March I fulfilled my promise to Mrs. Walker and took Loreen and the girls to the Great America Amusement Park in Santa Clara, and we made a day of it. Lisa was excited and wanted to ride all the different roller coasters, and was running from one to the next to the next. I told her she shouldn't be running here, but if she was going to run, I would run circles around her. She said, 'No way!' But I did it."

Lisa, who was there at the reunion with her husband Robert, had joined them while they were talking. Lisa said, "Yeah, I remember having a really good time that day. I could see that my mom was having a good time too; she was laughing and smiling—something I hadn't seen her doing much of in recent days."

"About that time, I had been listening to a song on the radio," Loreen said, "and I heard the words in a different way: 'I will survive! I've got all my life to live, I've got all my love to give.' I thought, *That's me . . . I've got all my life to live, all my life stretching out before me, and I will survive. I've still got all my love to give.* It was sort of an awakening. I've noticed that sometimes songs can touch my emotions and say what I am not yet able to put into words."

Matt continued, "Mary and Lisa got to ride all the rides they wanted, and Loreen rode most of them too. On the way out of the park, the evening breeze from San Francisco Bay had picked up and it was getting cold. I could see that Loreen wasn't dressed for the cold, was shivering, and walking to my car, I put my arm around her. She didn't pull away. The girls, walking just behind us, went, 'Oooooh!'"

Lisa said that she could see something was going on between them, and she liked it.

Matt said, "Loreen invited me to stay for dinner that evening. She had made lasagna, which just happens to be one of my favorites, and all she had to do was reheat it and make a simple salad, slice some French bread. When I finished eating, I picked up my plate and licked it clean to show I liked it, putting the girls into a fit of giggles. It had been a good day for me, much better than I had imagined."

"I remember him licking his plate," Lisa said. "I'd never seen an adult do that before."

Matt went on, "The next time I saw Loreen was at the awards ceremony in late April for Crews 6 and 11 at the hangar. It was to honor those who were in the accident and those who had helped with the rescue. Loreen came with Ken and Sara Smith, and Admiral Prindle presented her the posthumous Distinguished Flying Cross for Jerry in a private ceremony up in Pete Cressy's office. They came down to the hangar area afterward for the larger ceremony, and I saw Loreen sitting in the audience. The Smiths and Loreen were starting to leave before I had a chance to talk to them that day, so I caught up with them, bringing pieces of cake for Loreen to take home for her girls."

THE SECRETARY OF THE NAVY

 WASHINGTON. D.C. 20350

The President of the United States takes
pride in presenting the DISTINGUISHED
FLYING CROSS posthumously to

LIEUTENANT COMMANDER JERRY C. GRIGSBY UNITED
STATES NAVY
for service as set forth in the following
CITATION:

For heroism while participating in aerial
flight as Patrol Plane and Mission Commander of
a P3C(U) aircraft assigned to Patrol Squadron
NINE Detachment Adak, Alaska on 26 October 1978.
While conducting a routine maritime patrol in
the North Pacific Ocean, Lieutenant Commander
Grigsby's aircraft experienced a catastrophic
propeller failure which ultimately left him
with no choice but to ditch the aircraft under
the most adverse conditions of weather, sea
state, and aircraft configuration. Exercising
outstanding leadership and airmanship, he

prepared his crew and aircraft for water entry and was able to expertly land the aircraft on the water in the face of gale force winds, reduced visibility, and fifteen to twenty foot seas. Once in the water and with complete disregard for his own safety, he positioned himself on top of the rapidly sinking aircraft to direct the evacuation of his crew members. Lieutenant Commander Grigsby's heroic actions both in the air and in the water were responsible for thirteen of his fourteen crewmen reaching life rafts and eventual recovery by a surface vessel. By his extraordinary airmanship skill, selfless bravery, and tenacious dedication to his crew in the face of extreme personal danger and supreme sacrifice, Lieutenant Commander Grigsby reflected great credit upon himself and upheld the highest traditions of the United States Naval Service.

For the President,

W. Graham Claytor
Secretary of the Navy

A Developing Relationship

"It's Now or Never"
May 1979|October 24, 2004

"The squadron went on a Ready Alert rotation after the awards ceremony, so my schedule really wasn't my own," Matt explained. "I realized that I wanted to start dating Loreen, that I had feelings for her. It wasn't until later in May that we finally got together, and I asked her out to dinner at the Good Earth restaurant in Santa Clara. As it turned out, that was one of her favorite restaurants and she hadn't been dining out much since the accident.

"She told me that evening that she wasn't emotionally ready to start dating and didn't want to get hurt; if I had any idea that I might have serious intentions, we could continue to see each other. We both felt awkward about our developing relationship—too many memories on both sides. She knew the squadron was getting ready to deploy to Misawa, Japan, at the end of June—this time a six-month deployment. That didn't give us much chance to really get to know each other, so it was sort of a 'now or never' situation. She also knew that I would be rotating out of the squadron after deployment and getting orders to who-knew-where.

"It was clear to me that I was starting to feel serious about her, so we continued seeing each other. Often we just hung out at Loreen's house with the girls, and I got to know them better during that time.

"Loreen's brother Doug, and his wife Becky, made plans to take Loreen and the girls to Disneyland and Knott's Berry Farm over Memorial Day weekend, and Loreen invited me to come along. I wore a Hawaiian shirt and was in a party mood while we were waiting in line to board the flight to the Orange County airport. I was sort of dancing around, jabbing my index finger in the air and mimicking the little Hughes Airwest jingle from TV. A few other people started singing along and laughing: 'Yes, nana, nana, nana, yes, nana, nana, nana, Hughes Airwest, top banana in the West!' In those days the planes had a bright yellow paint scheme. Loreen and the girls were laughing too. It was good to see them smiling; I liked it when I made Loreen laugh.

"We spent a full day and a half at Disneyland, and Doug wanted to have chicken dinner at Knott's Berry Farm, a happy memory from his childhood, and to celebrate his graduation from the University of Washington. I rented a Chevy Monte Carlo with room for six, and I drove it like a madman across Orange County to get to Knott's in time for chicken dinner. We finally got there through the crazy rush hour traffic; Doug said the dinner was every bit as good as in his memories. We rode rides there until the park closed.

"Loreen and I got together as often as we could, and I remember going to movies, going to a play up in San Francisco, going out to eat. I flew home to visit my parents before I left on deployment and shared with them a photo of Loreen and the girls. I introduced them as my 'special friends,' and that raised some eyebrows, but they didn't press for details."

"In June, Matt sat through two and a half hours of dance

recital," Loreen said. "A lot of little girls wearing tutus and dancing to songs like 'I'm a Little Teapot' and 'Drip, Drip, Drop Little April Showers.' Mary had dropped out of dance by then, but Lisa still liked it. Her number this time was 'Sugar Shack.' The white blouse to her costume had large pink and black polka dots. The dance director had all us moms glue pink or black sequins around each of those circles, and it seemed like an endless task to me. In the end it was worth it because I could see Lisa's ear-to-ear grin and glowing face while she performed.

"Matt was cool with the whole thing, and I remember thinking this might be a match made in Heaven. I was feeling more comfortable with our relationship by then. At first, I wondered how I could love Matt if I still loved Jerry—had guilty feelings about it, like I was being disloyal—but realized I had room in my heart for them both."

"In June it was time to sell my condo in San Jose and put my things in storage for the duration of the deployment, knowing I would be transferred at deployment's end," said Matt. "We wrote to each other and enjoyed several transpacific phone calls, which were more than a little expensive back then. Our budding relationship survived the test of separation and continued to grow."

Loreen added, "I remember how much I enjoyed those phone calls despite the unbelievable cost. I loved the sound of his voice. I was lonesome, but not interested in dating anyone else."

"When my crew got R&R leave in early November, I flew commercial back to San Francisco, picked up a couple of brides' magazines at the airport, and asked Loreen to go ring shopping with me. This was a little more than a year after the accident.

"We picked out an engagement ring for Loreen and rings with tiny diamonds for the girls. We announced our engagement, and they became my three-ring circus."

Lisa remembered her little ring, lost long ago. She also remembered feeling excited about the marriage, thinking life would be one party after another with Matt as her stepdad; that is what it had seemed like to her during the whirlwind courtship—Sharkey and Jaws, Chuck E. Cheese, Great America, Disneyland, Knott's Berry Farm, movies . . .

"I was ready to settle down and had never wanted anything more in life then to get married and have children, and this had given me a head start on making my dreams come true." He could tell that Paula and Cindy were touched.

Loreen said Matt had missed one of the important parts of their story: "Back at the pool party and barbecue when we first met, something strange and unexplainable happened. I had noticed Matt playing with the girls in the pool like their uncles did, and was amused by it, but nothing more.

"Later when he came over to talk with me one-on-one for the first time, a sudden feeling came over me that I already knew him and had been wondering where he was: 'Oh, there you are . . . I was wondering . . .' It was all very irrational. I had never met him before or wondered where he was, so I pushed that thought out of my mind. Anyway, I *thought* I had pushed that thought out of my mind, but it kept coming back, especially during the next spring.

"And another thing that happened: Lisa asked me almost immediately after the accident if I thought I could marry Mr. Gibbons. A shocking question at that time, and not an idea I could even think about, nor a thought I could handle. Now here we are . . ."

Cindy said, "That sounds like the voice of God!" Loreen admitted she felt that way also—that some things, no matter how unlikely, were meant to happen.

Matt called his parents and told them about his engagement to Loreen. This was the first time he had talked to them about Loreen since showing them the picture of his special friends. His mother was ecstatic, happy for him; his father a little more thoughtful: "This is serious business, son. Are you sure you're not doing this just because you're lonesome? Marriage is a lifetime commitment, you know. Taking on two children at the same time will not be easy."

Matt sat down and wrote a long, heartfelt letter to his parents expressing all his feelings for Loreen: easy to talk to, enjoyable to be with, good mom with good kids, strong woman. She had won his respect, and he thought they would have a wonderful future together.

"I also wrote them a letter telling them what a wonderful, thoughtful man Matt was, how my daughters liked him, how he made me laugh, how he breathed new life into our family," said Loreen. "His parents were deeply touched by these letters, and there were no more concerns or hesitation.

"My parents were happy for me when I told them," she continued. "They knew how lonesome and sad I had been feeling, and my mom had met Matt after the accident and thought he was 'a nice young man, sensitive and considerate.' My mom, who always has something to say about everything, said, 'Are you sure, Loreen? He seems awfully young . . .' Yes, he was young, but that was the only hesitation and nothing else ever came up. Even the Grigsby family was happy for me."

Matt continued the story: "I went on ahead to my new duty station at Ohio State, but Loreen wanted to finish her degree at San Jose State. It was once again a long-distance relationship.

"We talked about buying a house, and Loreen told me what she wanted. I went out looking and narrowed the search to a few top choices. She flew out for a long weekend, and we decided on one to buy that was located reasonably close to Ohio State in the suburb of Upper Arlington, which had

top-rated schools. In early June, right after she graduated, she
had Navy-sponsored movers pack up her furniture and other
possessions and sent them off to Upper Arlington.

"Our wedding date was set for July 5, 1980, in Seattle—I
wanted two nights of fireworks, and she wanted one more day
of independence! Loreen's dad had passed away three weeks
before the wedding, so Loreen and the girls stayed with her
mom until the ceremony. It was a small wedding with Loreen's
closest relatives; my family flew out from New York. We had
both a Methodist minister and a Catholic priest officiating,
and then it was off to Puerto Vallarta for our honeymoon.

"Mary and Lisa flew out to stay with their Grigsby relatives in Oklahoma during the honeymoon," Matt explained,
"and we picked them up on our way across the country from
California in Loreen's VW camper. That was when Mrs.
Grigsby told me she considered me to be like another son to
her, which was very humbling to me."

"I had always wanted three children," Loreen said, "so
fifteen months later, we had Erin—to the delight of everyone. Mary and Lisa doted on her and were like a pair of extra
mothers; no child had been more loved."

The Amazing Part of Their Rescue

The Soviets React Favorably

Bruce Forshay and Ed Caylor came over again with fresh drinks just as Captain Arbuzov arrived for the happy hour event, and they were all surprised. He looked younger and taller than they had imagined; he had a sophisticated and vibrant strength about him. They talked about this with Matt for a few minutes.

Matt had held a stereotypical image in his mind of a short, stocky older man, perhaps with a weather-beaten face and a beard. His wife and teenage granddaughter were quite charming and friendly. Grateful survivors quickly surrounded the Arbuzov family. The interpreter was helping with introductions. There were plenty of smiles and much shaking of hands. This was shaping up to be a great reunion!

"Toward the end of our time in the rafts, I was beginning to think I might not make it to morning," said Matt.

Bruce said, "Matt, we were all thinking that."

"I was drifting in and out of consciousness and had some irrational thoughts," Matt went on. "I remember thinking that I couldn't die because I had house and car payments to make back in San Jose . . . Then along came Captain Arbuzov and the *Synyavin*."

"This is one of the truly amazing parts of our story, that the Soviets would react favorably and so rapidly, and Captain Arbuzov would come in search of us," Ed said. "He put his crew members over the side in those heavy seas in a covered lifeboat; his men had to physically pull each of us out of the rafts. The two rafts were drifting miles apart in miserable sea conditions; it's a miracle they were able to do it!

"I remember being carefully lifted aboard the *Synyavin* and immediately brought below where I was stripped in a steam room, wrapped in a warm blanket, and given hot tea with honey to drink," Ed continued. "Later they gave me some bread and jelly with more hot tea, and they put me in a hot shower. I was warmed from the inside out—just exactly what I needed. The Russian fishermen treated us like one human being to another, not like adversaries in a cold war.

"The effort to swim and push that raft toward Jerry took away all my energy for the rest of the event. I am sure Randy's, Jim's, Rich's and John's body temperatures, and mine, were the lowest of anyone in our raft at the thirty-minute mark. Over the final hours, all I could concentrate on was trying to help Jim Brooner stay awake, and not going unconscious myself."

Matt looked at his watch. "Got to go meet my family for dinner. Guess I'll have to wait until tomorrow to meet Captain Arbuzov. See you all tomorrow afternoon." He had invited his large Irish Catholic family from upstate New York to share in the reunion festivities with him. He had invited them after learning the reunion committee might not meet the minimum attendance required by Bally's for group events. He was on the planning committee and knew they had chosen Bally's because their numbers requirement was lower than other major casinos; he was happy some of his family members could share this event with him.

Kapitan Aleksandr
Alexeyevich Arbuzov

October 25, 2004

Matt and Loreen headed back to the hospitality suite for more visiting the next afternoon, leaving the family to continue sightseeing on their own. This afternoon would be a little different. John Ball's son, Matthew Orion, was making a video of the men sharing their memories of the ditching and rescue. He called small groups aside for interviews in the next room.

Captain Arbuzov spoke through his interpreter and said that for the rescue he didn't think about the magnitude of what was going on between America and Russia. He was only focused on rescuing the people in the severe weather. He didn't want to injure his own people in the heavy seas, so he put his most experienced men in the lifeboat. An American plane guided them to the first raft. The battle against time was a critical factor: the men had already been in the water for several hours by the time he was contacted. He didn't expect there would be many survivors, if any.

Bill Porter noted, when it was his turn, that the *Synyavin* crew was at first confused when he contacted them. "They thought we were trying to say that we were gonna land in the water, so we explained it's not our airplane; it's someone else in the water. Then they wanted to know who was in the water, so we told them friends were in the water. We traded names, and that is why the Captain knew my name. He must have been in the radio room at the time.

"At one point, I was saying to Manislov, 'You speak good English.' He came back and said, 'Bill, you speak good English too.' When he said that, it just lightened the whole thing and we all laughed: it made us feel better."

Bruce Forshay spoke next. "Well, that was excellent with all the participants involved, but one of those dominoes was the Air Force, and if they hadn't found us, there would be nothing to find. The airplane from the Navy finally got there, and had the 'Ready Alert,' as we call it. Then the Coast Guard guided the ship, stayed on station, and brought it back to us when there was nobody else to pick us up. Now I can thank them all for that because everybody had a participation or part in this. The guy who reached out and grabbed me out of the water was Russian, so that's where my thanks is, primarily. Thank you!

"They put their most experienced people over the side for us," Bruce continued. "Keep in mind that these guys have been out at sea for eleven months and have a full ship of fish. They've done a great job, they're going to be rich, they're almost home, and then we land in their laps. They turn around to come save us in a bad storm. I'm confused; my brain isn't working well because of the hypothermia, and I am concerned about my next phase of survival. I think, *Okay, we're going to the Russians, and I've been taught what that means.* Now, of course, I couldn't be more grateful. Thank you, Captain Arbuzov!"

Then it was Ed Flow's turn to speak. "I sort of assumed that since they had taken the time to come get us that they weren't gonna shoot us or anything right there. Once they got us on board the ship and ran us through hot showers and put us into bunks with blankets to warm us up, I was just glad to be alive and warm and dry."

"I think it speaks a lot about Captain Arbuzov and what he did pretty much with his own initiative," Matt said. "I mean, you're out there on the open ocean as in a commercial boat, or a Navy ship, or, you know, a P-3 flying around hundreds of miles from land." This was an informal session with prompting, but nothing scripted, nothing practiced. His emotions were triggered by the discussions, getting the best of him, and he was having trouble expressing himself.

"I mean, you're pretty much your own boss; there's nobody telling you what to do. There are all kinds of messages coming in and going out, but it's your judgment on the scene, and the fact that he turned around and went back into the storm he was trying to outrun says a lot about him. The fact that the State Department, the Pentagon, and the Carter administration, they did not flinch, did not hesitate to contact the Soviets for help."

Loreen was next. "That evening a friend from the squadron came to my home and said he wanted me to know there had been an accident, but it appeared that everything was okay—told me that right away—said that, you know, everyone seemed to be accounted for in life rafts. Of course, that's what I wanted to believe, so I believed it. Three days later, I saw official black Navy sedans pull up in front of my house. I was looking out the window, and by that time I realized what they were going to say, and it had just taken me the whole three days to come to grips with it because I kept thinking, *As long as there's hope, I'm going to have hope.*"

Now it was Bud Powers's turn to speak. "I was there at the Moffett TSC when they did ditch. I was there and heard Matt's last transmission. I heard part of it, and then we confirmed it with the Elmendorf Airways Radio people up in Alaska, that yes, the aircraft had ditched. When I heard about the aircraft in the water, I thought my career was over, I really did. I told Paula I was done, so we'll finish out this tour if they let me, and then go on to other things. I started thinking of what I wanted to do next because I knew I wasn't going to be in the Navy much longer. I was very much aware of the long-standing Navy tradition that the Captain is responsible for everything. As the sole Commanding Officer within Patrol Wings Pacific to lose a crew and aircraft, I realized I was now the lowest ranked among my peer squadron Commanding Officers."

His wife, Paula, said she didn't know at first that he thought that. "I saw great strength in the man I married, and I knew it was there when I saw him fight like he had to for his guys. This was at great expense to himself and his career, which who cares at a time like that when you've got men down overseas, got an international incident. He was fighting to bring them back because that was the most important thing—to get your guys back here—and there's no time to think about anything else."

Bud continued, "But it was the worst nightmare to know that you have a crew that just put one down, especially up there, I mean. Chances of survival, in those seas at that time of year, with those winds—and there was a very slim chance, very, very slim chance, of even putting the aircraft down in the water without just having it come apart—chances were very, very slim. So the whole thing, just, it was almost you thought the crew wouldn't make it, and the aircraft was gone when it happened."

Dennis spoke next, "I remember sprinting for my aircraft to get the inertial navigation systems going, and to fire up the radios. The entire Ready Alert crew ran out to the aircraft as fast as they could. Iron Mike Harris ran out to the plane as the SAR kit was delivered and gave us the latest position updates, unaware that I was already on the radios copying the minute-by-minute updates. Conway chimed in, 'We're gonna move heaven and earth to get airborne ASAP, just pass us the address we are heading for.' I knew the inertials still had about five or six minutes to go, but I just jumped on the radio to say, 'Hey, we're rolling now. We're gonna be looking for you.' Now I know that they had that on the PA system in the aircraft, so they all heard me talking, and I guess that helped morale a lot. It was just one of those times where I thought, *I'm gonna tell a lie, and I don't care that I'm telling this lie.* I guess it helped, and that's what's important."

Howie Moore added, "There were so many key events throughout; one key event was a great man who was able to power a crippled airplane onto the sea—which had never been done with this type of aircraft. Other great men who enabled me to survive in my life raft: John Ball held my head up and kept me alive. Great men, even during the Cold War times, are just men like us. They came to our rescue and showed that humanity is not just your neighbor back home; it is worldwide."

Thank You, Captain, My Friend

A Chance for a One-on-One

It was time for a break, and everyone went out to the hospitality suite for some much-needed refreshment. Matt was glad to have the interview session behind him, and ordered a beer. Loreen asked for a white wine; everyone around them was already visiting and enjoying the afternoon. Matt knew that all the survivors and everyone involved in the rescue would get a turn for interview sessions.

He caught up with Ron Price, Jim Dvorak, and Larry Carr, who were visiting together. Matt was surprised to learn that both Ron and Jim had sons who became P-3 pilots, carrying on the family tradition.

Matt thanked Ron for departing from Shemya for Adak to make his aircraft available for the next crew to continue searching for Jerry. Matt had read about the Shemya control tower closing the runway due to excessive crosswinds, visibility below minimums, and threatening to file an FAA flight violation against Ron, the pilot in command, if he took off. Ron had refueled at Shemya, planning an immediate return to Adak to switch crews and continue the search with this aircraft. The crosswinds at Shemya were gusting higher than allowable for the Air Force RC-135s or C-130s that usually flew from there, but they were below the maximum for the P-3—a fact the men in the tower apparently did not know. When Ron consulted with Pat Conway, his TACCO, Pat told him, "I can see the runway just fine; let's get the hell out of here." Without a takeoff clearance, they set takeoff power anyway and climbed away from Shemya in a hurry.

An FAA flight violation was serious business; had that violation gone through, it would have ended Ron's flying career. His commitment to continue the rescue effort was extraordinary in the face of these circumstances.

Dave and Pam Reynolds joined the group. Dave reminded Matt that he had switched places during the preflight with Gene Cummings, the regular Crew 6 Ordnanceman, making Gene one of the luckiest men alive. Gene had not had enough crew rest and asked Dave to take his place on the flight, so it was Dave, and not Gene, who spent that night freezing in a raft. It was great to see Dave and to meet Pam for the first time. Dave was just as positive as ever, thoroughly enjoying reconnecting with everyone. They joked about how Gene ended up flying that day anyway—had flown with the SAR crew—and was instrumental in dropping the SAR kit right next to the raft Dave was in.

Matt turned to John Hampel, who had photographed the XF675 crew rehearsing the drop of the massive SAR kit by the main cabin door of their plane. The crew dropped smokes and sonobuoys to confirm the wind direction and made a few practice runs. The actual drop went off like clockwork, splashing within mere feet of the twelve-man raft. Matt enjoyed reconnecting with John and meeting his wife, and thanked him for finding the MYS *Synyavin* on radar.

Matt spotted Ed Flow, Don Tullar, and Jim Kovach, three flight engineers with a combined sixty years of experience pushing the power levers of the mighty P-3. They had all been good friends with Butch Miller. Listening in on their shoptalk, Matt found that the three were discussing the overspeed. Based on later incidents, where parts could be examined in depth, they felt confident that the initial propeller overspeed was most likely caused by a hairline crack in the propeller control. The crack was between the increase pitch and decrease pitch lines, most likely caused by swelling of the O-ring seal. This new and improved O-ring was 4/1000th of an inch thicker (roughly the thickness of a sheet of paper), just enough to stress the assembly that it was designed to protect; the seal may have already been degraded before the plane took off that morning. It was certainly plausible but could never be proven given that the parts in question were scattered 14,000 feet deep in the North Pacific.

The good news was that with better training, updated emergency procedures, and more advanced propeller rebuild processes, the incidents of overspeeds had become extremely rare. All the crews involved in subsequent overspeeds had been able to get their crippled planes back to base safely—including one where the propeller did detach from the number one engine. Back in 1978, the P-3 cockpit simulator could not reproduce the indications they saw during that flight. A significant change to the emergency checklists came about a few months later.

Jerry had been caught in an emergency where he was expected to use his conscious thought processes to find the way out, and the conscious mind has a somewhat limited processing capacity. Matt remembered reading about this. With repetitive training and clearly stated emergency procedures, the information would have gone into the subconscious mind, which has an expanded capacity, a long-term memory, the ability to manage thousands of events at a time, and can process an average of four billion bits of information per second. In dealing with a compound propeller emergency, neither Jerry nor Butch had these new emergency checklists at their fingertips, so to speak.

Ed Caylor had said: "Jerry didn't have several hours to sit back and think it over, and his split-second decision-making was analyzed in detail. Pilots who do not survive an accident almost always shoulder some blame. The people who develop the checklists, maintain the aircraft, purchase the parts, approve the design changes, and train the pilots rarely seem to be found at fault—no matter how egregious their mistakes." There was widespread agreement on this point. Ed Flow mentioned that even though he, Butch Miller, and Jerry Grigsby had completed the Instructor Flight Engineer and Instructor Pilot training, this overspeed/immediate decouple/pitchlock scenario had never been discussed. Every single survivor, to a man, hailed Jerry as a hero for the decisions he had made given the training he had received at that time.

Matt was thinking about the "Safety Stand Down" in December of 1978 as he sipped his beer—this reunion was bringing back long-submerged memories. The crew was in demand to be on stage for a portion of that annual event held at the Moffett Field base theater. There was great interest and more than a little curiosity about the accident and its lessons learned. The theater that afternoon was packed, there was a moderator, and there were many questions from a panel. There was a palpable buzz in the audience. This was not going to be another boring safety meeting about safe driving over the holidays.

Matt had vivid memories of Captain George Phillips, the WINGSPAC Chief of Staff to Admiral Prindle, asking him how the survival equipment had performed. It struck a raw nerve within him: "Our Navy has let the VP community down. There are helicopter pilots flying five miles from aircraft carriers, and rarely more than fifty miles from any ship. They all have survival radios in their life vests. We fly hundreds of miles from anywhere—out in the middle of nowhere—often times over extreme open-ocean conditions, and none of us has a radio. That's something we've got to get fixed—yesterday. If we had had personal radios, that SAR kit could have been dropped next to the seven-man raft—and there would be three more survivors up here on stage with us this afternoon."

Matt remembered that you could have heard a pin drop as the audience stared back in disbelief. He did not intend to slam Captain Phillips at all—it just came out that way. The front rows of squadron leadership glared back at him— dismayed at his unvarnished candor and speaking truth to anyone who would listen. Farther back in the audience, he saw glimmers of recognition that he had made his point. The worldwide Navy P-3 fleet of more than four hundred aircraft and five thousand aviators were not equipped with personal survival radios. Maritime patrol aviators flew with empty radio pockets on their life vests, rarely giving it a second thought. No one had seriously considered how to maintain communications between the three orange rafts nor did they seriously consider what would happen if the emergency sonobuoy sank with the aircraft.

In May 1979, Commander Pete Cressy asked Matt to join him in a Sunday morning conference with the Naval Reserve Captains Study Group that met monthly at Moffett Field. This group contained aviators as well as Surface Warfare and Submarine Warfare senior leaders. It was something like a think tank for Bay Area Naval Reserve senior officers. Most of them had completed at least one tour of Pentagon duty. Cressy wanted to make certain that the safety recommendations the survivors had identified would make their way through the Pentagon acquisition process and not just end up buried in a file cabinet. Cressy knew that this group had the experience and connections to make things happen.

After playing a brief excerpt of the Mayday audiotape, Cressy invited Matt to be as candid as he was during his post-accident interviews, so Matt explained in detail how the survival equipment they had was inadequate and inappropriate for their missions. The audiotape and his insights got their full attention, and they agreed to take up the project. The Surface Warfare and Submarine Warfare panel members were surprised to learn that the aircraft had no radios that could talk directly to commercial ships. Their ships usually talked to P-3s on encrypted UHF channels. The carrier-based aviators were shocked to learn that the crews carried no personal survival radios out over the open oceans.

Military budgets are always driven by many competing priorities. The challenge for these Captains was to build awareness to ensure that these recommendations received the green light for future funding. Matt felt a measure of satisfaction that his crewmates had not died in vain.

Four months later, in September 1979, the Naval Aviation Safety Center monthly magazine *Approach* covered the ditching as its lead article. Even though it was short, and written by a non-aviator journalist, it ended with a bulleted list of the seven items that combined their main recommendations. While on deployment in Misawa, Japan, Matt and the other survivors felt like the Navy leadership was waking up to the issues, and that improvements would be coming soon. The Captains' involvement was beginning to show progress as the recommendations worked their way through the Budgeting Officers at the Fleet Commanders, Naval Safety Center, and Naval Air Systems Command.

While Matt was thinking about all of this, Captain Arbuzov came into the hospitality suite, having finished his video interview with Matthew Ball. Matt was finally getting his chance for a one-on-one with the man. He walked over, introduced himself, and expressed his gratitude for the rescue. Matt thanked him for making the decision to return into that major gale-force storm, thanked him for the skillful piloting of the *Synyavin*, and thanked him for selecting his most experienced crew to go out into those monstrous waves in a lifeboat.

Arbuzov smiled as Lana translated, and asked which raft he was in. When Matt answered that he was in the first raft with the red flare, the Captain said they could see it from the bridge very clearly and were able to tell the lifeboat crew which course to steer. Matt said in very basic Russian, (phonetically) "*Spasibo, Kapitan, moy tovarich*" (Thank you, Captain, my friend).

Arbuzov was the man of the hour, and through his interpreter, was already involved in another conversation. Many were curious about his first impressions of Las Vegas. Through Lana, he said he had never seen so many lights and that his granddaughter needed another suitcase to bring more jeans back home. Everybody got a good laugh over that answer.

Dennis and Cindy came by and they talked about the reunion and Matthew Ball's video project. It felt good to reconnect with old friends who shared this life-changing experience together—friends who understood the emotions of it all.

Cindy asked why Matt had left the Navy after seven and a half years, giving up a good career. Dennis had stayed on active duty for twenty years; they had made a lot of great friends, enjoyed a deep level of kinship and camaraderie, and traveled the world together. Dennis was now getting a monthly retirement benefit.

Matt said, "I did what I felt was best for my family at the time; Loreen and the girls had already been through enough.

Back in those days no one spoke much about grief counseling; no one recommended it to the families or to the survivors. Counseling in general lacked credibility and was thought to be an inexact science.

"Everyone was expected to keep a stiff upper lip and carry on. Family counseling could have been a big help at the time because Mary was quiet about what she was feeling, was generally a calm and quiet girl anyway. She was always 'daddy's little girl' and was very close to Jerry. She had developed a strong bond helping him with household projects and doing other activities with him. It appeared Mary had adjusted quite well, but the opposite was true—she had imagined all along that a Korean ship had rescued her dad and that the Koreans were holding him. She thought if he were released, he wouldn't be able to be with us because Loreen had married me."

Loreen said, "That was my fault. After the accident, I couldn't give up hope, and I thought maybe the Koreans could have rescued Jerry. Later, when I realized that was just magical thinking on my part, I didn't know Mary was still holding on to that hope. In retrospect, I should have talked to her about it. Much later, she told me that her memory of that time was that it rained every day, which of course didn't happen. Her good friend Shirin Etessam moved away and she lost interest in her activities, dropping out of them one by one. Her grades started falling, and that had never happened to her before."

Everyone was looking down, as though this information was too heavy, listening quietly. It was a sad aspect of the story, and Matt wanted to lighten the mood. He hadn't meant for the conversation to get so heavy, so he said, "Now you know the rest of the story, as Paul Harvey used to say."

Jerry Grigsby Survival Training Center

"My Dad Is a Hero"

John Branchflower—known as "Branch"—had joined the group. Branch of big personality. Branch of life-of-the-party fame. Branch who had occasionally brought a life-sized inflatable doll as his date to squadron parties. He had "Ms. Babette" with him here today—even though he was now happily married. He was always up for a joke or prank. The conversation switched automatically to a lighter tone. Loreen always enjoyed people who could make her laugh.

Branch had been a pilot on Delta Foxtrot 704, the second Ready Alert, at the time of the ditching, and had continued in the Naval Reserves until his retirement with the rank of Captain. He was now an airline Captain. He had been listening to the conversation and wanted to know why Matt never joined the Naval Reserves.

Matt explained that by the time he got out of the Navy in 1982, he hadn't seen a single safety improvement introduced to the fleet, and, frustrated, he was inclined to get as far away from the Navy as possible. The squadron had completed the

1979 Misawa deployment and the 1980 Iceland deployment without personal survival radios or improved exposure suits. (Ironically, the recommended safety improvements started trickling in by 1983.) In 1982, it was a time to focus on building a stable family life and a civilian career. He had moved back to California after two and a half years as an NROTC Instructor/Recruiter/CACO at Ohio State, had gotten an MBA, and had worked hard to make up for lost time. The girls, including his young daughter, Erin, had the opportunity to make long-term friends and go continuously to the same school system without the disruption of frequent Navy moves. Throughout the 1980s his association with former shipmates was reduced to a dozen or so close friends.

"In 1987, Bruce Forshay called and invited us to come up to Moffett Field and see the airplane and all the safety improvements that had finally been implemented," Matt explained. "It was great to see that the NATOPS Manual Emergency Chapter had been completely updated. It even included instructions on the life vest handheld survival radio. This was just what I needed to see. We had a nice day visiting and catching up with Bruce and Pattie. I was finally able to let go of the disappointment and frustration I carried; I finally found comfort that the loss of my crew had turned into something positive. I realized that my feelings impacted me way more than they impacted the Navy, and I was finally able to just let it all go."

Lisa and her husband Robert came up to the group, and Matt introduced them to Branch, adding that Lisa was Jerry's daughter. "It is so good to meet you!" Branch said with hardy sincerity. "I thought your dad was a great man and a real hero, and I see you have inherited his red hair and blue eyes. I was happy when I learned the new survival training center in Pensacola was named after him."

Matt said that it was quite a pleasant surprise. "Two squadron mates of Jerry's from his seaplane days submitted the 1979 *Reader's Digest* article, 'We Are Ditching, Ditching, Ditching,' to nominate Jerry to the naming committee in 1982. After all those years, they still thought so much of him. Jerry truly was someone special."

In 1983, Commander Everett Alvarez Jr., the Navy's longest-held prisoner of war in Vietnam, had served on the survival training center naming committee. He and Jerry had become good friends during their time together at the Naval Postgraduate School. They were project partners in their operations research major. Everett was able to speak in detail to the committee about Jerry as a person, and that is how this honor came to be.

"The facility was a huge improvement in Pensacola, and the training syllabus was greatly expanded—John Wagner was there, and you should ask him about it," said Branch.

"Yes, I will," Lisa replied. "I'm proud of my dad and the courage he showed. My sister Mary and I went to the dedication ceremony, and we gave a short speech together. My mom helped us write it and practice it. Mary and I didn't know what to expect; we thought we would be nervous. Our Grigsby grandparents were with us, and so were Aunt Dona and Uncle George. It was a small informal ceremony with people standing around listening outdoors along with the assembled staff of instructors in dress white uniforms standing in formation. It wasn't so overwhelming after all, something kids like us could handle. We were given a tour, and I was impressed."

Lisa and Robert were also joined by Ed and Carol Flow who caught up with them to express both their gratitude for what Jerry had done and their sorrow that Ed had not been able to help save him, could not get a lifeline to him. "The raft did not have an actual lifeline, so I had improvised and used the tethered PRT-5 radio beacon," Ed explained. "As I prepared to heave the beacon out to Jerry, who was about six feet away, a large swell knocked me off-balance and the beacon fell short. By the time I could reel it back into the raft and try again, your dad was even farther from the raft and still swimming frantically." Ed was one of the last people to see Jerry alive.

Lisa, always the empathetic one, said that she hoped he did not feel survivor's remorse, that she understood that everyone had done all that they could to save her dad.

Ed said that he still carried regret that when he stood and opened the cockpit overhead emergency escape hatch to exit the plane, it caused the rapid venting of the air inside the aircraft to escape, allowing water to fill the plane more quickly, and causing the plane to sink even faster. With 20/20 hindsight, he later realized he could have gone out the cockpit side exit.

Matt expanded on the theme, adding that each survivor carried some degree of regret. With the power of 20/20 hindsight, many actions could have possibly led to different and better outcomes. He finally understood why the portside raft was so hard to release when he realized that the lower edge of the port overwing exit was only six inches above the main cabin flooring, while on the starboard side it was fifteen inches above the floor. This explained that so much more ocean was coming in right at Randy. Matt felt that had he gotten up with his shroud cutter in hand he would have been able to quickly cut the retaining straps to get the life raft, water jugs, and emergency buoy out of the aircraft. It never occurred to him in those precious few seconds; it just wasn't engrained in their ditching drill training. It was just another "woulda, coulda, shoulda," moment that could have worked out differently, another one of many lessons learned the hard way.

Lisa went on to thank Ed for his part in helping to bring the plane down safely onto the waves and enabling Matt to come into her life as her stepdad. She felt fortunate to be loved and supported by three families; she was happy that she had been welcomed into the warm and friendly Gibbons clan and that Matt had been welcomed into the Grigsby family as another son.

She said, "I always knew I was loved. Sometimes other families are broken apart because of a lack of love: I am loved; my dad was loved. My dad is a hero who helped save many lives. I live today knowing his purpose in life was fulfilled and he was called back to be an angel. My faith in God may not be loud, but it is solid. That was all part of God's plan."

They stood around talking for a bit and then Lisa said that Mary was sorry she couldn't make it to the reunion, but she was at home taking care of her four young children. Also, Erin was taking architectural engineering classes at Cal Poly, and the curriculum was too dense to allow her to take the time off to come to this midweek event. Then it was time to go to dinner—the relatives were meeting up in the hallway.

To Jerry!

You Are in Our Hearts
Last Evening of the Reunion

The next evening, October 26, 2004—twenty-six years exactly after the ditching—was the high point of the reunion: a cocktail hour, a formal dinner, a celebration, and a remembrance. Reverend Wayne Brown began the program with a prayer followed by Gordy Alder, from Scone 92, playing "Amazing Grace" on his bagpipes.

After dinner, Matt got up out of his seat to go to the "Remembrance Table," a table with a black tablecloth set with a folded flag and a place setting left open for each of the crew members—"Forever young, still on station, still wearing their Wings of Gold." When Matt began to speak, Dennis Mette came over, kneeled on the floor beside Loreen, and put his hand on her shoulder. He knew this would be hard for her.

Matt spoke of each of those lost, including Jerry. He spoke of Jerry's heroism, his leadership, his airmanship, his tenacious dedication, his deep caring, his kindness and patience, his humility; he spoke of how Jerry was approachable and accessible, humble, and unassuming.

Loreen listened, filling in Matt's talking points in her mind with personal memories of Jerry and what he had meant to her. This was not a time for her to cry—Jerry wouldn't have wanted her to—though her eyes did tear up, and it did help her that Dennis held his hand on her shoulder.

The survivors presented commemorative plaques to the search and rescue team members, and they presented cobalt-blue and gold leaf reunion coffee mugs to all the attendees. Captain Arbuzov was presented with an honorary membership from the "World Famous Golden Eagles of Patrol Squadron Nine," and in turn Captain Arbuzov presented each survivor with a wall clock symbolizing the "gift of time."

What followed next was a series of toasts: For Butch, Jim, Randy, and Rich "still on station," for the crew of Scone 92, for the crew of X-ray Foxtrot 675, for the crew of Coast Guard 1500, for Captain Arbuzov and his crew of the MYS *Synyavin.*

Larry Carr, the pilot who had worked for Jerry in the safety department, approached the Remembrance Table. He told how, for twenty-six years, he had saved a bottle of Crown Royal gifted to him by Jerry back in 1978, in the summer before the ditching; he thought this evening would be the right time to open it. Casino staff served small shots of Crown Royal to the guests, and Larry toasted Jerry, "Here's to a loyal friend, a trusted mentor, and the history-making P-3 Naval Aviator who saved lives: To Jerry!"

To Jerry—you are in my heart and in my soul, and part of who I am is due to your loving influence: I am a better person because of you. You told the girls and me to hold you in our hearts where you would stay forever, and there you stay. Now I know how, for those who love, time is eternity and love is what we remember. Portions of I Corinthians flow gently through my mind:

Love is patient and kind, never boastful or proud, never haughty or selfish or rude. Love does not demand its own way. . . . We can see and understand only a little about God now, as if we were peering at his reflection in a poor mirror; but someday we are going to see him in his completeness, face to face. Now, all that I know is hazy and blurred, but then I will see everything clearly. . . . There are three things that remain—faith, hope, and love—and the greatest of these is love.

Epilogue: Search and Rescue Serendipity

One Year After the Accident

Throughout 1979, the surviving crew and their families got busy with business as usual. In preparation for their next six-month deployment to Misawa, in northern Japan, new crews were assembled. With an overseas deployment of the entire squadron heading to the Seventh Fleet area of responsibility, manpower replacements received a higher priority.

Crew 7 would be led by Ed Caylor as Patrol Plane Mission Commander, and Crew 11 would be led by Matt Gibbons as Patrol Plane Mission Commander. Newcomers joined their crews as "old-timers" departed. Crew readiness qualifications occupied most of the first half of the year.

The "TransPac to WestPac" was uneventful, all nine aircraft and a full complement of twelve crews quickly settled into the new home base for six months. The squadron conducted patrols in the western and northern Pacific, the Sea of Japan, the Sea of Okhotsk, and the northern edges of the South China Sea. Seventh Fleet exercises were conducted with the USS *Midway*'s carrier battle group.

In October 1979, President Jimmy Carter, in full support of the United Nations High Commission for Refugees, ordered Seventh Fleet units to begin searching for tens of thousands of Vietnamese "boat people." These refugees from the former South Vietnam were fleeing the harsh brutality of "reeducation camps" as they took to the ocean to escape in small coastal fishing craft.

Once again, Navy planners were called upon to improvise a large-scale search and rescue mission over a vast expanse of tens of thousands of square miles. There was widespread concern that these refugees were ill-equipped for open ocean conditions as they attempted to cross hundreds of miles in boats designed for fishing in coastal waters. Nobody knew where they were, where they departed from, or where they were headed. Searching for and locating small wooden vessels would be a long shot at best; and once found, could a nearby ship be persuaded to alter their route to assist?

Crews 7 and 11 were detached from Misawa to Naval Air Station Cubi Point, Philippines, led by Ed Caylor and Matt Gibbons. At first, everyone involved was "winging it"—trying to figure out how to overcome the challenges presented by this mission. The first challenge of how to effectively communicate with a merchant vessel was overcome by issuing each mission a handheld VHF FM radio to talk to any ship in the event refugees were sighted.

On their first "boat people" patrol, Crew 11 was tasked with conducting a ladder search in a large rectangular area halfway between Vietnam and the Philippines. Flying at 5,000 feet, copilot Wayne Roberts called out, "There they are!" Nobody else in the cockpit could see them, so he called, "My aircraft," and initiated a gradual descent to 500 feet—heading straight toward them. About a minute later, the rest of them could see what he was seeing. Wayne had extraordinary eyesight, better than 20/10 vision.

Now the fun began. Leveling off at 500 feet, they dropped a smoke float to better mark the location as they rocked the wings to let the refugees know they had been spotted, trying to give them some hope of rescue. As soon as they reported refugee contact, all hell broke loose on the teletype printer, as the military, State Department, even the UN High Commission for Refugees had a million questions. All they knew was where they were and that there were many men, women, and children apparently out of fuel and drifting mid-ocean.

Climbing away from their position, the crew expanded their radar search horizon, trying to find a ship that could render assistance. Thirty miles to the north they found one and attempted to communicate. In order to use the handheld VHF radio, they had to stand at the wide-open main cabin door as the aircraft circled the ship trying to speak with the ship's Master. Fortunately for all involved, especially the refugees, the ship altered course and proceeded directly to the position given to them.

Returning to the refugees, they rocked the wings again and dropped additional smokes to guide the ship and provide a visual reference of the wind direction. The ship arrived nearly two hours later, and based on the decrepit condition of the refugee vessels, they agreed to deliver the refugees to the next port. Without a doubt, it was one of the most fulfilling missions the crew had ever flown. Via the handheld radio, the ship's Master was able to answer many of the previously raised questions for the crew to relay back to Cubi Point.

Returning to Cubi Point, they were congratulated for their first rescue of 289 boat people. The rest of the mission debrief focused on what worked well and what could be improved. Bruce Forshay suggested that they develop Vietnamese-language leaflets that could be air-dropped to the next refugees instructing them to retrieve a sonobuoy microphone and use it to answer the top twenty questions needed to satisfy all interested parties. The leaflets were a huge improvement.

The second boat people flight yielded no refugee sightings. The crew had now experienced both the "thrill of victory as well as the agony of defeat" when trying to save lives. The planners at Cubi Point then changed the search area farther to the west. Their third mission was another huge success, and this time a United States Navy ship came to the rescue. Things were looking up in late October as both crews celebrated the first anniversary of their own rescue with the successful rescues of more than one thousand boat people. The BOQ at Cubi was the scene of an impromptu first anniversary celebration with Cubi Dogs, San Miguel beers, Cubi Specials, and a ceremonial dip in the pool.

Search and rescue had come full circle for the survivors, and it felt far more fulfilling to be a rescuer than the ones being rescued by others.

The Rescuers

In order of appearance

SCONE 92 USAF RC-135S COBRA BALL

CAPT Cliff Carter, First Pilot, Aircraft Commander
CAPT Bob Rivas, Copilot
CAPT Bruce Savaglio, Navigator One, Lead Navigator
CAPT Gordie Alder, Navigator Two
CAPT Alan Feldkamp, Tactical Commander,
ICBM Reentry Data Collection
1LT Rick Stotts, Raven One Instructor, Telemetry Collections
CAPT Bud Irons, Raven One, Telemetry Collections
CAPT Bob Carlson, Raven Two Instructor, Telemetry
    Collections
CAPT Greg Cummins, Raven Two, Telemetry Collections
1LT Bruce Carson, Raven Four Instructor, Electronic
    Intelligence Collections
CAPT Ron Hood, Raven Four, Electronic Intelligence
    Collections
MSGT Hank Lees, Manual Tracking Specialist for Optical
    Cameras
MSGT Tom Youngblood, Photographer, Large-Format
    Optical Cameras

SSGT Dennis Grundhauser, In-Flight Electronics Technician
MSGT Antonik, Airborne Mission Supervisor
SSGT Alexander, Airborne Maintenance Technician
SGT Miller, Operator Four, Russian Linguist
SGT Swank, Operator Two, Russian Linguist

X-RAY FOXTROT 675 USN P-3C CREW

Lieutenant Ron Price, Patrol Plane Commander
Lieutenant Pat Conway, Patrol Plane Tactical Coordinator/
    Mission Commander
Lieutenant (junior grade) Randy Lueker, Copilot
Lieutenant (junior grade) Van Gamble, Third Pilot
Lieutenant (junior grade) Dennis Mette, Patrol Plane
    Navigator/Communicator
AD1 Len Northrop, Flight Engineer
AW3 John Hampel, Sensor Three, Radar and Electronic
    Support Operator
AW3 Pete Geldard, Sensor One, Lead Acoustic Sensor Operator
AWAN Bill Rattenni, Sensor Two, Acoustic Sensor Operator
AT1 Hugh Littlejohn, In-Flight Technician
AO3 Gene Cummings, In-Flight Ordnanceman, Photographer

CG1500 USCG HC-130H CREW

Lieutenant (junior grade) Bill Porter, Aircraft Commander
Lieutenant (junior grade) Rick Holzshu, Copilot
AT1 Barry Philippy, Navigator
AT3 Ray Demkowski, Radio Operator
AM1 Daryl Horning, Flight Engineer
AD3 Butch Miconi, Scanner
AM2 Ken Henry, Loadmaster
SN Dan Malott, Scanner

Glossary

Over the years, military jargon has evolved into a language all its own. It is a curious blend of acronyms, abbreviations, contracted names, and places. We hope the list below will provide some color and background for the reader and a warm welcome into the salty world of reading how a sailor talks.

ALFA—A (ALPHA)
Alfa Foxtrot 586—the call sign assigned to the operational mission on 26 October 1978. Operational P-3 Orion missions typically flew with a five-character alphanumeric call sign.

ATC—Air Traffic Control; issues departure, enroute, and approach permissions to proceed with a flight routing.

Attitude—the aircraft's position of the nose and the wings relative to a level horizon. Composed of pitch (nose up or down), roll (wings level or not), and yaw (nose left or right of the tail).

Aviation Engineering Duty Officer—a Restricted Line Naval Officer assigned to duties involving research and development projects, not focused on Unrestricted Line command opportunities.

BRAVO—B

Bingo Fuel—an attention-grabbing callout that an aircraft needs to return to base as the amount of fuel on board is critically low considering the distance to return back to base.

Bureau number—the sequential Navy tracking number assigned to each aircraft. It represents the order in which the Navy accepted the aircraft from the manufacturer. PD-2 Bureau Number 159892 was the 159,892nd aircraft accepted by the Navy under this numbering convention and the 447th P-3 Orion accepted by the US Navy.

CHARLIE—C

C-130 Hercules—a four-engine turboprop cargo aircraft operated by the USAF, USN, USMC, and USCG.

CACO—an acronym for Casualty Assistance Calls Officer. The person assigned to the family of a deceased sailor to coordinate funeral arrangements and initial government claims applications.

Call sign—a radio address between bases, aircraft, and ships to specify who is talking to who, e.g., Alfa Foxtrot 586, Scone 92, Coast Guard 1500, Elmendorf, etc.

Charlie—the verbal representation of the letter "C" that was carried over from the Morse code days when "C" was shorthand for Correct.

CO/XO/CMC—abbreviations for the leadership team of a Navy squadron. Commanding Officer, Executive Officer, Command Master Chief. Together they represent the "front office" in charge of the organizational unit.

COMNAVFORJAPAN—the abbreviated form of Commander, Naval Forces, Japan; the regional administrative support command for Naval personnel in Japan.

Crypto—short for cryptographic materials; typically paper or electronic circuit cards that provide a degree of information security by scrambling the data.

DELTA—D
Decouple—a propeller emergency where the jet turbine engine is no longer connected to the propeller assembly.

Detachment—a sub unit of a squadron-level command. In Adak, for six months during 1978, three aircraft, three or four aircrews, and fifty or more maintenance personnel were rotated weekly between California and the Aleutians.

DIFAR—short for Directional Frequency Analysis; a type of sonobuoy that points in the direction toward the sound frequencies generated by the target of interest.

Dilbert Dunker—a simulated cockpit used for underwater aircraft egress training after a steep vertical drop plunging into a large training swimming pool.

Due regard—an Air Traffic Control status typically used on open-ocean surveillance missions where a properly equipped aircraft could assume responsibility for their own safety of flight traffic separation.

DWEST– short for Deep Water Environmental Survival Training; water-based training on aircraft evacuation and the proper use of life vests and life rafts.

ECHO—E

ELINT—a contraction for Electronic Intelligence; collecting military-related electronic signals for real-time and post-flight analysis.

Elmendorf—a major US Air Force base near Anchorage, Alaska.

ESM—Electronic Support Measures; a system on the P-3 Orion to capture and analyze electronic signals—typically search or tracking radars.

Extremis—an emergency that has turned extremely serious, where death is possible.

FOXTROT—F

FE—abbreviation for Flight Engineer. In the Navy, typically a senior enlisted systems expert with a background in aircraft systems. Typically a flying role for jet engine mechanics, aviation electricians, or aviation structural mechanics. A tight-knit brotherhood of hands-on subject matter experts.

Flash Precedence—a message speed identifier to get a Naval message sent as quickly as possible.

GOLF—G

Geedunk—refers to a ship's store, an aviation hangar snack bar, and a base mini-mart where snacks are available for purchase.

Gouge—an old Navy slang term for inside information, aka the straight scoop.

HOTEL—H
HF—short for High Frequency; a band of radio channels capable of long-distance, over the horizon voice, data, and teletype communication.

INDIA—I
IFT—short for In-Flight Technician; responsible for trouble-shooting and resetting onboard electronic systems.

Iron Mike—the shipboard equivalent of an autopilot used on long ocean voyages.

JULIET—J
JAG—short for Judge Advocate General; the legal department of the military.

KILO—K
knots/mph/kph—one knot is one nautical mile per hour. 100 knots equals 115.1 mph, or 185.2 kph.

KRIVAK—a class of smaller Soviet destroyer-style warship—sometimes referred to as a frigate. Approximately 400 feet long, it is equipped with both guns and missiles.

LIMA—L
LOFAR—the common omnidirectional type of sonobuoy Low Frequency Analysis and Recording; designed to detect the sound frequencies generated by the target of interest. Once found, a DIFAR buoy would be positioned nearby to point toward the target.

Loiter—the routine shutdown of one engine to conserve fuel. In the P-3 Orion, the number one engine was selected.

If conditions were favorable, the number four engine could also be shut down to extend mission duration even further.

MIKE—M
MAD boom—the distinctive tail stinger that contains a sensitive magnetic anomaly detector. A sensor device that can detect large metallic objects like submarines.

Mayday—the aviation radio code word you never want to say or hear—declaring an extreme in-flight emergency. Derived from the French phrase for "Help me!"

Master Chief—the Senior Noncommissioned Officer rank (E-9). Someone who really knows how to get things done.

MK12—the twelve-man life raft carried on the P-3 Orion. Equipped with a tarpaulin cover, it provided better protection than the smaller uncovered seven-man rafts. The survival equipment actually available on board this raft was far less than advertised during DWEST training and in the aircrew training manuals.

MK7—the seven-man life raft carried on the P-3 Orion. Neither seven-man raft carried covers, exposing their occupants to bitter cold wind chills. The survival equipment actually on board this raft was far less than advertised during DWEST training.

Morse code—a radio alphabet system based on dots (short) and dashes (long) signals.

MYS *Synyavin*—a 300-foot Soviet Far East Fisheries stern trawler. Directly translated to Cape Sinyavin, a port city on

Sakhalin Island in the Sea of Okhotsk. Named for Dmitry Senyavin, a Russian Imperial Navy Admiral during the Napoleonic Wars. Many towns across the Soviet Union are named for him. He is the Russian equivalent of Admiral John Paul Jones in the US Navy.

NOVEMBER—N

NARF—Naval Air Rework Facility; a shore-based maintenance command providing engineering, heavy maintenance, and major overhaul support as well as logistics inventory. NARF Alameda was repurposed to civilian use as indoor pickleball courts in 2023.

NATOPS—acronym for Naval Air Training and Operating Procedures Standardization; a very detailed flight and operation manual containing system descriptions, diagrams, and procedures. Three years after the ditch, on December 15, 1981, Interim Change 32 was introduced, expanding the Ditching Procedures pages of the Section 5 Emergency Procedures Chapter.

Naval Aircrew—the enlisted aviation ratings that form the crews on Naval aircraft.

Naval Aviator—the official designation of a Navy Pilot.

NAVCOMM—the Navigator/Communicator on a P-3 Orion crew.

Navy Ranks—the hierarchy of a Navy enlisted career. Trainees/Apprentices/Airmen (E1-E3); Petty Officers/Noncommissioned Officers (E4-E6); Chief Petty Officers/Senior Noncommissioned Officers (E7-E9).

Navy Rates—the Naval Enlistment Code that defines a military occupational specialty. An enlisted sailor's training, career progression, and promotions are based on personnel policies and head count targets, e.g., AD: Aviation Engine Mechanic; AE: Aviation Electrician; AW: Anti-Submarine Warfare Operator; AO: Aviation Ordnanceman; AT: Aviation Electronics Technician; PR: Parachute Rigger; RM: Radioman.

NFO—Naval Flight Officer; flying officers specializing in tactics, weapons systems, and navigation.

OSCAR—O
Ordnanceman—the enlisted crewman responsible for loading external search stores and weapons as well as deploying internal search stores as required. Usually doubles as photographer and occasional cook.

PAPA—P
P-2V Neptune—the 1947 designed predecessor to the P-3 Orion, the Neptune was smaller with two propeller engines and two small jet engines. After retiring from military service in 1979, many went on to become medium-sized firefighting aircraft.

P-3 Orion—in continuous frontline service since the Cuban Missile Crisis, it is one of the very few aircraft to serve the military for more than sixty years. A four-engine turboprop design typically carried a crew of ten to twelve on missions of between nine and twelve hours duration. Based on the 1950s-era Lockheed Electra turboprop airliner.

P-5M Marlin—a 1948 twin-engine seaplane designed with a flying boat hull that carried a crew of thirteen. It retired from Naval service in 1969.

PARPRO—short for the Peacetime Airborne Reconnaissance Program; after World War II, flights along the periphery of the Soviet Union, China, and North Korea. These flights were routinely flown to gather intelligence and gauge responses. Between 1946 and 1992 more than 150 US Air Force and US Navy personnel were lost in this highly classified aspect of the Cold War. Extensively declassified in 1994.

PATWINGSPAC—short for Commander Patrol Wings Pacific; the headquarters command over all maritime patrol squadrons in the Pacific.

PD—Papa Delta; the tail code painted on VP-9 aircraft since the 1960s.

Pinnacle—a very high-priority message in which the content is routed to the highest level.

Pitchlock—a propeller emergency when the blades are locked in a fixed angle other than fully feathered.

PQS—Personnel Qualification System; an individualized tracking system to ensure that the trainee demonstrates his or her understanding to a mentor who initials and dates successful knowledge completion.

PRT-5—a survival beacon located in P-3 Orion's life rafts. Once activated, it broadcasts a repeating tone on UHF frequency 243.0 MHz (UHF Guard) and 8.364 MHz (HF Guard), allowing search aircraft to home in on the signal.

Prudent limit of endurance—the point at which an aircraft should return to the home base based on fuel, distance, and headwinds remaining.

QUEBEC—Q

QD-1—the Quick Donning anti-exposure suit was a nylon fabric, rubber-coated one-size-fits-all dry suit coverall. It was widely used throughout the 1960s until its retirement in 1987. Well suited for temperate weather conditions, it was eventually recommended for use only in the tropics. The QD-1 dry suit was proven completely inadequate in the North Pacific in October 1978. Better cold weather suits superseded it fleetwide by 1987.

ROMEO—R

RAINFORM—a Navy-wide message classification system for multiple types of subjects. The RAINFORM PURPLE was the standard post-mission summary report completed after every maritime patrol flight.

RC-135—a family of USAF long-range high-altitude four-engine jets designed to collect various types of intelligence. In service since 1962, it continues flying to this day.

SIERRA—S

SATCOM—short for Satellite Communication; an extremely high-frequency line of sight long-distance communication system for encrypted data sent up to a satellite and then down to the recipient.

SERE—short for Survival, Evasion, Resistance, and Escape; the realistic training program to introduce all officer and enlisted aviation personnel to the distinct possibility of detention and/or capture by an adversary government. After a few days of living off the land, the trainees experience a simulated prisoner-of-war camp where they quickly learn that the Navy is not a job—it's an adventure. A truly unforgettable experience.

Shemya—a remote USAF base on the far western end of the Aleutian Islands.

Shooter—the nickname for an aircraft carrier Catapult Officer who oversees the launching of carrier-based planes.

Skyking—a communication overwatch monitoring organization that oversaw PARPRO operations.

SWO—short for Surface Warfare Officer; the designation for officers who are assigned to surface ships.

TANGO—T
TACCO—short for Tactical Coordinator; the Naval Flight Officer in charge of developing the big picture from the sensor operators and instructing the pilots on where to position the aircraft in order to transition from initial search to localization, tracking, and ultimately into resolving attack criteria to fully prosecute a submarine target.

TSC—Tactical Support Center; the ground-based activity responsible for briefing the missions before a flight and for evaluating the crew performance after a flight.

UNIFORM—U
UHF—Ultra High Frequency; typically relatively low-powered short-range, line of sight radio channels designed for voice, encrypted voice, and encrypted data communications.

URT-33—a two-way survival radio stored in the second seven-man raft. On 26 October 1978, it sank within the MK-7 raft that was not launched.

VICTOR—V

VHF—Very High Frequency; typically relatively low-powered short-range, line of sight radio channels designed for voice communications. Very common between aircraft and airports.

VP/VQ—Navy squadron designations as Fixed Wing Patrol or Fixed Wing Reconnaissance, like VF for Fighter squadrons or VA for Attack squadrons or VFA Fighter/Attack squadrons.

WHISKEY—W

Wings of Gold—the gold badge worn by Naval Aviators, Naval Flight Officers, enlisted Naval Aircrew, and Navy Flight Surgeons. One of very few communities in the Navy where enlisted personnel wear gold badges same as the officers. In most Navy communities, the enlisted badges are silver.

YANKEE—Y

Yankee Air Pirates—a frequent insult from SERE school interactions—designed for shock value.

ZULU—Z

Zulu—a time zone reference to Greenwich Mean Time. The time zone where all 24-hour clocks begin their day.

Bibliography

Boyne, Walter J. 2001. "The Early Overflights." *Air and Space Magazine*, June.

Burrows, William E. 2001. *By Any Means Necessary: America's Secret Air War in the Cold War*. Farrar, Straus and Giroux.

"Centennial of Naval Aviation—The Shadow Warriors." 2011. *US Naval Institute Blog*, November 27.

Dvorak, James A., and Powers, Byron L. 1978 Patrol Squadron Nine JAG Investigation Report, Aircraft Accident 26 October 1978, P-3C(U) Orion Aircraft BUNO 159892.

Everette, Dennis. 1983. "New NASC Building Named for Former Aviator." *GOSPORT*, CNET Public Affairs Office, October 28.

Jampoler, Andrew C. 2003. *Adak: The Rescue of Alfa Foxtrot 586*. Naval Institute Press.

Johanson, Robert L. 1978. "Participation in SAR Case following Ditching of Navy P-3C PD-2 AF 586." *US Coast Guard Aviation History*, October 26.

Martin, Gary L. 1979. "P3 Crew Recovery; Destination Yokota." *All Hands, The Magazine of the U.S. Navy*, February.

Martin, Gary L. 1979. "Touch and Go, Soviet Rescue," *Naval Aviation News*, October.

NFO/AIRCREW NATOPS Flight Manual, Navy Model P-3C Aircraft. NAVAIR 01-75PAC-1.1, Naval Air Systems Command.

Porter, Bill. "Manislov . . . This Is Bill." 1979. *Barometer, The Newspaper of CGAS Kodiak*, April

Selby, Earl, and Miriam . 1979. "We Are Ditching! Ditching! Ditching! Drama in Real Life." *Reader's Digest*, September.

Spink, Captain Tom. 2022. *Pacific Patrol: A History of Patrol Aviation During the Cold War in the Pacific.* Kindle Publishing.

Tart, Larry, and Robert Keefe. 2001. *The Price of Vigilance: Attacks on American Surveillance Flights.* Ballantine Books.

Reference Videos on YouTube and Other Links

ADAK AF586 Ditch and Rescue 1978
https://youtu.be/tdsUKdnwkds?si=WQ3C-32mpeRFFOpV

Matt's Final Call by Bill Porter
https://youtu.be/rl6Kza-vBMg

VP9 Ditch Reunion Part 1 by John Ball
https://youtu.be/ZcSidRWCDE0

VP9 Ditch Reunion Part 2 by John Ball
https://www.youtube.com/watch?v=5-pqBHYChoM

VP9 Ditch Reunion Part 3 by John Ball
https://youtu.be/SA0mG5SGtCw

VP9 Ditch Reunion Part 4 by John Ball
https://youtu.be/5RD8A_gQauU

Hickory Aviation Museum's P-3 Orion Walkaround
https://youtu.be/MPPnpug8aF4?si=dznX8sTKGzgkJg

C-SPAN.org "Adak Book Talk" by Andrew C. A. Jampoler
https://www.c-span.org/video/?319027-2/
book-discussion-adak-rescue-alfa-foxtrot-596

For more photos and background, please visit
www.loreengibbons.com

Acknowledgments

I could not have written this book without the help and support of my husband Matt. Although I lived through, and knew, the story, I did not know it in enough detail to write it into a book form. Profuse thanks, Matt, for your hours upon hours of filling in the gaps of my knowledge, and for reaching out to fellow survivors and rescuers. Thank you to my daughters, Mary, Lisa, and Erin, for your input that gave this book the shape it has today.

Ed and Janet Caylor, thank you for encouraging me in my earliest draft. Ed Caylor and Ed Flow, thank you for enlightening me about what was really happening in the cockpit. Thank you to all of the survivors for your collective memories that made this a more human story. John Ball, Bruce Forshay, Howard Moore, Dave Reynolds, and John Wagner: you are all my heroes. For the crew lost that day, Butch Miller, Jim Brooner, Randy Rodriguez, and Rich Garcia, and most especially to my greatest hero, Jerry Grigsby you will always be remembered for your bravery and devotion to the crew's survival.

My book club gave me much-needed encouragement with early drafts when I wasn't even sure I knew how to write a book. You kept me from giving up. Thank you, Mary Bristow, Kathy McElroy, Janel Hornbeck, Sue Masters, Virge Perelli-Minetti, Nancy Tostevin, and Linda Vrijenhoek.

Cindy and Dennis Mette, your inputs were invaluable. Bud Powers, Andy Pease, Bill Porter, Barry Philippy, Dan Malott, Alan Feldkamp, Cliff Carter, Van Gamble, Larry Carr, Pat Conway, John Hampel, Eddie Angel, Rick Burgess, Bob Masoero, Tom Adair, Darrel Whitcomb, Everett and Tammy Alvarez—I owe you all a huge debt of gratitude.

To Nina Solomita, you made me aware of the need to simplify the narrative. Louise Lane, your insights were right on centerline and glidepath. Sheila Trask, your editorial insights really polished the manuscript.

To the crews of Delta Foxtrot 704, Coast Guard 1600, Coast Guard 1601, Coast Guard 1602, Victor Bravo 760, Sierra Whiskey 608, Alfa Delta 275, Air Force Rescue 95825, Rescue 804, Rescue 805, and the Coast Guard Cutter Jarvis: thank you all for racing to SAR area, battling the stormy weather, and continuing the search for Jerry—keeping my hopes alive.

To the members of the California Writers Club–Central Coast community, I learned a lot from you about the craft of writing as well as the ins and outs of getting published. Special thanks to J.T. Rethke, Nicki Ehrlich, Mary Smathers, Nancy Middleton, Christine Sleeter, and Julie Tully. Thank you, Jerry Miller, for your skilled photo restoration and enhancement. Andy Jampoler, your *Adak* book was a valuable resource and a catalyst for our reunions. Thank you to Susan Brook and Bill Hamblett for permission to use the Map and Crew Seating Diagram from *Adak: The Rescue of Alfa Foxtrot 586*. To Tom Benner and Elizabeth Sessler, thank you for your skillful narration of the audiobook version.

To our extended family supporters Margaret Sullivan, Jim Gibbons, Connie Henry, Mary Beth Gibbons, Mary Anne Gibbons, Don Lynch, Joe Lynch, Joe Gibbons, Clare Gibbons Murphy, Nancy Chimara, Janet Grinstead, James Smithhart, Bev Smithhart, Rob and Judy Walker, Doug and Becky Walker,

Mitzie Miller, and Golda Kae Grigsby Young: thank you for your support. Also, I'm grateful to the many, many unnamed supporters along the way who encouraged me to keep writing even when I thought this book would never get off the ground.

To Fauzia Burke and Cassidy Ault thank you for your patience, guidance, and insights in developing my author platforms.

Last, but far from least, thank you to the She Writes Press team for bringing this story from the storm-tossed Aleutians to the public. Brooke Warner, Julie Metz, Addison Gallegos, Sheila Trask, Katie Caruana, Chas Hoppe, Tabitha Lahr, and Krissa Lagos.

And especially to the young men and women of Maritime Patrol Aviation, stay safe and take care of each other as you patrol the far flung fringes of freedom.

About the Author

A former Navy wife, remarried widow, and retired teacher, Loreen Gibbons lives with her husband Matt in the beautiful hill country of California's Central Coast. Her debut book, *All Eternity Lies Before Me*, started out as letters written to her older grandchildren so they would come to know the grandfather they never got to meet.

Author photo © Matt Gibbons

Looking for your next great read?

We can help!

Visit www.shewritespress.com/next-read
or scan the QR code below for a list
of our recommended titles.

She Writes Press is an award-winning
independent publishing company founded to
serve women writers everywhere.

Chicken Soup for the Soul®

Devotional Stories of Resilience and Positive Thinking

101 Devotions with Scripture, Real-Life Stories & Custom Prayers

Susan M. Heim
Karen Talcott

Chicken Soup for the Soul, LLC
Cos Cob, CT

Changing your world one story at a time ®
www.chickensoup.com